The Origins of Modern Mexico

Laurens Ballard Perry,
General Editor

Growth Against Development

The Economic Impact of
Railroads in Porfirian Mexico

John H. Coatsworth

Northern Illinois University Press   DeKalb 1981

About the artist: The scenes depicted on the jacket, frontispiece, and in the details throughout the book are from original artwork created by Mario Pérez Orona especially for the Origins of Modern Mexico series. Mario Pérez has exhibited his paintings, collages, and drawings in more than twenty-five exhibitions throughout Mexico in the past fifteen years.

Parts of chapter 6 are reprinted with permission of the *Hispanic American Historical Review* from John H. Coatsworth, "Railroads, Landholding, and Agrarian Protest in the Early *Porfiriato*," 54 (1974):48–71; portions of chapters 3, 4, and 5 are reprinted with permission of the *Journal of Economic History* from John H. Coatsworth, "Indispensable Railroads in a Backward Economy: The Case of Mexico," 39 (1979): 939–60; and map 2.1 is reprinted with permission of Sergio Ortiz Hernán Lozano from his work *Los ferrocarriles de México, una visión social y económica* (México: Secretaría de Communications y Transportes, 1970).

Library of Congress Cataloging in Publication Data

Coatsworth, John H   1940–
  Growth against development.

  (The Origins of modern Mexico)
  Translation of Crecimiento contra desarrollo, with a new introduction and many revisions in the English version.
  Bibliography: p.
  Includes index.
  1. Railroads—Mexico—History. I. Title.
II. Series: Origins of modern Mexico.
HE2818.C5613   385'.1'0972   80–8662
ISBN 0–87580–075–0

Copyright © 1981 by Northern Illinois University Press
Published by the Northern Illinois University Press
DeKalb, Illinois 60115
Manufactured in the United States of America

for Patricia Ann Sopiak Coatsworth, with love

Contents

List of Tables and Figures

FIGURES

Acknowledgments

The author wishes to acknowledge the support of the Henry and Grace Doherty Foundation, the Lincoln-Juárez Fellowship Program, and the University of Wisconsin which provided funds for more than a year's residence in Mexico; and to the Social Sciences Division and the Latin American Studies Committee of The University of Chicago for research assistance and travel grants required to complete this book. This study has benefited from the assistance of Peter Lindert, Morton Rothstein, and Jeffrey Williamson, who read the entire manuscript as a doctoral dissertation and made numerous contributions to its improvement. In addition, Albert Fishlow, Robert W. Fogel, Friedrich Katz, Donald McCloskey, and the members of the Economic History and Comparative Social History Workshops of The University of Chicago offered helpful comments on parts of this work. My research was aided by the advice, hospitality, and encouragement of Cedric Belfrage, Mary Belfrage, Rondo Cameron, Enrique Florescano, Eric Lampard, Alejandra Moreno Toscano, Moïsés González Navarro, Manuel Gollás, Ellen Gollás, Adrián Lajous Vargas, Arthur P. Schmidt, Jr., Enrique Semo, Anthony D. Tillett, Elizabeth Tillett, Gabriel Tortella Casares, Victor Urquidi, and Josefina Zoraida Vásquez. To each of these friends I am indebted still. For courteous and efficient assistance the author wishes to thank the staffs of the libraries of the University of Wisconsin–Madison, The University of Chicago, the Latin American Collection of The University of Texas, the Colegio de México, the Departamento de Investigaciones Históricas of the Instituto Nacional de Antropología e Historia, the New York Public Library, and the Biblioteca Nacional of Mexico, as well as to those of the Hemeroteca Nacional of Mexico, the Archivo Histórico of the Secretaría de Comunicaciones y Transportes, and the Archivo General de la Nación. Research assistance was provided by Paul Krause and Eugene Wiemers. None of those mentioned is responsible for the errors that may remain in this work.

J.H.C.

Abbreviations

AHSCT	*Archivo histórico* of the *Secretaría de Comunicaciones y Transportes*
DyE	*Demografía y Economía*
EEH	*Explorations in Economic History*
EHR	*Economic History Review*
HAHR	*Hispanic American Historical Review*
HM	*Historia Mexicana*
JEH	*Journal of Economic History*
MF	*Memoria* of the *Secretaría de Fomento*
MH	*Memoria* of the *Secretaría de Hacienda*
MSCOP	*Memoria* of the *Secretaría de Comunicaciones y Obras Públicas*
TE	*Trimestre Económico*

Note: Unless otherwise indicated, the symbol $ in this text refers to Mexican pesos. In 1910, $1.00 exchanged for approximately fifty U.S. cents.

Chapter 1
Introduction

From Backwardness to Underdevelopment

During the first half century of its independence from Spain, Mexico very nearly fell apart. The disintegration of the colonial economy had already reached an advanced stage in the eleven years of internal strife that preceded independence in 1821. By the 1830s, political and social instability became endemic, crushing all possibility for a revival of the colonial economy. Between 1836 and 1848, foreign aggressors seized half the national territory. In the 1860s, the country came close to losing its independence altogether when the French army installed a Hapsburg "emperor" and managed to pacify most of the country. The restoration of the Republic in 1867 solved none of Mexico's problems, and made some of them still worse—new *pronunciamientos*, continued bankruptcy, bitter Indian revolts, and more foreign threats.

Then, almost as suddenly as it had come, Mexico's time of troubles ended. In 1877, General Porfirio Díaz seized power in what appeared to be just another cynical coup d'etat. Within a few short years the country was at peace, its economy growing, its government stable, and its borders recognized by all the major powers. For thirty-three years, the country stayed on course. By 1911, the old Mexico was no more. The economic transformation of Mexico in the Porfirian period is the subject of this book. Its magnitude can best be perceived in contrast to the half century that came before.

In 1800, the colony of New Spain was twice as large as the new United States of America. At the time of independence, the territory claimed by the Mexican state measured 4,444,718 square kilometers, still much larger than its northern neighbor despite the latter's acquisition of Louisiana and several smaller areas including the Floridas from Spain. In the decades that followed, Mexico lost more than half its national territory. In the treaty of Guadalupe Hidalgo, in 1848, Mexico formally ceded sovereignty over enough of its territory to make its northern neighbor the colossus it has been ever since. Altogether, the territories seized by the United States measured more than 2.4 million square kilometers, and included all of Texas, Upper California, and the entire New Mexico region. By mid-century (after the Gadsden Purchase of 1853), the Mexican Republic was reduced to 1,987,324 square kilometers, an area only one fourth as large as that occupied by the United States.[1] The magnitude of the resources lost came dramatically to light less than a year after the 1848 treaty. The California Gold Rush began in 1849. In a few short years, that lost territory was producing more precious metals than all the legendary "silver mountains" of old Mexico. By the early twentieth century, the mineral output (including oil) of the lost territories exceeded by far the total gross national product of the Mexican nation.[2]

In 1800, the Spanish colony of New Spain had a population of some 5.8 million, half a million more than the United States. By 1810, the U.S. population, growing at a faster rate, had already passed that of Mexico, but the Spanish colony still had more citizens to count than the slaveholding republic to the north. By 1910, Mexico's population had not quite tripled to 15.1 million, while that of the United States had increased more than twelve times to 92.4 million. Mexico's population grew at a rate of approximately 0.6 percent per year until the 1860s, jumped to 1.1 percent between the 1870s and the 1890s, and increased again to 1.4 percent between 1893 and 1910. The U.S. population meanwhile was growing at an annual average rate of 2.6 percent per year, two and a half times the overall

1. Data on U.S. territorial expansion is found in the U.S. Bureau of the Census, *Historical Statistics of the United States, Colonial Times to 1957* (Washington, D.C.: Government Printing Office, 1960), p. 236.

2. In 1850, total U.S. production of gold and silver amounted to U.S. $55.1 million, nearly all of it produced in California (Bureau of the Census, *Historical Statistics*, p. 371). In the same year, Mexico produced an estimated $19.4 million. At its apogee, the Mexican mining industry produced some $27.1 million in 1804—approximately 37 million pesos of 1900 (Manuel Orozco y Berra, *Informe sobre la acuñación en las Casa de Moneda de la República;* document printed in vol. 2 of Secretaría de Fomento, *Memoria de la Secretaría de Estado y del Despacho de Fomento, Colonización, Industria y Comercio de la República Mexicana escrita por el ministro del ramo, C. Manuel Siliceo, para dar cuenta con ella al Congreso Constitucional* (Mexico, 1857), pp. 15, 22–34; hereafter cited as *MF, 1857*. The output of minerals produced mainly in the former Mexican territories (petroleum, copper, lead, zinc) are found in Bureau of the Census, *Historical Statistics*, pp. 360–69.

nineteenth-century Mexico rate of 1.0 percent. Not until well into the twentieth century, when immigration to the United States slowed to a trickle and modern disease prevention measures became available to most Mexicans, did Mexico's population begin to grow more rapidly than that of the United States.[3]

In economic terms, despite its larger population and territory, the total output of New Spain (excluding the northern territories later lost) amounted to only about half that of the United States in 1800, and slightly less than half in per capita terms.[4] Had this ratio of per capita income persisted through the nineteenth century—that is, had the Mexican economy grown as fast as that of the United States— Mexico would have reached its 1950 level of per capita income at about the turn of the century.[5] Between 1810 and the late 1870s, however, Mexico's economy stood in place while its income per capita fluctuated around an average of roughly fifty to sixty pesos of 1900. By 1860, Mexico's total product had dropped in relative terms from one half to less than one quarter that of the United States. By the early 1880s, just as the Porfirian boom was taking off, the Mexican economy produced about 2 percent of the total output of its northern neighbor. In per capita terms, the decline was almost as drastic. From a per capita product equal to roughly 45 percent that of the United States in 1800, Mexico's output per inhabitant dropped to 10 percent of the U.S. level by the 1870s.[6] This relative decline in both population and per capita product was due chiefly to Mexico's eco-

3. For Mexican population estimates between 1790 and 1867, see Marcelo Bitar Letayf, "La vida económica de México de 1824 a 1867 y sus proyecciones" (Mexico: Tesis de licenciatura, Universidad Nacional Autónoma de México, 1964), chapter 2. For population estimates between 1877 and 1911, see El Colegio de México, *Estadísticas económicas del Porfiriato: Fuerza de trabajo y actividad por sectores* (Mexico: El Colegio de México, n.d.), p. 25. U.S. population data are found in Bureau of the Census, *Historical Statistics*, p. 7.

4. See John H. Coatsworth, "Obstacles to Economic Growth in Nineteenth Century Mexico," *American Historical Review* 83 (1978):81–83.

5. In 1950, Mexico's per capita income equaled roughly $207 in pesos of 1900. In 1900, U.S. per capita income equaled approximately U.S. $231 or 462 pesos. Taking 45 percent of this 1900 U.S. per capita figure yields 207 pesos, Mexico's per capita income fifty years later. Mexico's 1950 per capita income is deflated by the price index in Leopoldo Solís, "La evolución económica de México a partir de la Revolución de 1910," *DyE* 3 (1969):1–24.

6. Coatsworth, "Obstacles," pp. 82–84.

nomic stagnation during a period of rapid growth in the United States. Mexico lost not only half its territory, it lost half a century's growth in productivity as well.

All these losses ended with the *Porfiriato*. By the 1880s, Mexico's per capita income was growing at a rate of perhaps 1.0 percent a year. Between 1893 and 1907, when more precise estimates of national income become available, the Mexican economy grew more rapidly than that of the United States. Total product advanced at a rate of 5.1 percent a year, or 3.7 percent in per capita terms. Had the economy of the United States stopped growing during the *Porfiriato*, Mexico would have recovered the major portion of the ground lost during the first fifty years after independence. In 1907, Mexican total product stood at 3 percent that of the United States and had recovered to approximately 17 percent of U.S. per capita product.[7]

The magnitude of the Porfirian transformation can be gauged from a brief list of its achievements. Most notable among them was the construction of more than 20,000 kilometers of railway which began with major foreign projects in the early 1880s. With cheap transportation available, the mining industry revived and expanded. Foreign capital transformed the industry, shifted its output increasingly to the production of industrial minerals (especially copper), modernized production with a myriad of new technical processes for extracting low grade ore, and built a new smelting industry from the ground up. While agricultural production for domestic consumption barely kept pace with population growth, the production of industrial and export crops advanced at rapid rates. Mexico became nearly self sufficient in cotton production and began to export large quantities of sisal, coffee, rubber, livestock, and other products. Industries producing for domestic consumption also grew rapidly during the *Porfiriato;* textiles, alcoholic beverages, food processing, and other light consumption goods industries, modernized with foreign financing, came to displace artisanal production with more efficient and larger scale operations, which used the new transport system to reach markets from one end of the country to the other. Economic growth

7. The Mexican economy suffered a recession reflected in the G.D.P. data between 1908 and 1910. Growth rates would be slightly lower if 1910 were used instead of 1907, as in the text.

and political stability combined to end the paralysis of public policy which had afflicted bankrupt Mexican governments since the mid-1820s; by the turn of the century, Mexican public debt issues were snapped up on the European and North American exchanges at rates of interest less than half that offered a scant two decades before.[8]

The Porfirian achievement had another side, however, one which the 1910 Revolution revealed more dramatically than the printed word. Two central issues, which still reverberate in Mexican political discourse, were raised by the Revolution: the issue of social justice, especially for the landless majority of the rural population, and the issue of foreign domination of economic life and public policy. The question of political democracy, the chief preoccupation of Francisco Madero and his immediate followers, served mainly to create a political environment in which these two central issues could be raised. Both concentration of landownership and the foreign presence in Mexico's economy increased substantially during the Porfirian period. In fact, the rapid rate of economic growth achieved in the late nineteenth century could scarcely have been attained without both of these changes. The marked increase in the concentration of landownership occurred because new incentives to agricultural production, especially export production, made land more valuable. The expropriation of the free Indian villages also provided an important stimulus to the formation of an agricultural and industrial proletariat in the center and north of the country. Foreign capital to construct the railway network and to build or rebuild mining and industrial enterprise was indispensable to Porfirian economic expansion. Foreign demand for primary products produced in Mexican mines and plantations provided an essential stimulus for the foreign investment that Mexico needed as well as for continued increases in output.

While social justice and national economic independence emerged as major issues in the Mexican Revolution, they have also preoccupied economists working on problems of development. Excessive concentration of wealth and income may retard the development of industry by restraining market growth. To the extent that such con-

8. For the sheer mass of data, the best single work on the Porfirian economy is still Daniel Cosío Villegas, ed., *Historia moderna de México: El Porfiriato, La vida económica,* 2 vols. (Mexico: Editorial Hermes, 1965).

centration is reflected in public policy (and it is frequently intensified by state intervention) suboptimal levels of investment in human resources occur. Poor health and nutrition and low levels of education and skills inhibit industrialization as much as (perhaps more than) lack of capital or even natural resources. Dependence on external financing may retard the development of domestic financial institutions, directing their growth to short-term financing for commercial operations complementary to the basic development financing provided from abroad. The flexibility of economic policymaking is reduced dramatically in contrast to more advanced economies at comparable levels of economic activity. Growth oriented toward exports attracts resources, human and physical, to an excessive specialization in the production of particular commodities on the basis of short run, static perceptions of comparative advantage in world trade. When terms of trade shift unfavorably over the long run, the economy may lack the capacity to mobilize domestic (or foreign) resources to new export products or to a growth path oriented more toward the development of internal markets. The depletion of natural resources, and the repatriation of returns to foreign investors, act as a brake on development with which the industrialized countries did not have to contend during their industrial revolutions.

This description fits rather well the Mexican case, and many others. The different structure of the growth paths followed by many Latin American countries in the late nineteenth century produced marked advance in the physical attributes of modernization. At the same time, however, foreign-financed export oriented growth created or intensified obstacles to economic development over the historical long run. This is not to say that backward economies prior to this period did not suffer from even more severe constraints on growth. Before the Porfirian period, the Mexican economy lacked basic transport and communications facilities as well as banks, capital, technology, and skills. Economic organization suffered from inefficiency, property rights were ill defined and often unenforceable, and fiscal policies did more harm than good by discouraging enterprise, fragmenting markets, and wasting public funds on unproductive expenditure. What the *Porfiriato* accomplished in these areas is scarcely an issue. The point is that the accomplishment was partial and even contradictory. Mexico could no longer be described as backward in

1910. Instead, thirty years of nearly uninterrupted growth had endowed the country with an economy whose structure and institutions were almost a caricature of the modern textbook description of underdevelopment.

By the last quarter of the nineteenth century, no plausible historical alternative to underdevelopment existed for Mexico and for most of the backward regions of the world. Since these regions followed a much different path from that of the already advanced capitalist countries, it is not likely that contemporary remedies based on linear stage models of earlier success stories will prove any more plausible. It is useful nonetheless to compare the different economic histories of the developed and underdeveloped regions in order to make precise statements about differences which have both historical interest and implications for assessing contemporary options. Mexico is once again passing through an era of sustained economic growth; many of the traumas and contradictions of the present period find familiar echoes in the *Porfiriato*.

Railroads, Growth, and Underdevelopment

The most celebrated technological innovation of the nineteenth-century industrial revolution was the railroad. Since nearly every product of industry, agriculture, and mining used transport, and railroads reduced transport costs, the effects of the new technology were felt throughout entire economies. Since railroads quickly came to be major consumers of iron and steel, they were credited with stimulating the development of basic industries. As large enterprises with heavy capital requirements, they pioneered the development of modern management techniques and had considerable impact on the evolution of modern capital markets. The social effects of cheap, rapid transport provided drama for historians of labor struggles, elite behavior, and migratory patterns. Military historians have noted the difference that railroads made in strategic and tactical planning.

Economic historians of several countries have recently produced an interesting cluster of monographs which have attempted to test the conventional wisdom about the magnitude of the railroad's effects on economic growth in the nineteenth century.[9] Most of these studies have focused on economies that are currently among the world's most advanced. None have raised questions which, in addition to the growth issue, bear directly on the different patterns of growth experienced in backward nations. This book attempts to do so by raising three general questions about the impact of railroads in Porfirian Mexico. The first is the question addressed by earlier studies: What was the measurable impact of railroad development on Mexican national income before 1910? The second and third relate to questions of primary interest to historians of backward regions. What difference did it make that most of Mexico's railroads were built by foreign corporations in an environment that permitted a relatively free flow of productive factors across international boundaries? And, what effect did railroads have on the distribution of land in the Porfirian era? These are not the only questions that might legitimately interest students and scholars who wish to know more about the impact of railroads in the *Porfiriato*.

A number of historians, both Mexican and foreign, have described the political and institutional history of railroad enterprise in the *Porfiriato*.[10] Several of these works have illuminated important aspects of the disputes over railroad concessions, the evolution of the administration and organization of the railroad companies, the history of railroad finance, and the like.[11] But, except in some comments in the final chapter, very few of the politicians and promoters who conspired to construct and operate Mexico's railroad network appear in the pages of this book.

9. See the works of Fishlow, Fogel, Hawke, North, and others cited below and in the Methodological Appendix.

10. John G. Chapman, "Steam, Enterprise and Politics: The Building of the Veracruz–Mexico City Railway, 1837–1880" (Dissertation, The University of Texas, 1971).

11. See, for example, David Pletcher, *Rails, Mines and Progress: Seven American Promoters in Mexico, 1867–1911* (Ithaca, N.Y.: Cornell University Press, 1958) and the chapters by Francisco Calderón on railroads in Daniel Cosío Villegas, ed., *Historia moderna de México* in the volumes subtitled *La República Restaurada, La vida económica* and *El Porfiriato, La vida económica*, vol. 1 (Mexico: Editorial Hermes, 1955–1965).

Some historians have directed their attention to the social history of Mexico's railroads, where, as in so many other countries (including the United States), railway workers are found among the most class-conscious and militant sectors of the new industrial proletariat.[12] Little reference is made in this work to the thousands of men and women who built Mexico's railways and made them run, and no mention is made beyond this page to their struggles to organize unions to protect their jobs and their livelihood. The reader will find reference to wage data in Chapter 5, which illustrate the discrimination suffered by Mexican employees (even on the "Mexicanized" *Ferrocarriles Nacionales*), but this data is used solely as an economic rather than a social indicator. Despite the rich primary sources available, a scholarly work on the history of railway workers and their organizations has yet to be written.[13]

A number of important books have been written on the history of Porfirian state policy toward infrastructural development and on the evolution of public policy toward the railroads from the first concession in 1837 to the Mexicanization of the country's major railroad companies in the last years of the Porfirian regime.[14] Chapter 2 of this book contains a summary of some important aspects of Porfirian transport policy, and the reader can find some comments on Mexicanization and other policy issues in the concluding chapter. The focus of this study, however, lies elsewhere.

12. See, for example, Marcelo N. Rodea, *Historia del movimiento obrero ferrocarrilero en México (1890–1943)* (Mexico: n.p., 1944).

13. The railroad materials filed in the *Archivo Histórico de la Secretaría de Comunicaciones y Transportes* (Tacuba 8, Mexico City), contain data on employees, their salaries and nationalities, as well as information on labor force recruitment, strikes, trade unions, and the like, company by company for the entire period of the *Porfiriato*. Materials in this archive are hereafter cited as *AHSCT*, followed by file number.

14. See, for example, Pablo Macedo, *Tres monografías que dan idea de una parte de la evolución económica de México* (Mexico: J. Ballesco y Cía., 1905); Fernando González Roa, *El problema ferrocarrilero en México y la Compañía de los Ferrocarriles Nacionales de México* (Mexico: Carranza e Hijos, 1915); Vicente Fuentes Díaz, *El problema ferrocarrilero en México* (Mexico: n.p., 1951); Carlos Villafuerte, *Ferrocarriles* (Mexico: Fondo de Cultura Económica, 1959); Sergio Ortíz Hernán Lozano, *Los ferrocarriles de México: una visión social y económica* (Mexico: Secretaría de Comunicaciones y Transportes, 1970).

The Theory

To measure the impact of railroads on Mexican national income, two concepts drawn from the body of contemporary economic theory are employed. The first is the concept of "social savings."[15] The second is the concept of "linkage."[16] Readers familiar with these concepts may wish to consult the Methodological Appendix for a discussion of the analytical issues involved in their use.

"Social" savings does not refer to money saved by individuals, but rather to resources saved by "society." Resources may be saved in many ways, but the most potent economic source of resource savings in the modern world has been technological innovation. Railroads saved resources because they transported people and goods at less cost than other means of travel. After railroads were constructed, resources no longer needed for transportation could be used to produce other goods and services. The amount of these freed resources is called the *direct social savings*. Under certain assumptions, discussed in the Methodological Appendix, the direct social savings of railroads represent additions to national income. Estimating direct social savings thus provides one measure of the railroads' stimulus to the economy as a whole.

Direct social savings are estimated by subtracting the total cost of rail transportation from the total cost of transporting the same quantity of goods or passengers the same distance by the cheapest alternative means of transportation. Complicated analytical issues are raised by the need to specify (1) the exact quantity of goods or passengers to use in constructing the measure and (2) the appropriate alternative mode of transportation on which to base the comparison. These issues are also discussed in the Methodological Appendix.

Considerable controversy has arisen over the use by U.S. economic historians of "counterfactual" propositions.[17] To estimate the direct

15. See Robert William Fogel, *Railroads and American Economic Growth: Essays in Econometric History* (Baltimore: Johns Hopkins Press, 1964), chapter 1; Albert Fishlow, *American Railroads and the Transformation of the Antebellum Economy* (Cambridge, Mass.: Harvard University Press, 1965), chapter 1.

16. Albert O. Hirschman, *The Strategy of Economic Development* (New Haven: Yale University Press, 1958), chapter 4.

17. See Methodological Appendix where the relevant literature is cited.

social savings of railroads, it is necessary to imagine a hypothetical economy without railroads and to compare the hypothetical costs of transporting a hypothetical number of goods and passengers with the actual costs of railroad transportation in the same year. Philosophical doubts about the use of the counterfactual method in economic history may cause skepticism in some readers. To these doubts, there is, I believe, a definitive reply. Every causal statement in historical work contains an implicit assertion about the course of history in the absence of the specified cause. To say that railroads caused an increase in national income, still more that they were the "fundamental and indispensable prerequisite"[18] for economic growth in Porfirian Mexico, implies directly that in the (hypothetical) absence of railroads national income would have been smaller. The most important contribution of what North American academic politicians have come to call the "New Economic History" has been to make such statements explicit in quantitative terms and to examine them more carefully, and more precisely, than earlier historians.

Linkages, in the economic sense, are relations between producing units. A forward linkage exists, for example, when railroads provide a necessary input (transportation) to other economic units. A backward linkage exists when railroads use the products of other industries (iron, steel, engineering, machinery, coal, wood, water, and the like) to produce transportation. Direct social savings are a measure of the strength of forward linkages. The greater the direct social savings produced by railroads, the stronger are the railroads' forward linkage effects on other industries. By reducing the cost of a necessary input to other industries, railroads stimulate output. The magnitude of this stimulus is equal to the direct social savings.

Estimates of direct social savings do not, however, measure the effect of backward linkages. Separate analysis is required to determine whether railroads caused an additional increase in national income, in an indirect way, by increasing demand for the products of other industries. Economists usually distinguish the direct social savings of the railroad's forward linkage effects from the *indirect social savings* due to backward linkages. In value terms, the indirect social

18. Fernando Rosenzweig Hernández, "El desarrollo económico de México de 1877 a 1911," *TE* 32 (1965):413.

savings are equal to the increment in the output of other sectors due to the increase in the demand for their products generated by the railroads. Economists usually attach special significance to railroad backward linkages that stimulate the development of modern industries.[19]

The Hypotheses

Mexico is a country where geography conspires against economy. Since the pre-rail transport system depended on overland movement using animal power or on foot, transport costs were high. In countries like the United States, Great Britain, the Netherlands, or even Tsarist Russia, relatively cheap water transport existed before the construction of railroads.[20] The higher costs of Mexico's pre-rail system suggest that railroads introduced greater savings in Mexico than elsewhere. The reduction in the unit costs of transportation (the cost of moving one passenger or one ton of freight per kilometer) should prove to be greater in the case of Mexico than in other countries where an inexpensive alternative to overland transport already existed before the railroads.

Before formulating any hypotheses, however, it will be necessary to consider other factors. In the case of passenger travel, the railroads saved not only resources, but time. The value of the time "wasted" in

19. See Fogel, *Railroads*, chapter 4; Fishlow, *American Railroads*, chapter 1.

20. See the studies of railroads in the United States (by Fogel and Fishlow, cited above); in England and Wales by Gary Hawke, *Railways and Economic Growth in England and Wales, 1840–1870* (London: Oxford University Press, 1970); in Scotland by Wray Vamplew, "Railways and the Transformation of the Scottish Economy," *EHR*, 2d ser., 24, no. 1 (1971):37–54; in Colombia by William Paul McGreevey, *Economic History of Colombia, 1845–1930* (Cambridge, England: Cambridge University Press, 1971), chapter 10; in the Netherlands by Jan de Vries, "Barges and capitalism. Passenger transportation in the Dutch economy, 1632–1839," *A. A. G. Bijdragen*, vol. 21 (1978): 237–44; in British India by John Hurd II, "The Economic Impact of Railways in India, 1853–1947," in *The Cambridge Economic History of India* (forthcoming); and in Tsarist Russia by Jacob Metzer, "Some Economic Aspects of Railroad Development in Tsarist Russia" (Dissertation, The University of Chicago, 1972), part 2.

travel depends on the productivity of the travelers. In high wage industrial countries, the railroad's greater speed made a difference. In less productive, low wage regions, like Mexico, the value of the time spent traveling was less. The output of travelers who saved time by riding trains may have been too small to have an impact on national product. The question, then, is whether the resources saved by transporting passengers by rail were large enough to make a difference. If the old overland system required large quantities of resources to carry passengers, such as carriages, horses, road building tools, and the like, then the railroad could have freed these resources for other uses. Most prerail travelers, however, walked to their destinations. Walking takes time, but uses little in the way of resources. Thus, there are grounds to suspect that the unit savings (if any) per passenger kilometer of railroad services were low.

Low unit savings may add up to large social savings, however, if enough units are produced. The question is whether the railroads attracted enough passengers to produce total savings in time and resources sufficiently large to have a significant impact on national income. The hypothesis tested in Chapter 3 is that they did not. In highly mobile, advanced countries, where railroads saved both resources and time, the direct social savings from passenger services were not high. In Mexico, it may be hypothesized, the direct social savings were lower still.

Freight transportation is another matter. It can be hypothesized that both unit savings and total savings were large. Large unit savings may be predicted because the alternative to the railroads—wagons and mule trains—were much more costly than the ships and barges available to pre-railroad shippers in other countries. The question is whether the railroads attracted sufficient freight to translate large unit savings into large social savings. In some parts of the underdeveloped world, where railroads were built by colonial powers for military or strategic reasons, or where independent governments miscalculated the railroads' potential impact on economic activity, expensive construction projects generated so little freight that direct social savings were small or even negative. In Spain, overbuilding of new rail links in the mid-nineteenth century diverted resources from other projects, failed to generate sufficient freight to justify their large costs, and contributed to bankrupting successive governments.[21] In the case of Mexico, however, a number of factors (including proximity to the United States and large, unused mineral resources) led to heavy use of the new transport system. The hypothesis tested in Chapter 4, therefore, is that the direct social savings from railroad freight services amounted to a large proportion of national income.

A second set of hypotheses, tested in Chapter 5, is suggested by the second of the three questions posed above. While the social savings estimates will capture the aggregate direct impact of railroads on national income, they abstract from the structural effect of the new technology on the composition of national production, or what economists call the "output mix" of the economy. The export sector of the Mexican economy grew more rapidly than the sectors producing for the domestic market during the *Porfiriato*. In this aspect, Mexico's economic growth in the railroad era resembled that of many other "underdeveloping" regions of the world. Chapter 5 begins by testing the hypothesis that railroads contributed to the structural imbalance of Mexican growth because their stimulus to new output was skewed. The forward linkage effects of the railroads, the direct savings they brought to freight transportation, were concentrated in the mineral and agricultural export industries.

Chapter 5 also considers some issues raised by the importance of foreign capital in the development of the railway network. The importance of foreign capital, and the low level of prior industrialization, suggest the hypothesis that backward linkages to Mexican industries were relatively small. In contrast to the large direct social savings, *indirect* savings are expected to be small. The backward linkages which might have stimulated the development of modern industries in Mexico, according to this hypothesis, leaked abroad to the already modern industrial establishments of the North Atlantic economies.

Chapter 5 concludes with a measure of the flow of railroad benefits out of Mexico in the form of payments for foreign inputs, the costs of imported consumption goods for the railroads' foreign employees, and the remittance of profits and interest to foreign investors. This chapter implicitly abandons the analytical perspective of the previous

21. Gabriel Tortella Casares, *Los orígenes del capitalismo en España* (Madrid: Editorial Tecnos, 1973), chapters 3–5.

ones which measured the benefits of railroads against a plausible hypothetical alternative. No attempt is made to measure the costs of foreign participation against some hypothetical alternative. To provide a definitive measure of the net costs (or benefits) of foreign participation would require a comparison of the actual costs of railroad development financed by foreigners with the hypothetical costs of railroad development financed in some other way. Nonetheless, the amount of the absolute loss due to foreign participation in an open economy is a significant descriptive statistic which permits comparison with other types of railroad development in other countries and regions. The hypothesis tested in Chapter 5 is that these absolute costs were high.

The final question addressed in this book concerns the impact of the railroads on the distribution of wealth and income in Porfirian Mexico. A complete analysis of the railroad's distributional effects (not to mention its social impact) would require more data and better theory than are presently available. Chapter 6 therefore focuses on a single dimension of the railroad's effect on the distribution of wealth, namely the impact on land tenure. This chapter tests the hypothesis that railroads contributed directly to the new concentration of landownership evidenced in the early years of the *Porfiriato* by providing a powerful and unexpected incentive for legal and illegal expropriation of rural properties by men of wealth and political influence. This incentive arose because of the railroad's effect on agricultural production possibilities and thus on land prices.

Additional hypotheses relating to the social and political consequences of the railroad are advanced in the concluding Chapter 7 as an agenda for further research. Chapter 7 also contains a summary of the conclusions reached in the preceding sections of the book.

Chapter 2
Transportation and Transport Policy in Mexico

Highways

Before the construction of Mexico's railroad system, people and goods traveled overland along an extensive network of roads and trails on routes largely inherited from the pre-Hispanic era.[1] During the first century after the Spanish conquest, viceregal administrations spent considerable sums on improving communications. Widening ancient trails and constructing bridges with tax revenues burgeoning in the boom years of the mining industry, colonial administrations facilitated the introduction of wheeled vehicular transport of goods between Veracruz, New Spain's only legal Gulf coast port, via Mexico City, the colony's commercial and administrative capital, to the mining regions in the north and northwest. With Mexico City at the center, new highways radiated in all directions. The Mexico City–Veracruz highway was the most heavily traveled route, despite the steep grades on lengthy sections descending the eastern escarpment of the Sierra Madre Oriental.[2] The *Camino Real de la Tierra Adentro* was the colony's longest road, originating in Mexico City and extending some 1,500 miles to the northwest through the mining regions of Zacatecas and Durango to the furthest outposts of the Spanish empire at Santa Fe and beyond. A second northern route left the *Camino Real* at Querétaro and ran due north through the colony's other great mining areas near Guanajuato and San Luis Potosí, continuing beyond to Laredo and the Texas missions. Additional highways were constructed running west from Mexico City to Guadalajara by way of Valladolid (now called Morelia), south down the western escarpment past Cuernavaca to Acapulco, and southeast via Oaxaca to Central America. Priority in the construction of roads was assigned

1. For a description of the pre-Hispanic communications network, see Robert C. West and John P. Augelli, *Middle America: Its Lands and Peoples* (Englewood Cliffs, N.J.: Prentice-Hall, 1966), pp. 250–51.
2. Ibid., p. 299.

to the routes uniting the mining regions and northern outposts to Mexico City and the latter to Veracruz. The road to Guadalajara was passable for wheeled vehicles in some sections, but the highways to Acapulco and Central America narrowed to mule trails not far from Mexico City.[3] Despite its great length, Mexico's highway system never came close to equaling the density or the quality of construction of contemporary European road networks.[4]

The need to transport bulky freight through relatively insecure frontier areas led to the modification of Spanish freight wagons and to the development of the unique Mexican *carro,* a huge two-wheeled wagon pulled by up to sixteen mules. Constructed of "heavy planking and studded with pikes and clamps, such *carros* could serve as rolling blockhouses for protection against the Indians."[5] Trains of thirty to eighty of these huge vehicles provided the essential long distance transport required by the developing mining industry in the sixteenth century and by the agricultural producers who supplied the mining regions with food, fibers, and drink.[6] Once mineral output began to falter and the prosperity of the sixteenth century gave way to "New Spain's century of depression," the highway network deteriorated rapidly. The revival of mining in the eighteenth century did not inspire a new era of transport improvement and innovation. In its declining years, the Spanish empire was beset by internal and international conflicts which consumed all the resources an increasingly voracious Crown could manage to extract. The disappearance of wheeled vehicles from most of the colony's roads was not reversed. By the end of the eighteenth century, the Mexico City–Veracruz highway "had degenerated into a perilous muletrack."[7] Only the road running north from Mexico City to Chihuahua via Zacatecas and Durango remained open to wheeled traffic over its entire length, and even here contemporary accounts emphasize the preponderance

3. Ibid., pp. 300–301.

4. Ibid., pp. 299–302. See also Alexander von Humboldt, *Political Essay on the Kingdom of New Spain,* trans. and ed. by John Black, 4 vols. (London, 1811–1822), for a description of the transport system late in the colonial era.

5. David R. Ringrose, "Carting in the Hispanic World: An Example of Divergent Development," *HAHR* 51 (1971):38.

6. Ibid., pp. 38–40.

7. Ibid., p. 49.

of mule trains over vehicular traffic. The *consulados* of Mexico City and Veracruz had begun the reconstruction of two separate routes between Puebla and Veracruz, but neither survived the devastation of the independence wars.[8]

The governments of independent Mexico did not command the resources required to restore and improve the highway system. Until the creation of the *Secretaría de Fomento* in 1853, the old viceregal highway system was administered by a dependency of the Ministry of Foreign Relations.[9] What little was spent on highway maintenance in the first three decades after independence (1821–1852) came mainly from tolls (*peajes*) collected from highway users by private contractors who agreed to use a part of the revenues for essential maintenance and repair work. The performance of these contractors, according to the new *Fomento* ministry's account, left much to be desired.[10] The organization of a new General Administration of Roads and Tolls in 1853 had little effect. The federal government in the first Juárez administration (1856–1862), asserted responsibility for eight major highway routes, reorganized the administration of tolls, and began to supervise maintenance work more closely. Repair and construction expenditures were limited, however, to the Mexico City–Veracruz highway, the road from the capital to Guadalajara, and short stretches of major routes in the vicinity of the Valley of Mexico.[11] Major highway projects (and railroad construction) were initiated by the French invaders after 1862, partly for military purposes.[12] During the brief tenure of the imperial government (1862–1867), rela-

8. Ibid., pp. 48–49; and Sergio Ortiz Hernán Lozano, "Caminos y Transportes en México a fines de la colonia y principios de la independencia" (Tesis de licenciatura, Universidad Nacional Autónoma de México, 1970), pp. 101–6, 258–62.

9. *MF, 1857*, p. 7.

10. Ibid., pp. 7–11.

11. "Noticia general sobre el estado que guardan los caminos y peajes consignados a la administración general del ramo: 1857," in ibid., pp. 1–40, contains, together with the reports and documents which follow, a description of the amounts spent and the repair and construction work undertaken by the *secretaría* during the years 1853 to 1857.

12. Ministerio de Fomento, *Memoria presentada a S.M. El Emperador por el Ministro de Fomento, Luiz Robles Pezuela, de los trabajos ejecutados en su ramo, el año de 1865* (Mexico, 1866), 501 ff; hereafter cited *MF, 1865*.

tively large expenditures amounting in 1865 to more than $1,200,000 were consumed in repair and improvement projects along the same routes which had been given priority under the republican administration.[13] Once restored, the Republic, too, allocated large sums for the highway network in 1868 and 1869, and even increased the list of routes eligible for federal funds.[14] But the lack of resources and the high cost of maintaining order in the face of repeated *pronunciamientos* and revolts paralyzed road work for months and years at a time until Porfirio Díaz seized power in 1877.

Inheriting a miserably primitive transport system, the Porfirian regime also began by allocating funds to highway improvements. Between 1877 and 1884, the federal government annually spent between $130,000 and $270,000 for repair and new construction.[15] Since tolls had been formally abolished by Juárez in 1867, it is impos-

13. Ibid., p. 501.

14. Compare the list of federal highways in *MF, 1857, MF, 1865,* and those contained in the *Memorias* of the Secretaría de Fomento in the period of the Restored Republic (cited below). For allocation of funds in 1868 and 1869, see Secretaría de Fomento, *Memoria que el Secretario de Estado y del Despacho de Fomento, Colonización, Industria y Comercio de la República Mexicana presenta al Congreso de la Unión, correspondiente al año trascurrido de 1º de julio de 1868 al 30 de junio de 1869* (Mexico, 1870), pp. 15–49; hereafter cited *MF, 1868–69.* During the two fiscal years ending 30 June 1872 and 1873, the Fomento ministry was paralyzed except for the irregular expenditure of small funds for repair work on major routes: Secretaría de Fomento, *Memoria que el Secretario de Estado y del Despacho de Fomento, Colonización, Industria y Comercio de la República Mexicana presenta al Congreso de la Unión, conteniendo documentos hasta el 30 de junio de 1873* (Mexico, 1873), p. 3; hereafter cited as *MF, 1872–73.* The next *Memoria* of the Fomento ministry was not published until 1877, after Díaz's coup d'etat. In the reports published here, ministry officials and federal highway directors indicate general paralysis of work on most federal roads during most of 1875 and 1876, with work on some routes still suspended as late as the fall of 1877: Secretaría de Fomento, *Memoria presentada al Congreso de la Unión por el Secretario de Estado y del Despacho de Fomento, Colonización, Industria y Comercio de la República Mexicana, Vicente Riva Palacio, correspondiente al año transcurrido de diciembre de 1876 a noviembre 1877* (Mexico, 1877), pp. 59–64, 74–232; hereafter cited as *MF, 1876–77.*

15. For data on actual expenditures, as opposed to sums budgeted but seldom appropriated or spent, the reports of the directors of the federal highways annexed to the *Memorias* of the Fomento ministry are indispensable. For the year ending 30 November 1877, see *MF, 1876–77,* cited above. For expenditures from 1 December 1877 to 31 December 1882, see Secre-

sible to say whether Porfirian expenditures really exceeded the combined expenditures of prewar contractors and ministries. Despite the growing list of federal "highways," the funds available were too small to be distributed throughout the system, and expenditures had to be limited to "the highways in the central states, and the ones which communicate with the principal ports."[16] Table 2.1 lists the roads for which the federal government had assumed responsibility by 1877, the year in which the federal highway system reached its greatest extension. As the table suggests, federal responsibility for roads may have represented a long-term commitment to improvements to restore or extend vehicular traffic, but the realities reported by the federal highway directors indicate how small had been the progress achieved during the decade of the Restored Republic.[17] More than half of all federal "highways" were suitable only for beasts of burden, while one stretch on the Ciudad Victoria–Matamoros highway consisted of a trail so narrow and broken that the road's director reported it usable for pedestrian traffic alone.[18] Recent accounts of the highway system in this era have suggested that vast sums and major expansions were undertaken. The evidence cited has consisted of (1) the increase in the list of routes approved by Congress as federal highways and (2) the proposed highway expenditure budgets submitted to Congress during the period.[19] In fact, listing routes did not

taría de Fomento, *Memoria presentada al Congreso de la Unión por el Secretario de Estado y del Despacho de Fomento, Colonización, Industria y Comercio de la República Mexicana, General Carlos Pacheco, corresponde a los años transcurridos de diciembre de 1877 a diciembre de 1882,* 4 vols. (Mexico, 1885), vol. 2; hereafter cited as *MF, 1877–82.* For highway expenditures from 1883 to 30 June 1885, see Secretaría de Fomento, *Memoria presentada al Congreso de la Unión por el Secretario de Estado y del Despacho de Fomento, Colonización, Industria y Comercio de la República Mexicana, General Carlos Pacheco, corresponde a los años transcurridos de enero de 1883 a junio de 1885,* 5 vols. (Mexico, 1887), 5:5–234; hereafter cited, *MF, 1882–85.*

16. *MF, 1877–82* 2:5.

17. Compare the number of federal highways listed in *MF, 1868–69,* pp. 15–49, with those in *MF, 1876–77,* pp. 60–64.

18. See the reports of the federal highway directors in the *Memorias* of the Fomento ministry already cited.

19. The most complete account of the federal highway system during the Restored Republic is in Calderón, *La vida económica,* pp. 572–608. Calderón's study suffers from the errors indicated above.

TABLE 2.1

*Federal Highways, 1877 Distances
(kilometers)*

Highway Route	Wheeled Vehicles	Mules Only	Total
1. México–Guanajuato	370.0	—	370.0
2. Guanajuato–Guadalajara	305.5	—	305.5
*3. Querétaro–San Luis Potosí	242.8	—	242.8
4. Cuautitlán–San Juan del Río	131.3	—	131.3
5. Dolores–Guanajuato	—	64.2	64.2
6. San Luis Potosí–Durango(a)	207.8	335.2	543.0
7. Ojo Caliente–Lagos	—	192.1	192.1
8. San Luis Potosí–Tampico(b)	342.4	120.8	463.2
9. Guadalajara–Manzanillo	285.3	30.1	315.4
10. Zacatecas–Mazatlán	406.2	131.5	537.7
11. Guadalajara–San Blas	285.9	—	285.9
12. Morelia–Zihuatanejo	58.7	423.2	481.9
13. Morelia–Cuitzeo	—	32.8	32.8
14. San Luis Potosí–Saltillo	——— NO REPORT ———		
15. Matehuala–Linares	—	261.5	261.5
16. Morelia–Guadalajara	228.6	515.9	744.5
17. Querétaro–Tampico	——— NO REPORT ———		
18. Saltillo–Matamoros	——— NO REPORT ———		
19. Saltillo–Piedras Negras	——— NO REPORT ———		
20. México–Palmillas	118.0	370.4	488.4
*21. México–Pisaflores	——— NO REPORT ———		
22. México–Toluca–Morelia	380.5	—	380.5
23. México–Puebla–Tehuacán–Esperanza	287.7	—	287.7
24. México–Tampico(c)	47.2	—	47.2
25. México–Tuxpan	51.3	272.1	323.4
26. México–Acapulco	39.0	472.2	511.2
27. Tehuacán–Oaxaca–Puerto Angel	—	472.9	472.9
28. Huaumantla–Nautla	—	179.8	179.8
29. Tula (Tamps.)–Matamoros(d)	—	533.1	533.1

TABLE 2.1 (*cont.*)

Highway Route	Wheeled Vehicles	Mules Only	Total
30. Jalisco–San Marcos	128.2	—	128.2
31. Amozoc–Veracruz	253.7	—	253.7
32. Guatemalan Border–Tonalá	— NO REPORT —		
33. Campeche roads	34.9	51.7	87.6
34. Yucatán roads	21.2	14.4	35.6
Totals	4226.4	4474.0	8700.4

Source: *MF, 1877–82*, passim.
Note: Totals may be off due to rounding.
*Indicates road suffers considerably during rainy season, usually for lack of proper drainage; suitable for vehicles only part of the year.
(a) Zacatecas–Durango stretch abandoned until 1881.
(b) Opened for wheeled traffic to Tantoyoquito, 1878.
(c) Part way by rail.
(d) 66.5 kilometers too rough for mules—human porters only.

change their condition and the *Secretaría de Fomento* normally spent far less than the sums budgeted for the road system.[20]

Federal road expenditures were supplemented by local resources in the form of state funds, labor contributed by municipalities, and, in at least one case, by an association of merchants and property owners who donated money and equipment.[21] The sum of these local

20. In fiscal 1876–1877, for example, the Fomento ministry budgeted an expenditure of $1,564,400 on the road system. The *Memoria* published in 1877, covering the period from 1 December 1876 to 30 November 1877, contains highway directors' reports which indicate actual expenditures of $72,812.09. *MF, 1876–77*, pp. 60–64, 73–153, 164–232.

21. A company of "property owners and merchants" of San Luis Potosí and Tampico, formed in 1870, donated nearly $40,000 to the costs of constructing a highway between San Luis Potosí and Tantoyoquito on the Río Tamesí, a distance of 212 kilometers. The Tamesí, after cleared of logs and debris, proved navigable for the small steamer which ran the remaining 120 kilometers to Tampico. *MF, 1876–77*, pp. 168–74, contains a summary history of the highway as well as the director's report on the progress of construction. The total cost of transforming the trails and short stretches of wagon road between these two points into a highway suitable for vehicular traffic came to $217,085.47, of which the federal government contributed

contributions probably far exceeded the outlays of the federal government, but their impact was for the most part confined to unarticulated stretches of road with little effect on long distance transport conditions. Occasionally, such contributions improved federal highways for short distances, but the motive and the effect of such activities did not go far.[22]

With the development of the railroads, federal highway expenditures dwindled. As soon as a rail link was forged between towns on a federal highway, state and local governments were required to assume responsibility for maintenance and repairs. By the mid-1890s, federal highway expenditures had diminished to less than $20,000 per year.[23] Ten years later, the annual reports of the *Secretaría de Comunicaciones y Obras Públicas* had begun to include a special section devoted to *"Revindicaciones de Caminos Nacionales,"* reporting legal efforts by federal authorities to recover sections of the national highway network which had been occupied (and frequently cultivated) by local residents.[24] Deterioration of the national roads advanced very far with the diversion of funds and attention to the development of railroads.

---

somewhat more than half, the private company over a quarter, and the state government of San Luis Potosí the remainder. The highway was completed early in 1878 and officially opened on the fifth of May. *MF, 1877–82* 2:13–14, 343–437.

22. There is no convenient account of the road building and maintenance activities of state and local governments. Their infrequent contributions to the improvement of parts of the federal highway system are mentioned in the *Memorias* of the Fomento ministry cited above.

23. Secretaría de Comunicaciones y Obras Públicas, *Memoria presentada al Congreso de la Unión por el Secretario de Estado y del Despacho de Comunicaciones y Obras Públicas, General Francisco Z. Mena, corresponde a los años transcurridos de 1° de julio de 1891 a 30 de junio de 1896* (Mexico, 1899); hereafter cited *MSCOP, 1891–96.*

24. The Ministry of Communications and Public Works commissioned an engineer in 1906 to undertake the *"revindicación"* of federal property illegally occupied. Accounts of this work are found in the *Memorias* of the ministry beginning in 1907: Secretaría de Comunicaciones y Obras Públicas, *Memoria presentada al Congreso de la Unión por el Secretario de Estado y del Despacho de Comunicaciones y Obras Públicas de la República Mexicana, Ingeniero Leandro Fernández, corresponde al período de 1° de julio de 1906 a 30 de junio de 1907* (Mexico, 1908), pp. 7–9; hereafter cited *MSCOP, 1906–07.*

Coastal Shipping

Mexico is almost completely lacking in navigable waterways. Lake traffic in the Valley of Mexico and on Lake Chapala near Guadalajara was significant only for local trade.[25] A portion of the Río Tamesí from Tantoyoquito to the port of Tampico was heavily used for a short time after the completion of the federal highway from San Luis Potosí in 1878, but the completion of a rail line in 1889 all the way to the port effectively eliminated this traffic.[26] Several other estuaries were navigable for short distances between the Gulf coast and the foot of the Sierra Madre Oriental, but a negligible portion of the nation's commerce made use of them. Along the Pacific coast, possibilities of water transport were eliminated by the absence of a coastal plain. The mountains rose directly from the sea, and the rivers that cascaded down their sides could not have been made navigable.[27]

Slightly more important was the development of coastal shipping. Very little information about this activity has survived. What evidence there is suggests that it played a small role in prerail Mexico. Although Mexican law reserved the coasting trade for Mexican vessels, the federal government, in its efforts to promote the country's international communications, granted subsidies to foreign-owned shipping companies willing to make regular calls at Mexican ports.[28] A substantial portion of the coasting trade apparently involved the distribution of imports to smaller ports in exchange for exports brought back for transfer to ocean-going vessels at the larger ports. Sisal from Yucatán, for example, was first transported to Veracruz largely in exchange for foreign goods unloaded there from ocean vessels. The beginning of regular service by ocean vessels at Sisal, and later Pro-

25. Matías Romero, *Geographical and Statistical Notes on Mexico* (New York, 1891), pp. 32–34.

26. *MF, 1877–82* 2:13–14.

27. Matías Romero, *Notes*, pp. 33–34.

28. Subsidies granted to international shipping companies are described in Calderón, *La vida económica*, pp. 543–59. Occasionally, the restrictions preventing participation of foreign-owned international steamship companies in the coasting trade were relaxed, always with deleterious effects on the coasting traders. See Ermilo Coello Salazar, "El comercio interior," in Cosío Villegas, ed., *Historia moderna de México: El Porfiriato, La vida económica*, vol. 2, pp. 779–80.

greso, reduced the coasting trade considerably.[29] Aside from the cost of transferring freight from coastal to ocean vessels, observers noted that coastal shipping rates were normally three times the rate charged by ocean vessels over equal distances.[30]

The coasting trade never accounted for a significant portion of Mexico's domestic commerce. Miguel Lerdo de Tejada listed a total of forty-seven small vessels with a total displacement of 3,332 tons involved in the coasting trade of the Gulf of Mexico in 1854.[31] In 1862, the number of vessels in the coasting trade in both the Gulf and the Pacific was estimated at eighty-six with an average displacement of slightly less than one hundred tons.[32] Thirty years later, the Mexican Railway's annual reports distinguished the quantity of freight shipped on the line which originated or was destined for the coasting trade. Between 1894 and 1910, this figure varied from over 8,000 to slightly under 20,000 tons. The total tonnage shipped by the Mexican Railway during these years was usually over fifty, and frequently more than one hundred, times as great as the tonnage of freight listed for the coasting trade.[33]

With most of the population concentrated on the plateaus and valleys of the Mesa Central, and lacking even one navigable river to either coast, water routes offered no alternative to overland transport. Certainly the coasting trade could not have absorbed more than a negligible quantity of the freight and passengers actually carried by rail during the *Porfiriato*. The patterns of railroad transport give little support to the hypothesis that railroads displaced coasting vessels in the carriage of freight within Mexico.

29. Miguel M. Lerdo de Tejada, *Apuntos históricos de la heróica ciudad de Vera-Cruz* (Mexico: Imprenta de Vicente García Torres, 1858) 3:54–55; Calderón, *La vida económica*, p. 554.

30. Calderón, *La vida económica*, p. 557.

31. M. Lerdo de Tejada, *Apuntos históricos*, pp. 55–56.

32. José María Pérez Hernández, *Estadística de la República Mejicana* (Guadalajara: Tip. del Gobierno, a cargo de Antonio de P. González, 1862), p. 168.

33. The data on the composition of freight on the Mexican Railway are found in the appropriate files of *AHSCT*, Mexico City.

Ocean Shipping

The railroad's contribution to the carriage of international freight between Mexico and the United States, however, is a somewhat different matter. There is evidence that the first of the major trunk lines from the Valley of Mexico to the U.S. border (the Mexican Central) initially established extremely low rates for international freight in order to divert goods from the water route through the Gulf of Mexico to Veracruz where the competing Mexican Railway linked the port with Mexico City. These low rates subjected the Mexican Central to scathing denunciation in the press, especially for charging lower rates on U.S. imports than for competing Mexican products, and resulted in the publication of a report by a Commission of the Ministry of *Fomento* charging the company with illegal rate manipulation.[34] Both the Central and the Mexican National, whose trunk line to the U.S. border was not completed until 1889, collaborated with their U.S. parent companies in evading Mexican rate regulations by fixing low through-rates for passengers and freight between shipping points in Mexico and the United States.[35] The Mexican Railway, which operated the line between Mexico City and Veracruz, suffered a rapid decline in traffic and was forced to reduce its rates drastically after completion of the Central's north-south trunk line in 1884.[36] The Central and the National may also have diverted freight previously carried by mule train or wagon from the central plateau to the smaller Gulf coast ports.

Table 2.2 indicates the percentage of exports that passed through the customshouses of Mexico in the period 1877–1878 to 1910–1911. The data suggest an initial diversion of traffic to the northern frontier from the Gulf ports, especially from Veracruz. Gulf ports account

34. See the report of the commission appointed by the Secretaría de Fomento to review the new classification and rate schedule proposed by the Central in 1884 printed in *MF, 1883–85* 2:559–70. The Commissioners estimated that the rates charged on the northern section of the line had been set illegally at a discount of up to 50 percent. Ibid., p. 564. Public controversy in the Mexican press over alleged favoritism to U.S. importers is reported in the *Mexican Financier* (Mexico City), 15 July 1884.

35. Ibid.

36. See appendix I, and "The Mexican Railway in 1885," *Railroad Gazette* (4 June 1886), p. 384.

TABLE 2.2
Distribution of Exports by Customshouse and Region, 1878–1911
(*Percent of Total Exports*)

	1878	1879	1880	1881	1882	1883	1884	1885	1886	1887	1888	1889
Veracruz	62.3	60.9	58.7	51.5	51.5	57.3	53.9	42.2	40.0	41.1	33.0	32.6
Tampico	3.6	3.4	5.4	4.2	4.0	3.1	2.3	1.9	2.0	1.6	1.5	1.1
All Gulf Coast Ports	77.3	79.2	77.9	73.7	74.2	75.5	72.0	58.9	55.7	57.3	53.3	50.3
Cuidad Juárez	0.1	—	0.1	—	0.3	2.1	5.4	21.1	24.3	21.6	24.7	25.9
Cuidad Porfirio Díaz	—	—	—	0.4	0.4	0.3	0.5	1.1	1.8	1.0	1.8	3.7
Laredo	0.1	0.8	1.3	0.8	0.9	2.9	4.3	3.1	3.1	2.9	2.5	3.8.
All Northern Frontier	1.3	2.4	2.5	2.4	2.4	6.5	12.6	27.6	31.1	27.7	31.1	34.7

	1890	1891	1892	1893	1894	1895	1896	1897	1898	1899	1900	1901
Veracruz	32.2	32.6	35.1	32.1	29.0	30.2	21.3	20.2	21.5	20.5	17.0	14.7
Tampico	1.2	1.7	4.8	10.1	13.8	17.1	22.8	26.9	28.3	29.4	26.7	29.5
All Gulf Coast Ports	51.2	51.6	53.1	56.0	56.1	59.7	56.6	58.8	62.8	67.0	65.9	59.6

TABLE 2.2 (cont.)

	1890	1891	1892	1893	1894	1895	1896	1897	1898	1899	1900	1901
Cuidad Juárez	24.2	22.7	22.4	19.2	19.9	15.8	18.7	16.1	15.2	10.3	11.5	14.4
Cuidad Porfirio Díaz	4.0	4.3	4.0	2.7	3.4	3.1	2.9	2.6	2.4	2.2	1.6	4.2
Laredo	4.9	5.3	6.4	7.5	5.8	3.3	3.1	3.3	3.2	4.7	3.6	4.7
All Northern Frontier	34.5	33.9	34.3	31.5	30.8	25.8	30.5	28.3	27.1	23.9	22.5	30.7

	1902	1903	1904	1905	1906	1907	1908	1909	1910	1911
Veracruz	15.7	20.5	20.7	18.0	24.3	19.6	18.5	16.8	15.3	18.3
Tampico	29.0	30.0	30.1	34.5	28.6	32.5	36.0	32.4	31.9	31.5
All Gulf Coast Ports	65.4	69.8	69.3	68.9	66.1	67.6	68.1	62.7	59.4	62.7
Cuidad Juárez	6.8	7.4	7.9	5.0	9.9	7.9	8.7	7.5	11.1	10.0
Cuidad Porfirio Díaz	3.7	4.0	3.1	3.4	6.6	6.0	5.6	5.8	8.6	7.2
Laredo	5.4	6.4	5.7	7.0	5.8	3.9	4.0	10.1	6.7	8.4
All Northern Frontier	27.0	24.8	22.5	22.2	27.9	24.3	23.9	30.0	24.9	32.6

Source: El Colegio de México, *Estadísticas económicas del Porfiriato: Comercio exterior de México 1877–1911* (Mexico: El Colegio de México, 1960), pp. 480, 485–86, 489, 491.

for 72.0 percent of all exports in 1883–1884. At the end of this fiscal year, the Central opened its direct line to the United States and the Gulf ports' share of exports dropped in the next twelve months to 58.9 percent. In the same period, the customshouses on the northern land border increased their share from 12.6 to 27.6 percent. Gulf ports lost about $6 million worth of freight, while an increase of $7 million was recorded by the northern customshouses. Initially, then, some freight which had previously been shipped overland to the Gulf coast was probably diverted to rail transport for its journey to the United States.

A closer examination of the data suggests, however, that most of the freight diverted from Gulf ports was freight which developed initially in response to construction activity on the two north-south trunk lines. Terms of the concessions awarded to the Central and National companies required that construction begin simultaneously from Mexico City and the northern border.[37] For the years from 1881 to 1883, export freight on the southern portion of these lines was shipped back to Mexico City and down the Mexican Railway to Veracruz.[38] Much of this freight, which could not have borne the cost of wagon or mule transport to Mexico City, represented a temporary increase in Veracruz exports, which revived for two years the old port's previously declining share of the nation's export trade. On completion of the Central, most of this new freight simply changed directions. The actual export data show a rapid expansion of exports through Veracruz from a low of $15.0 million in 1881–1882 to a high of $25.1 million in 1883–1884. From this high, exports through Veracruz declined for two years to $17.4 million in 1885–1886, a level still higher than before the north-south construction had begun, despite the sharp reduction in world trade which reached a cyclical low point in mid-1885 and did not recover until the following year.[39]

37. Mexican Central Railway Company, Ltd., *Introductory Report, Massachusetts Laws, Mexican Concessions, By Laws* (Boston, 1881); and Secretaría de Fomento, *The Main Concession (September 13, 1880) of the Mexican National Construction Company (Palmer-Sullivan Contract) as reviewed and modified by the law of January 11, 1883* (Mexico, 1882).

38. For comments on this increase in traffic, see Mexican Railway Company, Ltd., *Annual Reports, 1881–1884* (London, 1882–1885).

39. The U.S. economy reached a trough in May 1885; Arthur F. Burns and Wesley C. Mitchell, *Measuring Business Cycles* (New York: National Bureau of Economic Research, 1946), p. 78.

Nevertheless, a permanent increase in the proportion of Mexico's exports which crossed the northern land border with the United States did occur. From less than 2 percent of all exports, the customshouses of the north increased their share to a high of 34.7 percent by fiscal year 1889–1890. It is not possible to estimate how much of this increased land commerce with the United States would have continued by shifting freight to water shipment from the Gulf ports in the absence of the railroads. This unanswered question is significant for the analysis of railroad social savings because it affects the specification of an appropriate alternative to the railroads. If a substantial portion of the railroad's freight should be expected to shift to using less land and more sea transport, then specifying an exclusively overland alternative to the railroads will bias the resulting social savings estimates by exaggerating the cost of the nonrail alternative.[40] Water transport was notoriously cheaper, even if slower, than either wagon or rail freight carriage.[41]

Fortunately, this problem is less serious than it appears because of evidence that indicates that by 1910, and perhaps as early as 1889, the quantity of overland freight services could not have been reduced by diversion of goods to sea transport. In 1889, the Central branch line to Tampico was completed, uniting the major population and production centers north of Mexico City with their nearest Gulf coast port.[42] From this year forward, the percentage of freight passing over the northern land border began to diminish. From a high of 34.7 percent of all exports, the share of the northern customshouses diminished slowly to 22.5 percent a decade later. At the same time, the share of the Gulf coast ports, which had dropped to its lowest level in the same year (50.3 percent in 1888–1889), began a recovery which peaked at a high of 67.0 percent exactly ten years afterward.

40. This observation implies the assumption of zero price elasticity of demand for transportation. In the nonzero case, the assumption of an exclusively overland alternative to the railroad would tend to overstate the reduction in demand for transportation in the hypothetical nonrailroad economy and thus yield less exaggerated savings figures.

41. For rail and wagon freight rates, see chapter 4. For nineteenth-century coastal shipping rates, see M. Lerdo de Tejada, *Apuntos históricos*, pp. 70–71.

42. The report of the opening of the Tampico branch is found in Mexican Central Railway Company Ltd., *Tenth Annual Report, 1889* (Boston, 1890), p. 5.

The shift back to the Gulf, and the dramatic increase in the importance of Tampico (see table 2.2) after 1889 suggests that when the railroads had finished replicating the major prerail highway links to the Gulf ports, all those shippers who could profitably use water transport to the United States hastened to do so. After 1889, the output of overland freight services could not have been reduced without reducing the quantities shipped because railroad transport patterns already reflected the desire of inland shippers to take advantage of cheaper water carriage whenever it was feasible. A permanent increase in overland traffic did occur in the north, largely because of the rapid development of the northern mining and cattle industries, but not because of railroad competition with Gulf shipping to the United States.

This conclusion is supported by the history of railroad pooling arrangements first attempted in 1892. The pools involved the four major carriers of international freight. In addition to the Mexican, the Central, and the National, the Interoceanic was included in the pools, having opened a second rail link between Mexico City and Veracruz in 1891.[43] Through-rates were fixed and freight apportioned between competing points in Mexico served by two or more of the companies and the Gulf ports through which European and United States goods entered.[44] A separate pool was attempted for exclusively overland freight originating in or destined to the U.S. Southwest.[45] The fact that the Gulf ports and land border pools were separated without any protest from the two companies (the Mexican and the Interoceanic) that had no land connections with the northern border suggests that little if any overland competition existed for freight from water shipment points in the United States by the early 1890s.

While the distribution of freight between overland and water shipment would not have been affected after 1889 by the disappear-

43. The report of the opening of the Interoceanic's line from Mexico City to Veracruz is found in Interoceanic Railway of Mexico (Acapulco to Veracruz) Ltd., *Annual Report, 1892* (London, 1893), p. 4.

44. Pool arrangements are reported in the *Economist* 52 (13 August 1892): 1033; 53 (1 June 1893):712; 54 (31 October 1896): 1421; and 57 (6 May 1899): 649; and the *South American Journal* (11 November 1893), p. 492.

45. *Economist* 57 (6 May 1899):649.

ance of Mexico's railroads, the magnitude of overland freight would certainly have diminished in the absence of rail connections with U.S. lines. A portion of the social savings attributed in this study to Mexican railroads hinged upon these U.S. rail links, because a large part of the Mexican traffic carried to the border would not have developed without rail links to points deep inside the United States. This fact raises no analytical difficulties, however, because Mexico's major border links were constructed by U.S.-based firms intimately tied to precisely those U.S. interests that had undertaken railroad construction through Texas to the Rio Grande.[46] Without the U.S. lines, the Mexican north-south trunk lines might have been delayed for years, or never constructed at all. Thus, it appears entirely reasonable to treat the connecting U.S. railroads as exogenous to the present study, since without them, the Mexican lines would not have been constructed in the first place.

The First Railroads

The first railroad concession granted by the Mexican federal government was awarded to a wealthy Veracruz merchant who promised, in exchange for a thirty-year monopoly on the Veracruz to Mexico City route, to carry mail free of charge and to pay $50,000 annually to the federal government after the first ten years of the line's operation.[47] After the initial concession was revoked for failure

46. On the U.S. connections of the Mexican Central and the Mexican National, see Arthur M. Johnson and Barry E. Supple, *Boston Capitalists and Western Railroads: A Study in the Nineteenth Century Railroad Investment Process* (Cambridge, Mass.: Harvard University Press, 1967), pp. 300, 302; Julius Grodinsky, *Transcontinental Railway Strategy, 1869–1893: A Study of Businessmen* (Philadelphia: University of Pennsylvania Press, 1962), pp. 162, 166, 214; *Railroad Gazette* (23 July 1880), p. 398; (26 November 1880), p. 637; (13 January 1888), p. 31. The Central was linked to the Atcheson, Topeka, and Santa Fe system, while the National initially formed part of the railroad empire of financier Jay Gould.

47. Francisco Arrillaga, *Proyecto del primer camino de hierro de la República desde el puerto de Veracruz a la capital de México* (Mexico, 1837), pp. 4–7; Vicente Fuentes Díaz, *El problema ferrocarrilero*, pp. 8–10; Chapman, "Steam Enterprise and Politics," chapter 2.

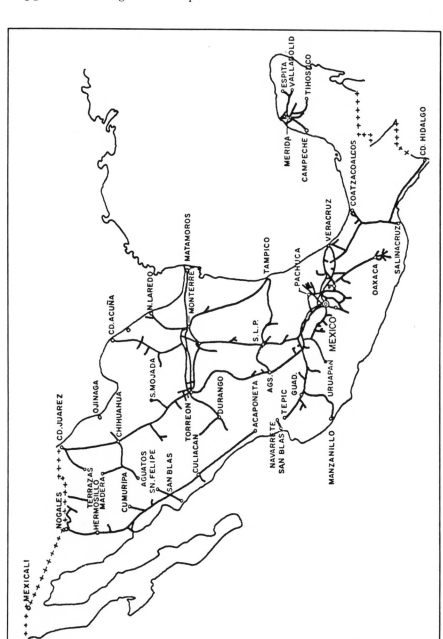

MAP 2.1
Mexican Railroad System, 1910

to begin construction by the stipulated time, a series of concessions for a rail link between Veracruz and the capital proved equally fruitless.[48] Not until 1873 was Mexico City finally linked by rail to Veracruz. The Mexican Railway, as the line was called, had cost more than twelve times the $5,000,000 estimated by the first concessionaire.[49] More than half the cost of constructing the line had been covered by subsidies paid to the company by the federal government.[50]

Mexico's railroad boom did not actually begin until 1880. In that year, two concessions for major trunk lines linking Mexico City with the northern border were awarded to competing groups of North American entrepreneurs.[51] The data in table 2.3 show clearly why the era of Porfirio Díaz has become synonymous with the era of the railroad in Mexican history.

When Díaz seized power in 1877, Mexico boasted no more than 640 kilometers of railroad track, of which 424 belonged to the Mexican Railway and another 114 employed mules rather than steam engines for motive power.[52] The governments of the Restored Republic had been unable to entice foreign investors with concessions Congress was willing to approve and unsuccessful in attracting substantial domestic capital to railroad construction.[53] For its first three years, the Porfirian regime proved equally unsuccessful. Without foreign capital, railroad progress was slow. The government adopted two methods of promoting construction in this period. First, public

48. Gustavo Baz and E. L. Gallo, *Historia del Ferrocarril Mexicano* (Mexico: Gallo y Cía., 1874), pp. 3–16; David Pletcher, "The Building of the Mexican Railway," *HAHR* 30, no. 1 (February 1950):26–62.

49. Estimates of the real cost of constructing the line from Veracruz to Mexico City have varied. Still more varied and controversial have been attempts to estimate the magnitude of public monies granted succeeding companies in subsidies. The best survey of the evidence is found in Calderón, *La vida económica*, pp. 631–35.

50. Juan C. Adorno, *Informe al Secretario de Comunicaciones y Obras Públicas* (MS, dated 1879 in AHSCT, 1/138); Calderón, *La vida ecónomica*, pp. 630–36.

51. See concessions cited in footnote 37 above.

52. Francisco R. Calderón, "Los ferrocarriles," in Cosío Villegas, ed., *Historia moderna de México: El Porfiriato, La vida económica*, vol. 2, p. 516. These figures omit urban and suburban lines under federal concession as well as all lines constructed under state concessions.

53. Calderón, *La vida económica*, pp. 698–732; Calderón, "Los ferrocarriles," pp. 488–504.

TABLE 2.3

Expansion of Railroads Under Federal Concession, 1873–1910

Year	Constructed During Year (kilometers)	Annual Increase (%)	Total (kilometers)
1873	—	—	572
1874	14	2.4	586
1875	76	13.0	662
1876	4	0.6	666
1877	34	5.1	684
1878	65	9.5	749
1879	144	19.2	893
1880	193	21.6	1,086
1881	575	52.9	1,661
1882	1,922	115.7	3,583
1883	1,725	48.1	5,308
1884	436	8.2	5,744
1885	122	2.1	5,866
1886	76	1.3	5,942
1887	1,738	29.2	7,680
1888	29	0.4	7,709
1889	599	7.7	8,308
1890	1,250	15.0	9,558
1891	306	3.2	9,864
1892	436	4.4	10,300
1893	165	1.6	10,465
1894	120	1.1	10,585
1895	20	0.2	10,605
1896	259	2.4	10,864
1897	666	6.1	11,530
1898	565	4.9	12,095
1899	374	3.1	12,469
1900	1,071	8.6	13,540
1901	908	6.7	14,448
1902	612	4.2	15,060
1903	978	6.5	16,038
1904	409	2.6	16,447

TABLE 2.3 (*cont.*)

Year	Constructed During Year (kilometers)	Annual Increase (%)	Total (kilometers)
1905	411	2.5	16,858
1906	577	3.4	17,435
1907	558	3.2	17,993
1908	545	3.0	18,538
1909	429	2.3	18,967
1910	238	1.3	19,205

Sources: Fernando González Roa, *El problema ferrocarrilera y la Compañía de los Ferrocarriles Nacionales de México* (Mexico: Carranza e Hijos, 1915), p. 30; Francisco Calderón, "Los Ferrocarriles," in *Historia moderna de México: El Porfiriato, La vida económica*, ed. by Daniel Cosío Villegas, vol. 1 (Mexico: Editorial Hermes, 1965), pp. 517, 541, 568, 629.

funds were invested directly in the construction of a short line between Tehuacán and Esperanza, the latter close to a station on the Mexican Railway.[54] Fifty-one kilometers in length, it used mules to pull small trains. The line cost under $6,000 per kilometer to construct, less than the cost of building a new highway between the two towns, and less even than the usual government subsidy to private entrepreneurs for the construction of steam trackage.[55]

More important, the government adopted a policy of granting railroad concessions to state governments. Some twenty states received a total of twenty-eight concessions for railroads between 1876 and 1880.[56] State governors usually received the concessions as the first step in efforts to bring together local capitalists who might be interested in such projects. As soon as sufficient capital had been pledged, a local company was formed to undertake the construction, and the concession then transferred to it.[57] In the four years during

54. Calderón, "Los ferrocarriles," pp. 488–502.
55. *MF, 1877–82* 3:717–18 and appended reports and documents, pp. 719–63; Manuel Téllez Pizarro, *Breves apuntes históricos sobre los ferrocarriles de la República Mexicana* (Mexico, 1906), pp. 17–18; Calderón, "Los ferrocarriles," p. 489.
56. Calderón, "Los ferrocarriles," pp. 491–502.
57. Ibid., pp. 491–500.

which this experiment was tested, eight of the twenty-eight concessions proved fruitful. Local companies constructed a total of 226
kilometers of track before North American capital arrived to construct the country's two major arteries.[58] The local companies demonstrated that Mexican capitalists, willing enough to participate in a
few small projects, could not be expected to risk their fortunes on the
kind of vast national construction programs that various foreign
groups promised. Still, some of the local lines had developed rapidly.
The railroad from Mexico City to Cuautla accounted for 96 of the
226 kilometers constructed by 1880, and an isolated stretch of 60
kilometers between Celaya and León had been built despite the cost
of transporting materials overland by wagon and mule from Mexico
City.[59] Two of the companies developed an ingenious way of tapping
the resources of small savers in a society almost entirely lacking in
financial institutions. The Mexico–Toluca–Cuautitlán and Mérida–
Progreso companies instituted railroad lotteries, selling lottery tickets
cheaply and applying to construction the excess of ticket revenues
over the prize monies distributed.[60] Nearly all of the local companies
ceased their activities shortly after the major concessions of 1880.
Several, including the Mexico–Toluca–Cuautitlán and the Celaya–
León lines, were simply absorbed by one of the new North American
firms.[61]

Railroad Growth in the *Porfiriato*

Descriptive accounts of Porfirian railroad growth abound, so there is
little need to give a detailed account here. On application to federal
authorities, railroad promoters received concessions that required
congressional approval.[62] The concessions usually indicated the ap-

58. Ibid., p. 500.

59. Ibid., pp. 494–95, 500.

60. Calderón, *La vida económica*, pp. 690–91; Carlos A. Echánove Trujillo,
ed., *Enciclopedia Yucatense*, 8 vols. (Mexico, 1944) 3:543.

61. Calderón, "Los ferrocarriles," p. 496.

62. After passage of the 1899 Railroad Law, congressional approval was
no longer required for each concession. Instead, the law specified new and
stricter conditions for the issuance of railroad concessions and established
priorities for the granting of government subsidies. "Ley sobre ferrocarriles," *Diario Oficial*, 13 May 1899.

proximate route to be followed, specified the amount and type of federal subsidy to be given, fixed time limits for the construction of sections of track, granted exemptions from most taxes (including import duties on construction materials and equipment), and set maximum tariffs for passengers and freight.[63] Other provisions established the right of the government to set and inspect construction and operating standards, the obligation of companies to supply free mail service and to carry official freight and passengers at low rates, a basis for condemnation proceedings for acquisition of rights of way, monopoly grants according to which the government agreed not to subsidize the construction of parallel lines for a stipulated period of time, the principle that the lines would revert to government ownership upon expiration of the concession (usually ninety-nine years), and limitations on the issuance of corporate stock and bonded debt up to a fixed maximum per kilometer of track. A large majority of the concessions issued were revoked for failure to begin construction within the stipulated time limits,[64] although the government could usually be persuaded to extend the time limits whenever the concessionaire appeared to have good prospects for initiating work soon.[65] The subsidies granted by the federal government were frequently supplemented by direct grants and other encouragements from state and local entities.[66] In addition to railroads constructed under concessions issued by the federal government, state governments frequently issued concessions for smaller lines, including urban trolley systems, short commuter lines from cities to nearby towns and villages, and feeder lines constructed by private firms and landowners.

63. Early railroad concessions are reprinted in the Fomento *Memorias* cited above. See also, "Ley de ferrocarriles," and Pablo Macedo, *Tres monografías*, pp. 206–7.

64. Calderón, "Los ferrocarriles," pp. 538–39; Fuentes Díaz, *El problema*, pp. 25–31.

65. Documents in the Fomento *Memorias* cited above include numerous decrees granting extensions of time limits. See also Calderón, *La vida económica*, p. 691.

66. No complete accounting of such grants is possible. Annual reports of the following companies indicate, often without specifying amounts, direct local or state assistance: the Central, National, Hidalgo y Nordeste, several of the Yucatán lines, and a number of smaller companies.

By 1910, commuter and feeder lines, many employing animal rather than steam traction, accounted for 7,850.6 kilometers of track.[67] In the same year, railroads under federal concession (excluding urban trolleys in the Federal District) totaled 19,738.5 kilometers in length.[68] This study is confined to the impact of the federal railroads. The state and local lines were not required to submit reports on their operations to federal authorities. While many of these lines no doubt provided a significant transport savings to their users, especially in the state of Yucatán where nearly a third of this local trackage was located, data on their operations could not be compiled without undertaking a research effort more costly than could be justified by anticipated results. These small lines had quite limited capacities for transporting freight or passengers and frequently, as in the case of Yucatán, spent most of the year idle.[69]

As table 2.3 indicates, railroad construction activity reached its highest point, both absolutely and relatively, in 1882. In the four years 1881 through 1883, the length of the railroad system increased from just over 1,000 to nearly 6,000 kilometers. High levels of activity can again be observed in 1887, 1890, and again in the four years beginning in 1900. After 1880, railroad construction hit low levels in 1885–1886, 1888, and 1893–1895. Toward the end of the *Porfiriato*, from 1904 to 1910, new construction diminished considerably in relative terms, although several hundred kilometers of track were built each year. Part of the reason for the slower rate of expansion lies in the untabulated efforts of several companies to complete double tracking and add sidings, but the addition of such efforts would not markedly affect the trend. It is possible, given the slower rate of growth of the export sector and of the economy as a whole, that by the early twentieth century, railroad expansion in Mexico had reached the point of diminishing returns. Export sector output provided the major portion of railroad freight.[70] Contemporary ob-

---

67. Secretaría de Fomento, *Boletín de la Dirección General de Estadística*, no. 1 (1912):64–65.

68. Ibid., pp. 55–63.

69. The local Yucatán lines were usually "portable," constructed chiefly for transportation of *henequén* on large plantations during harvest seasons.

70. See below, chapter 4.

servers, including responsible government officials, frequently commented upon the tendency of the railroad companies to concentrate their investments in certain regions where overbuilding of parallel lines resulted in "excessive" competition along favored routes while vast areas of the country remained isolated.[71]

Estimates of the output of the railroad industry show a similar slowdown in the last decade of the *Porfiriato*. Table 2.4 contains estimates of the total gross revenues earned by all steam-powered federal railroads for the years 1873 to 1910. Unfortunately, current peso data are not easily translated into constant peso equivalents. Three price indices are available for use, but none reflects the costs of producing rail transport adequately. All three indices were constructed by the Colegio de México's Seminar in the Modern History of Mexico.[72] The Mexico City Wholesale Price Index covers 1877 and 1886–1910. The Wholesale Price Index for the entire republic covers 1885–1908. The Export Price Index covers fiscal years ending 30 June from 1877 to 1911. The Export Price Index is used in table 2.4 as the basis for extrapolating the Mexico City Wholesale Price Index from 1878 to 1885, on the assumption that movements in the latter were proportional to movements in the export index lagged six months. The result of these attempts to derive 1900 constant peso estimates of railroad output is to deflate the apparently sizable increase in railroad revenues in the first decade of the twentieth century and to replace them with small to substantial declines in seven of the eleven years from 1900 through 1910. Volume estimates of freight traffic in Chapter 4 tend to confirm these results and lend support to the hypothesis of diminishing returns.[73] Mexico's short-lived railroad boom ended nearly a decade before the Porfirian regime fell to the revolutionaries in 1911.

71. Secretaría de Hacienda, *Memoria de Hacienda y Crédito Público correspondiente al año económico de 1º de julio de 1898 a 30 de junio de 1899 presentada por el secretario José I. Limantour al Congreso de la Unión* (Mexico, 1902), pp. 401–15 (hereafter cited *MH, 1898–99*) and Macedo, *Tres monografías*, pp. 208–23.

72. El Colegio de México, *Estadísticas económicas del Porfiriato, Comercio exterior de México, 1877–1911* (Mexico: El Colegio de México, 1960), p. 155; and El Colegio de México, *Estadísticas: Fuerza de trabajo*, pp. 156, 172.

73. See below, tables 4.3 and 4.4.

TABLE 2.4
Total Output of Mexican Railroads, 1873–1910
(in pesos)

Year	1	2	3	4
1873	1,848,336			
1874	2,387,262			
1875	2,489,804			
1876	2,265,883			
1877	2,844,826			4,140,940
1878	3,048,632	4,473,386		
1879	3,457,769	5,048,513		
1880	4,067,402	5,938,610		
1881	5,679,193	8,283,714		
1882	9,033,506	13,071,460		
1883	11,193,811	16,052,432		
1884	10,164,691	14,694,534		
1885	9,823,381	14,432,712	12,115,665	
1886	10,409,086		13,970,052	13,362,113
1887	12,249,695		16,462,432	17,804,790
1888	14,951,272		18,545,363	18,458,360
1889	17,485,146		21,894,748	19,983,024
1890	19,489,575		22,942,407	22,848,270
1891	22,280,478		22,612,888	26,274,149
1892	24,071,852		21,581,363	24,638,538
1893	24,270,166		24,517,796	22,961,368
1894	25,211,276		26,995,691	27,050,725
1895	27,651,774		28,894,225	29,701,153
1896	29,490,598		29,680,554	28,855,771
1897	34,915,413		39,266,097	33,964,410
1898	37,014,123		44,185,415	41,823,867
1899	44,315,641		48,940,520	51,831,159
1900	49,677,526			
1901	51,112,136		49,580,011	41,622,260
1902	56,282,991		51,456,382	46,591,880
1903	67,183,127		67,324,509	53,447,198
1904	70,070,573		64,456,419	65,609,151
1905	74,670,391		59,990,672	61,558,442

TABLE 2.4 (*cont.*)

Year	1	2	3	4
1906	83,314,199		66,428,161	61,305,518
1907	96,903,534		77,232,434	72,370,078
1908	89,094,381		67,649,492	67,546,915
1909	93,113,117			64,842,003
1910	103,544,884			62,489,368

(1) Current pesos
(2) Deflated by adjusted Export Price Index (1900–1901 = 100)
(3) Deflated by national Wholesale Price Index (1900 = 100)
(4) Deflated by Mexico City Wholesale Price Index (1900 = 100)
Source: Appendix I.

Porfirian Transport Policy

Initially, railroad development in Mexico served chiefly to fortify the new political regime by contributing mightily to the reduction in unemployment (and underemployment) of manpower and resources. Factors of production habitually combined for military and political strife were diverted to the construction of a modern infrastructure. The concession and regulatory policies pursued by Mexican governments in the 1880s united to the Porfirian regime the interests of *hacendados,* mine owners, and the most important merchants, many of whom had long lamented the lack of adequate transport facilities. In the political and social environment of Mexico at that time, the least dangerous concession policy from the point of view of the government was one that pledged public subsidies to almost any project no matter what its proposed route. In this way, the distribution of the benefits of transport development to the nation's property owners proceeded on the basis of private rather than official allocation. A government that granted concessions pledging public monies to the construction of almost any railroad proposed to it could not be faulted for the frequent failure of promoters to raise the necessary capital for construction. To the extent that the government acted on any priorities at all, it devoted its energies to a misguided search for private capitalists, domestic or foreign, willing to complete a line across the Isthmus of Tehuantepec.[74]

Liberality in the granting of concessions was a policy defended easily on grounds of its dramatic results. Thousands of kilometers of track were built and placed in operation within a very short span of years. The policy, as its official proponents asserted, involved a reliance on market forces and private, frequently foreign, institutions to determine the pattern of Mexico's transport development. The perceptions of foreign capitalists, and especially those of North American entrepreneurs projecting extensions of their U.S. interests, involved estimates of prospective private returns from investments in Mexico which could be harmonized with their previous commitments elsewhere.

By the end of the 1880s, railroad development had proceeded so far as to induce the establishment, in 1891, of a separate ministry responsible for Communications and Public Works. The creation of the new *secretaría* and the resulting increase in regulatory vigilance reflected the government's increasing awareness of the extent to which the nation's new export-oriented prosperity depended upon the railroads. Increased efforts were made to balance railroad returns with the necessary profitability of the growing export industries which the railroads served. The report of Finance Minister José Yves Limantour in 1898 on the nation's communications system proposed still more government intervention to provide better supervision over the existing rail network and to orient public incentives according to planned priorities for future railroad construction.[75] The need to harmonize the transport sector with the requirements of the na-

74. On concession policies see Calderón, "Los ferrocarriles," pp. 542, 569–70; Fernando González Roa, *El problema*, pp. 19–24, 27–37; and Limantour's comments in *MH, 1898–99*. On the history of the Tehuantepec line see Angel Peimbert, *El Ferrocarril Nacional de Tehuantepec, reseña histórica y resumen general de los trabajos llevados a cabo durante la administración de los señores S. Pearson and Son, Ltd., hasta el 31 de diciembre de 1906* (Mexico: Tipografía de la Dirección General de Telégrafos, 1908); Edward B. Glick, *Straddling the Isthmus of Tehuantepec* (Gainesville: University of Florida Press, 1959); Fred W. Powell, *The Railroads of Mexico* (Boston: Stratford Co., 1921), pp. 145–56.

75. *MH, 1898–99*, pp. 401–15.

tion's developing export industries, and the desire to maintain the nation's prosperity by extending transport innovation to more remote regions received major emphasis in Limantour's report.[76] The result of the minister's interest was a new railroad law, issued by the president after congressional authorization in the following year.[77]

An important consequence of the new law was the creation of a special Tariff Commission within the Communications and Public Works ministry. The commission's president and four regular members were appointed by the minister. The four appointed members were selected with a view toward adequate representation of shipping, especially export shipping interests. In addition, the commission included two railroad representatives, one representative chosen by the National Association of Chambers of Commerce, and one representative of the leading *hacendado*-dominated Agricultural Society. Only the regular members of the commission were allowed to vote on tariff revisions.[78] The commission's recommendations were almost invariably followed by the ministry in its dealings with the railroad companies.[79] Increased formal representation of shipping interests in the determination of railroad tariffs may help to explain why railroad revenues per ton kilometer declined sharply in 1901–1902 and failed to return to previous levels thereafter.[80]

Less than five years after the enactment of the 1899 Railroad Law, the Mexican finance minister again sought to increase government intervention in the railroad industry. In a series of actions between 1903 and 1910, the government negotiated purchase of a controlling interest in the nation's largest railway companies and absorbed a number of smaller firms in the process. The history of the "Mexicanization" of Mexico's railroads has conventionally received major em-

76. Ibid., pp. 410–14. See also Limantour's later comments in Secretaría de Hacienda, *Informe del Secretario de Hacienda y Crédito Público a las Cámaras Federales, sobre el uso de las facultades conferidas al Ejecutivo de la Unión por la ley de 26 de diciembre de 1906 para la consolidación de los Ferrocarriles Nacional de México y Central Mexicano* (Mexico, 1908), pp. 12–14.

77. "Ley sobre ferrocarriles."

78. Fuentes Díaz, *El problema*, pp. 36–44; Powell, *Railroads*, pp. 173–75; González Roa, *El problema*, pp. 35–37.

79. Powell, *Railroads*, p. 175.

80. See below, table 4.6.

phasis in the works of historians of the *Porfiriato*.[81] Limantour first moved to acquire a majority of shares in the nearly bankrupt Interoceanic line in 1903, then used Interoceanic stock and the proceeds of a foreign loan to secure control of the National in the same year, negotiated to achieve a controlling interest in the Central through another foreign loan and manipulation of the company's stock in 1906, and finally, in 1907, organized a new company, the National Railways of Mexico (*Ferrocarriles Nacionales de México*), to take charge of the Mexicanized lines. With the addition of lines acquired by the new company after 1907 and several previously owned by the government but operated independently, more than two thirds of Mexico's steam railroads under federal concession had been Mexicanized by 1910.[82]

At the beginning of the *Porfiriato*, the railroads had been viewed as indispensable initiators of growth. Once the rapid growth of the country had begun, the railroads came to be viewed as critical to continued success. In the early years, railroad companies had been beneficiaries of government policies designed, willy-nilly, to encourage investment. By the early 1890s, the very success of the railroads in stimulating foreign investment in other activities had created powerful interests which welcomed government control as an assurance of reasonable rates and efficient service. Mexicanization, as Limantour pointed out repeatedly in his reports, guaranteed rates established in conformity with overriding "national" interests as well as economies in management and improvements in the condition of equipment and service.[83] Mexicanization coincided exactly with the general economic policy orientation of the Porfirian regime, which saw in foreign capital and export markets the key to economic growth and the nation's newfound political stability.

81. John H. McNeely, *The Railways of Mexico: A Study in Nationalization* (Southwestern Studies, Monograph no. 5, El Paso, 1964), pp. 17–20.

82. Secretaría de Comunicaciones y Obras Públicas, *Memoria presentada al Congreso de la Unión por el Secretario de Estado y del Despacho de Comunicaciones y Obras Públicas de la República Mexicana, Ingeniero Leandro Fernández, corresponde al período transcurrido de 1º de julio de 1909 a 30 de junio de 1910* (Mexico, 1911), pp. 81–83; hereafter cited as *MSCOP, 1909–10*.

83. Secretaría de Hacienda, *Informe del Secretario*, pp. 50–59.

Chapter 3
Railroad Passenger Services: Resource Savings and Internal Migration

The Problem

Railroad passenger services save both money and time. Money is saved when passengers travel the same distances at less cost. The lower price of rail transportation in comparison to prerail modes of conveyance reflects the smaller quantity of resources which railroads use to transport people. The resources no longer needed for transport are employed elsewhere in the economy and the result is an increase in total output. Time is saved when people waste less of it to get where they are going, because railway travel is faster. Nevertheless, only if the time saved traveling by rail actually increases the time put to productive use can we speak of an increase in social product due to the railroad's greater speed. The same may be said, of course, for resources saved due to the railroad's greater efficiency; only if the resources that would have gone to the transport sector are actually employed productively in other sectors does the economy benefit. In the resource case, however, all that is needed to assure this result is a functioning market for resources, or rather for that portion of the nation's resources which existing markets would otherwise have channeled into mule trains, freight wagons, stagecoaches, and the like. In the case of time saved, however, the existence of a market for labor does not guarantee that travelers will use the time they save productively. People, unlike resources, can consume as well as produce. The time saved by rail travel may just as easily be converted to leisure, or to any one of a number of socially necessary activities — for example, housework, gardening, childrearing, food preparation — which do not conventionally appear in economists' national product accounts. Tourists, children, housewives not gainfully employed, people living on "unearned" investment incomes or rents, victims of unemployment, pilgrims to religious shrines, and the like may all benefit from the speed as well as the comfort of rail travel, but this addition to "consumer's surplus" does not affect the productivity of the economy in measurable ways.

In his study of North American railroads, Albert Fishlow argued against measuring the time savings in passenger travel at all.[1]

> That travelers could go their ways more comfortably by railroad enhanced their satisfaction; their support of the railroad from the beginning indicates that they valued such comfort highly. Still, from the social point of view, the traveler who arrives wearied after a longer journey does not reduce the economy's capacity to produce—except to the extent that longer periods on conveyances meant shorter periods at work, etcetera. These latter offsets do not come to much because the average passenger trip was typically short.

The logic here is correct, but the conclusions are wrong. In the case of Mexico, the maximum average stagecoach speed over the best roads was reported to have been fifteen kilometers per hour between Mexico City and Veracruz.[2] But even this report appears to have been an exaggeration, the result of dividing three and one half eleven-hour days (38.5 hours) into the total highway distance to Veracruz. In fact, the Mexico City–Veracruz stagecoaches traveled part of the way at night and probably averaged, as one contemporary has it, closer to eight kilometers per hour in the mountainous stretches between Jalapa and Veracruz and slightly over eleven kilometers per hour on the relatively flat plateau from Perote to Puebla.[3] In the United States, where road conditions were generally superior to Mexico in the nineteenth century, Wells Fargo stages averaged close to five miles (less than nine kilometers) per hour.[4] Even if the high figure is accepted, the difference between a railroad journey of sixty-seven kilometers (the average distance traveled in 1910) and the same trip by stagecoach is at least three hours (assuming a minimum

---

1. Fishlow, *American Railroads,* p. 90.

2. Calderón, *La vida económica,* p. 603.

3. Waddy Thompson, *Recollections of Mexico* (New York: Wiley and Putnam, 1847), pp. 11–12, 15.

4. J. Hayden Boyd and Gary M. Walton, "The Social Savings from Nineteenth-Century Passenger Services," *EEH,* 2nd. ser., 9 (1972):243.

rail speed of forty kilometers per hour).[5] While a relatively comfortable railroad journey of an hour and a half could well have been accomplished without affecting a passenger's working time, a stagecoach trip of more than four and a half hours could easily have had the effect of removing travelers from the work force for an entire day. The delays, uncertainties, infrequent departures, small and rigid maximum loads, greater risks, and discomfort associated with stagecoach travel, and the greater sensitivity of coaches to weather, road conditions, and the designs of bandits support this view. It is likely, therefore, that the additional time required by stagecoach constitutes an *underestimate* of the total loss of working time by gainfully employed travelers.[6] In the case of travelers who could not afford to travel by stage and had to walk to their destinations (the majority in prerail Mexico), the necessity of taking into account the railroad's greater speed is even more compelling. What the railroad accomplished in a matter of an hour or two would have taken the foot traveler two full days.

While it is important to take the time costs of travel into account, it is still true that for many passengers the economic opportunity cost of time spent traveling was close to zero. Unfortunately, there is no way to estimate the number of conventionally "unproductive" travelers on Mexico's railroads. If this were a study of railroad passenger savings in a high income country, the lack of such data would be problematical. This is so because in high income areas, "time is money." In two cases where attempts have been made to estimate passenger savings (the United States and England/Wales) they were found to be fairly high relative to freight savings and to the gross national prod-

5. Government inspectors reported average speeds of forty kilometers per hour between stations on the Central as early as 1884. *MF, 1883–85* 2:773. Later reports indicate even better speeds.

6. For a similar account of stagecoach travel couched as advice to tourists, see the famous Terry's Guide, T. Philip Terry, *Terry's Mexico* (Cambridge, Mass.: Houghton Mifflin, n.d.), pp. xxxvii–xxxviii. For such travelers of course, "Pedestrianism in Mexico is thus far unknown, excepting the ascents of the lofty volcanoes." Alfred R. Conkling, *Appleton's Guide to Mexico* (New York: Appleton and Co., 1884), p. 15.

uct.[7] In a low income country like Mexico, however, the absolute value of the output lost from extra time spent traveling may be expected to be low. It may also be expected that effective demand for rail passenger travel will be lower in per capita terms both because incomes are smaller and because the railroad's speed (rather than its money savings) will not constitute its chief advantage over prerail modes of transport. The hypothesis is therefore advanced that passenger services contributed little in a direct way to Mexican economic growth because the railroads carried relatively fewer people and because the value of the time they saved was lower. If this hypothesis is true, the social savings estimate should be so low that interpretation will not depend on a precise estimate of the number of productive passengers.

Considerable internal migration took place during the *Porfiriato*, mainly from the center of the country to the north. The hypothesis of low passenger social savings suggests that the railroads' contribution to this redistribution of the labor force was correspondingly small. We will return to this question later. For the moment it is enough to note that the passenger social savings estimate will only reveal whether the economy benefited *directly* from the availability of rail transportation to migrants as well as to the other people who made use of it. That is, the savings figures will only tell us how much the economy would have lost if rail passengers had been forced to use some other means to reach their destinations. It will not capture the indirect gains which the economy may have derived from the greater productivity of workers who were persuaded to move to new areas by the availability of rail passenger travel.

Alternatives to Railroad Passenger Travel

The chief difficulty in estimating social savings due to passenger services lies in the selection of the appropriate prerailroad costs to be used in the calculation. Four alternatives faced prerailroad travelers:

7. Fishlow, *American Railroads*, pp. 90–93; Boyd and Walton, "Social Savings," pp. 237–40; Hawke, *Railways*, p. 188. Cf. de Vries, "Barges and capitalism," pp. 237–44.

stagecoach (*diligencia* or *carruaje*), litter (*litera*), horse, mule or donkey back, and traveling on foot. Contemporary observers reported that only the rich could afford to travel by stagecoach, while most of the poor walked.[8] Stagecoach fares were high, and litter fares even higher.[9] Stagecoaches could be used only by passengers traveling between points located on well-constructed federal highways. Litters carried passengers between points located on roads not passable by stagecoach, and occasionally competed with stagecoaches on highway routes because they were believed to have a lower holdup rate.[10] Wages were low among the poor, so walking, a mode of transport where time costs are the only relevant price, was cheap.

Fortunately, it is not necessary to rely solely on travelers' accounts and indirect evidence to estimate the distribution of travelers by mode of conveyance. On 30 September 1877, the Secretary of *Fomento*, General Vicente Riva Palacio, issued a circular to the directors of the twenty-two federal highways requesting bimonthly reports on road use.[11] The reports were slow in coming, but by the publication of the ministry's *Memoria* for the years 1877 to 1882, road use data had been submitted by most of the federal highway directors.[12] The reports cannot be considered accurate for direct use. Some were carelessly formed, and all purported to measure traffic between distant points by head counts and rough freight estimates at a single checkpoint along the route. Only one of the highway directors submitted reports for all of the five years covered in the ministry's reports, and several submitted none at all. By the publication of the ministry's next *Memoria* in 1885, most of the directors had ceased counting, as railroads penetrated larger and larger areas of the country.

The reports contain no data on the length of the journeys of the travelers passing the checkpoints. It is likely that a much higher proportion of foot travelers consisted of local, short-distance travelers than did that of stagecoach passengers. At the same time, it is also likely that a large number of foot travelers walking between localities

8. Thompson, *Recollections*, chapters 2 and 3.
9. Ibid., p. 10.
10. Ibid., pp. 10–11.
11. *MF, 1876–77*, p. 20.
12. *MF, 1877–82*, vol. 2.

where no checkpoints had been set up went unreported. While the precise numbers may be inaccurate and unsuitable for direct use, the proportions of travelers reported as stagecoach passengers, mounted travelers, and walkers is still a useful index of prerailroad traffic.

Table 3.1 shows the number of travelers reported to have passed checkpoints on fourteen of the federal highways between 1877 and 1882, grouped by type of conveyance. The proportion of stagecoach passengers fluctuated from zero to 33.2 percent of the total. The average for all roads is 6.5 percent. The number of foot travelers varied from 28.6 to 90.3 percent, while the proportion for all roads was 68.4 percent. These data confirm the contemporary observation that the alternative to railroads, for most travelers, was walking.

Although most travelers walked, and only a small minority could afford stagecoach travel, a significant number of people chose mounted travel. Mounted travelers accounted for between 6.9 and 64.9 percent of the total for all roads. Mounted travel was more comfortable and less tiring than walking. Horses were probably twice as fast as walking, and donkeys equal to foot travel in speed. Whatever the animal, mounted travel was less comfortable and slower than stagecoach. The choice of mounted over foot travel appears to have been affected by the length of the journey. The proportion of mounted travelers is lowest in the reports of traffic between such nearby towns as Puebla and Cholula, Mexico City and Toluca, and Mexico City and Cuernavaca. The proportion of foot travelers along these routes was higher than the average, too. More generally, the proportion of mounted travelers is inversely related to the proportion of foot travelers.[13] No clear relationship can be discerned between the proportion of stagecoach passengers and that of mounted travelers.[14] The inverse correlation between mounted and foot traveler proportions suggests that some substitution was taking place. The absence of correlation between stagecoach and mounted traveler proportions indicates that if any substitution took place between

13. A simple regression of the proportion of mounted travelers on the proportion of foot travelers yielded $r^2 = .508$, significant at the 1 percent level.

14. No correlation was found between the proportion of mounted and stagecoach travelers ($r^2 = .076$, not significant at any acceptable level).

TABLE 3.1
Passenger Traffic on Federal Highways, 1877–1882

High-way	Rte.	Year of Report	Stage-coach	(%)	Mounted	(%)	Foot	(%)
1.	a′	1881–1882	3,816	(5.8)	17,843	(26.9)	44,648	(68.3)
	a″	1881–1882	3,425	(4.3)	14,439	(18.1)	62,080	(77.6)
	b′	1879–1880	6,193	(4.4)	23,906	(17.1)	109,427	(79.0)
	b″	1879–1880	6,400	(3.5)	22,343	(12.1)	154,218	(84.3)
2.	a′	1881–1882	3,958	(6.8)	18,152	(31.2)	35,974	(62.0)
	a″	1881–1882	9,938	(8.7)	25,108	(55.5)	16,156	(35.8)
3.	a	1879–1880	17,879	(2.8)	43,752	(6.9)	570,289	(90.3)
	b	1878–1879	3,044	(6.5)	8,528	(18.1)	35,570	(75.4)
	c	1878–1879	6,360	(6.4)	20,546	(20.7)	72,264	(72.9)
	c	1879–1880	3,138	(2.8)	17,615	(15.9)	89,968	(81.3)
	d	1878–1879	445	(2.6)	7,370	(43.2)	9,321	(54.2)
	e	1879–1880	414	(6.1)	1,996	(29.0)	4,398	(64.9)
4.	a	1878–1879	25,538	(11.5)	64,454	(29.1)	121,557	(59.4)
5.	a	1878–1879(1)	4,496	(4.2)	28,262	(26.3)	74,516	(69.5)
	a	1879–1880	3,628	(6.1)	15,444	(26.1)	40,201	(67.8)
	a′	1881–1882	1,886	(10.0)	4,234	(22.5)	12,279	(67.5)
	a″	1881–1882(2)	1,074		4,234	(sic)	12,279	(sic)
6.	a	1879(2)	2,968	(15.6)	3,611	(20.9)	11,001	(63.5)
	a′	1880(2)	2,203	(13.2)	3,821	(22.9)	10,649	(63.9)
	a″	1880(2)	2,578	(15.1)	3,673	(21.4)	10,902	(63.5)

TABLE 3.1 (*cont.*)

High-way	Rte.	Year of Report	Stage-coach	(%)	Mounted	(%)	Foot	(%)
	a	1880–1881	9,772	(22.1)	15,079	(22.1)	43,334	(63.6)
	b′	1881–1882	878	(4.3)	5,378	(26.4)	14,121	(69.3)
	b″	1881–1882	961	(4.7)	4,926	(23.8)	14,778	(63.6)
7.	a	1878	2,407	(9.0)	8,908	(33.4)	15,338	(57.6)
	a	1879(2)	1,262	(8.8)	4,658	(32.3)	8,477	(58.9)
8.	a	1878	5,849	(4.3)	42,076	(30.8)	88,699	(64.9)
	a	1879(2)	1,466	(3.8)	12,153	(31.1)	25,375	(65.1)
	b	1878–1879(2)	4,021	(4.6)	28,762	(32.5)	55,587	(62.9)
9.	a	1877–1878(2)	767	(2.0)	6,219	(16.0)	31,840	(82.0)
	a	1878–1879(2)	1,613	(4.0)	7,505	(18.7)	31,005	(77.3)
	a	1879–1880	1,624	(2.8)	10,687	(18.3)	46,137	(78.9)
	a	1880–1881	970	(1.4)	11,442	(17.0)	55,041	(81.6)
	a	1881–1882	1,494	(1.5)	26,287	(27.2)	68,943	(71.3)
10.	a	1877–1879(2)	1,412	(1.6)	11,578	(13.4)	73,363	(85.0)
	a	1878–1879	171	(1.6)	1,020	(9.5)	9,545	(88.9)
	a	1879–1880	278	(1.7)	2,560	(16.0)	13,141	(82.3)
	a′	1881–1882(2)	3,623	(8.2)	13,018	(32.8)	23,445	(59.0)
	a″	1881–1882(2)	3,161	(12.2)	12,602	(48.6)	10,171	(39.2)
11.	a	1878–1879(2)	—		1,201	(15.6)	6,480	(84.4)
12.	a	1878(2)	1,584	(3.4)	11,084	(23.7)	34,081	(72.9)
	a	1878–1879	23,731	(8.6)	88,009	(32.0)	163,215	(59.4)

	Year						
a	1879–1880(2)	79,424	(17.3)	88,868	(19.4)	289,465	(63.3)
a	1881–1882(2)	37,878	(11.4)	64,279	(19.3)	229,920	(69.3)
b	1878(2)	1,172	(5.9)	6,617	(33.5)	11,978	(60.6)
b	1879(2)	2,221	(8.9)	10,266	(41.1)	12,467	(50.0)
b	1880(2)	1,084	(8.5)	4,011	(31.5)	7,648	(40.0)
c	1878(2)	1,043	(5.9)	7,518	(43.3)	8,826	(50.8)
c	1881–1882(2)	3,785	(5.1)	27,231	(37.0)	32,525	(57.9)
d	1878(2)	100	(7.7)	459	(15.4)	736	(56.9)
d	1880(2)	2,332	(2.4)	17,240	(17.8)	77,319	(79.8)
e	1878(2)	440	(9.3)	1,572	(33.3)	2,704	(57.4)
e	1879(2)	823	(9.7)	2,849	(33.7)	4,772	(56.6)
f	1879(2)	3,214	(12.0)	8,770	(32.7)	14,855	(55.3)
f	1881–1882(2)	4,203	(2.6)	54,746	(34.4)	100,118	(63.0)
g	1881–1882(2)	17,385	(33.2)	15,719	(30.1)	19,215	(36.7)
h	1878(2)	124	(1.6)	2,076	(26.4)	5,674	(72.0)
h	1881–1882	1,297	(5.8)	5,008	(22.4)	16,091	(71.8)
i	1878(2)	6,114	(7.9)	22,065	(28.5)	49,127	(63.6)
j	1878(2)	2,976	(4.5)	24,469	(36.7)	39,296	(58.8)
j	1880(2)	1,357	(20.6)	3,277	(50.8)	1,842	(28.6)
k	1881–1882(2)	8,803	(5.8)	49,294	(32.5)	93,346	(61.7)
l	1881–1882(2)	4,200	(7.3)	16,018	(27.8)	37,341	(64.9)
a	1878–1879(1)	5,787	(3.7)	80,760	(51.3)	70,805	(45.0)
a	1880(2)	3,516	(3.4)	40,344	(38.6)	60,720	(58.0)
a	1881–1882(2)	15,609	(3.7)	54,856	(36.8)	250,737	(59.5)

13.

TABLE 3.1 (*cont.*)

High-way	Rte.	Year of Report	Stage-coach	(%)	Mounted	(%)	Foot	(%)
	b	1881–1882(2)	4,179	(7.2)	20,601	(35.6)	33,058	(57.2)
	c	1881–1882(2)	56	(0.0)	34,678	(54.1)	29,362	(45.9)
	c′	1878–1879(2)	3	(0.0)	29,879	(40.8)	43,330	(59.2)
	c″	1878–1879(2)	3	(0.0)	31,245	(40.0)	46,880	(60.0)
	d′	1878–1879(2)	84	(0.5)	9,866	(64.9)	5,258	(34.6)
	d″	1878–1879(2)	100	(0.6)	8,845	(53.0)	7,751	(46.4)
	d	1881–1882(2)	396	(0.5)	27,549	(36.9)	48,836	(63.3)
	e	1881(2)	6,055	(7.3)	32,608	(39.6)	43,746	(53.1)
	f	1881(2)	1,453	(2.9)	17,003	(33.5)	32,254	(63.6)
14.	a′	1879–1880	—		6,997	(20.0)	27,921	(80.0)
	a″	1879–1880	—		7,271	(20.8)	27,621	(79.2)
Totals			393,371	(6.5)	1,509,297	(25.1)	4,113,267	(68.4)

Notes: Fiscal years ending 30 June are indicated by hyphenated dates. Calendar years are indicated by single dates. (1) Indicates reported data for more than a total of one year. (2) Indicates coverage of less than a full year, but more than three months. Reports based on less than three months of observation are not included. Highway number key is below. Routes are indicated by lowercase letters. A primed letter indicates traffic going toward the first-named point in the route description; double-primed letters indicate one-way traffic in the opposite direction. Unprimed letters indicate total traffic in both directions.

TABLE 3.1 (*cont.*)
Highway Number Key

1. México–Morelia–Las Barrancas
   a. México–Morelia
   b. México–Toluca
2. México–Querétaro–Guanajuato
   a. México–Querétaro
3. México–Tehuacán via Puebla
   a. Puebla–Cholula
   b. Tehuacán–Esperanza
   c. Tehuacán–Esperanza–Orizaba
   d. Tehuacán–Puerto Angel
   e. Tehuacán–Oaxaca
4. Amozoc–Veracruz via Puebla
   a. Puebla–Amozoc
5. San Luis Potosí–Querétaro–Aguascalientes
   a. San Luis Potosí–Querétaro
6. Zacatecas–Mazatlán via Durango
   a. Zacatecas–El Refugio
   b. Zacatecas–Durango
7. Ometusco–Tuxpan via Tulancingo
   a. Ometusco–Tulancingo
8. México–Tampico via Pachuca and Ometusco
   a. Ometusco–Pachuca
   b. Tizayuca–Pachuca
9. San Luis Potosí–Tampico
   a. San Luis Potosí–Ciudad del Maíz
10. México–Acapulco
    a. México–Cuernavaca

11. Huaumantla–Nautla
    a. Huaumantla–Nautla
12. Guadalajara–Guanajuato
    a. Guadalajara–Zapotlanejo
    b. Zapotlanejo–Tepatitlán
    c. Tepatitlán–Jalostoitlán
    d. Jalostoitlán–San Juan de los Lagos
    e. San Juan de los Lagos–Lagos
    f. Lagos–Silao
    g. Lagos–Puente de Cuarenta
    h. Silao–Guanajuato
    i. León–Silao
    j. San Pedro section
    k. Puente de Tololotlán
    l. Lagos–León
13. Guadalajara–Manzanillo
    a. Guadalajara–Santa Ana Acatlán
    b. Zocoalco–Sayula
    c. Tonila–Colima
    d. Colima–Manzanillo
    e. Guadalajara–Tepic
    f. Tepic–San Blas
14. Morelia–Cuitzeo
    a. Morelia–Guanajuato

Source: *Memoria de Fomento, 1877–1882,* vol. 2, passim.

stagecoach and mounted travel it must have been on a smaller scale than the substitution between mounted travel and walking.[15] This evidence tends to confirm the contemporary observation that most mounted travelers on Mexican roads in this era were Indians riding donkeys.[16]

In estimating savings on passenger services, we will assume that the alternative for first class passengers was stagecoach travel. In 1910, 29.0 percent of all passengers carried by rail were first class passengers.[17] This contrasts with the much smaller proportion (6.5 percent) of stagecoach passengers in the prerail era. In fact, the percentage of first class rail passengers is much closer to the combined proportion of stagecoach and mounted travelers (31.6 percent) reported in table 3.1. This would suggest that a significant number of first class rail passengers might have shifted to mounted travel in the absence of the railroad. Recent studies of the elasticity of demand for passenger transportation suggest that elasticity increases with increases in the luxury component of the transport services offered.[18] Robert Fogel has suggested that the demand for passenger services may be divided into two separate demand functions: a relatively inelastic demand for basic transportation and a highly elastic demand for luxury while traveling.[19] Any increase in the price of a luxury-intensive mode of travel, given other means of basic transport at lower levels of luxury, will cause a shift from the more to the less luxurious carriers. Since the reverse would also be true, it suggests that the decrease in the price of luxury-intensive travel with the substitution of first class rail for stagecoach transportation induced some mounted travelers to shift to first class rail travel.

We have eliminated mounted travel as an alternative to first class

15. The case of the Guadalajara–Guanajuato highway between Guadalajara and Zapotlanejo appears to be the only exception to this generalization which may be seen from an inspection of the traffic data reported. See table 3.1.

16. See, for example, Manuel Payno, *Los bandidos del Río Frío* (México: Impreso M. León Sánchez, 1928), vol. 1, pp. 440–41.

17. See below, table 3.2 and text.

18. See the discussion by Boyd and Walton, "Social Savings," pp. 240–41.

19. Robert Fogel, "Comments on chapter 2 of Gary Hawke's Dissertation," (Chicago: Xerox, 1968), p. 2. I am indebted to Professor Fogel, who kindly made these comments available to me.

rail service for two reasons. First, the rather small percentage of stagecoach passengers in the years 1877 to 1882 was due in part to road conditions which would have improved in the absence of railroads. The poor and frequently impassable condition of even the federal highways in the prerail era reduced the proportion of stagecoach passengers considerably. Seven of the highways with the smallest proportions of stagecoach passengers listed in table 3.1 were reported impassable or in extremely poor condition by their directors in reports submitted along with the traffic data, while those showing above average proportions in the table were usually the best maintained.[20] Stagecoach travel was further reduced by the seasonal character of road maintenance. The risk of floods and landslides during the rainy season caused fluctuations in the monthly data on road use among the proportions of stagecoach passengers on several roads. Rather than risk prolonged delays at intermediate points, some travelers apparently preferred to make their entire journeys by horse.[21]

Second, many of the 1910 first class rail passengers traveled between points inaccessible by stagecoach in the prerail era.[22] A portion of the travelers between these points would have traveled for part of their journeys along routes served by stagecoach, but would have chosen to make their whole trip by horse because of the inconvenience or impossibility of hiring horses at points where their itineraries diverged from stagecoach routes. A general improvement in the number and quality of federal highways in the absence of the rail-

20. The exception to this generalization was the well-maintained Mexico City–Toluca highway where the small proportion of stagecoach passengers was due to the large numbers of foot travelers and donkey riders going to and from Mexico City, the marketplace for the produce and amusement of the densely populated nearby countryside.

21. On the seasonality of highway conditions, see Calderón, *La vida económica*, pp. 588–89. Seasonal fluctuations in the number of stagecoach passengers and their proportion of total travelers may be observed in some of the highway directors' road use reports where monthly traffic breakdowns are given. The reports are in *MF, 1877–82*, vol. 2.

22. Although rail routes tended at first to duplicate the prerail highway network, by 1910 the number of towns and villages with rail communications which had been inaccessible to wheeled vehicles in the prerail era must have been considerable. The 1910 rail network was more than three times as large as the prerail federal highway system.

roads would have reduced the inconvenience as well as the costs of traveling by stage and removed an important limitation on the supply of stagecoach services. It is still true, however, that eliminating mounted travel as an alternative for first class rail passengers probably introduces an upward bias in the social savings estimates, by exaggerating somewhat the cost of the alternative conveyance.

First class rail and stagecoach travel also offered a roughly comparable mix of luxury and basic transportation. Comparable mix does not, of course, imply comparable service. Stagecoach travel was much less comfortable as well as slower than first class rail travel. Even second class rail travel was more comfortable than stagecoach. While the difference in time costs of first class rail and stagecoach are estimated below, there is no practical way to evaluate the "psychic" cost of the discomfort which the railroads eliminated. Greater comfort, however, does not increase the economy's capacity to produce, and it is the railroad's contribution to economic growth that is to be measured.

In the calculation of social savings for second class passenger services, it is assumed that the nonrail alternative was foot travel. The elimination of the mounted travel alternative for second class passengers is reasonable, because the difference in the cost of walking and the cost of riding a donkey was no doubt very small. Second class passengers were more likely to have switched to donkeys than horses because of the lower purchase price and trifling maintenance costs involved.[23] Donkeys also served as beasts of burden. Using them for carrying people added nothing to their upkeep and cost nothing when there was no other work to be done. That donkeys were used more than horses can be confirmed with data from the livestock census of 1878. The census reported a population of some 1.5 million horses and at least 11.5 million donkeys.[24] It is unlikely that more than a small minority of mounted passengers in prerail Mexico were horsemen.

23. The price of a donkey in the 1870s was about half that of a horse. See El Colegio de México, *Estadísticas: Fuerza de Trabajo,* p. 84, where output and value of horses and mules for 1878 is estimated. Horses required more care than donkeys, which could be expected usually to feed themselves along the roadside.

24. Luis Cossio Silva, "La agricultura," in Cosío Villegas, ed., *Historia moderna de México: El Porfiriato, La vida económica,* vol. 1, p. 177, reports on the

Passenger Transport in 1910

Terms of concessions and regulatory legislation required Mexican railway companies to submit annual reports containing up-to-date financial as well as operating statistics.[25] Most of the reports submitted by Mexico's railway companies for the period of nearly forty years ending in 1910 have been preserved.[26] In 1910, reports for fifteen smaller lines and one medium-sized company were found to be missing. The total length of these lines was listed by the Ministry of Communications and Public Works at 869 kilometers, or 4.4 percent of the total of 19,205 kilometers of federal steam railroad lines in the country.[27]

A direct calculation of total passenger kilometers produced by Mexican railways in 1910 has been made from the annual reports of the thirty-four companies which owned 95.6 percent of all steam railroad trackage in that year. Figures for total passenger kilometers for each line were derived by multiplying total number of passengers times average distance carried as indicated in the company reports. Unfortunately, the division of passenger kilometers between first and second class could not be calculated directly owing to the failure of the reports (with two exceptions) to distinguish average distance carried by class. The calculations then were made by multiplying the number of first or second class passengers carried by the average distance traveled by all passengers on each line. The results of these calculations are reported in table 3.2.

Total revenue from passenger traffic has also been calculated directly. Fourteen smaller lines, which carried some 7.7 percent of all reported passenger kilometers in 1910, failed to distinguish first and

Census. The number of donkeys in the country is estimated by assuming that the proportion of total population to output is the same as that reported for horses in the Census, and calculating the total from donkey output estimates in El Colegio de México, *Estadísticas: Fuerza de trabajo*, p. 84. The Census also reported a population of about 200,000 mules. The value of these animals in industry and for freight transport made their selling price as high as that of horses.

25. The texts of all railway concessions and legislation are contained in appropriate numbers of the *Diario Oficial*.

26. In the *AHSCT* files.

27. *MSCOP, 1909–10*, pp. 81–83.

TABLE 3.2

Passenger Kilometers of Mexican Railroads, 1910

Company	First Class	Second Class	Total
Mexican	22,546,639	88,900,457	111,447,096
Tehuantepec National	1,728,088	9,558,979	11,287,067
Sonora	4,881,693	13,017,589	17,899,282
Interoceanic	17,038,521	103,423,219	120,461,740
National Railways	161,822,282	519,335,820	681,158,102
Veracruz	613,906	2,480,262	3,094,169
United of Yucatán	5,933,086	35,855,253	41,788,339
Monte Alto – Tlalnepantla	153,204	1,066,414	1,219,618
Mexican Northern	52,724	249,606	302,330
Toluca – Tenango	633,700	3,642,070	4,275,770
Esperanza – El Xúchil	(1)	8,658	8,658
Coahuila and Zacatecas	409,822	1,461,314	1,871,136
Jalapa – Teocelo	(1)	1,751,954	1,751,954
Cazadero – Solís	(1)	41,304	41,304
San Juan – El Juile	(1)	59,930	59,930
San Marcos – Huajuapan de León	163,938	854,544	1,018,482
Occidental of Mexico	904,816	846,820	1,751,636
Ixtlahuaca, Mañi and Presa Grande	(1)	118,930	118,930
Torres – Minas Prietas	46,060	111,600	157,660
San Rafael – Atlixco	1,376,708	7,088,657	8,465,365
San Luis Potosí – Río Verde	(1)	137,153	137,153
Parral and Durango	132,907	1,388,926	1,521,833
Mineral of Chihuahua	166,417	767,081	933,498
Nacozari	509,567	1,380,523	1,890,089
Kansas City, Mexico and Oriente	252,339	1,491,702	1,744,041

TABLE 3.2 *(cont.)*

Company	First Class	Second Class	Total
Pan American	1,115,954	4,748,773	5,864,727
Tlalnepantla–Mexico	100,315	724,821	825,137
Inter-California	28,374	560,532	588,907
Tultenango–Yondesé	237,803	936,999	1,174,802
Zitácuaro–Joconusco	7,067	31,735	38,802
South Pacific of Mexico	6,950,211	16,762,130	23,712,340
Minatitlán	75,452	181,402	256,854
Northwestern	2,025,081	11,552,656	13,577,737
Totals	229,906,677	830,537,814	1,060,444,491

Note: (1) No first class passengers carried.
Totals may be off due to rounding.
Source: Appropriate files in *AHSCT*.

second class passenger revenues in their reports. The missing data were estimated by assuming the first class tariff was double that for second class travel (as it was approximately for all the other lines). Passenger revenue data is reported in table 3.3.

One further manipulation was required to obtain both passenger kilometers and revenues. In four cases involving more than half the revenue and passenger kilometers of Mexican railroads in 1910, company reports covered fiscal years ending 30 June, rather than calendar years, as was the case for the remaining thirty lines. For two of these companies, the Interoceanic and the San Marcos to Huajuapan de León, the figures reported in the tables are averages of the total reported by the companies in their annual reports for fiscal 1909–1910 and fiscal 1910–1911. In the case of the remaining two, the government-controlled National Railways of Mexico and the Mexican International, a merger was involved. The International filed its last annual report for the fiscal year ending 30 June 1910. Its operations were included in the report of the government line for fiscal 1910–1911. The figures reported in the tables for these two lines are condensed and reported as for the National Railways Com-

TABLE 3.3

Passenger Revenues of Mexican Railroads, 1910
(current pesos)

Company	First Class	Second Class	Total
Mexican	1,131,926	1,021,226	2,153,152
Tehuantepec National	44,698	220,330	265,028
Sonora	254,771	206,081	460,852
Interoceanic	706,771	1,341,210	2,047,981
National Railways	5,336,294	7,139,426	12,475,720
*Veracruz	24,363	49,215	73,578
*United of Yucatán	205,316	615,723	821,039
Monte Alto–Tlalnepantla	5,479	20,744	26,223
*Mexican Northern	2,993	7,985	10,079
Toluca–Tenango	17,061	49,026	66,087
Esperanza–El Xúchil	(1)	231	231
Coahuila and Zacatecas	16,298	35,075	51,373
Jalapa–Teocelo	(1)	46,128	46,128
Cazadero–Solís	(1)	985	985
San Juan–El Juile	(1)	1,265	1,265
*San Marcos–Huajuapan de León	7,987	10,055	18,041
*Occidental of Mexico	14,734	6,895	21,629
Ixtlahuaca, Mañi and Presa Grande	(1)	1,155	1,155
*Torres–Minas Prietas	3,948	4,782	8,730
*San Rafael–Atlixco	36,285	93,416	129,701
San Luis Potosí–Río Verde	(1)	2,267	2,267
*Parral and Durango	2,912	15,217	18,129
*Mineral of Chihuahua	8,084	18,631	26,715
*Nacozari	33,458	45,322	78,780
Kansas City, Mexico and Oriente	12,495	39,376	51,872
Pan American	56,581	113,266	169,848
Tlalnepantla–Mexico	3,393	11,650	15,043
Inter-California	1,149	16,752	17,901
Tultenango–Yondesé	9,140	20,978	30,118

TABLE 3.3 *(cont.)*

Company	First Class	Second Class	Total
*Zitácuaro–Joconusco	280	628	908
South Pacific of Mexico	403,277	424,553	827,830
*Minatitlán	4,505	5,415	9,920
*Northwestern	109,077	311,038	420,115
Totals	8,453,275	11,895,149	20,348,424

Notes: (1) No first class passengers carried. * Passenger revenues not reported by class, estimated assuming ratio of first to second class rate is 2:1.
Totals may be off due to rounding.
Source: Appropriate files in *AHSCT*.

pany. They represent the average of the sum of the operations of both, in the two fiscal years 1909–1910 and 1910–1911.

The calculations described above show that a total of 15,821,921 passengers were carried an average distance of 67.0 kilometers each at an average cost of $0.019 per kilometer on Mexico's railroads in 1910. First class passengers numbering 4,590,561 traveled approximately 229,906,677 kilometers at an average fare of $0.037. Second class passengers numbered 71.0 percent of the total (11,231,360) and traveled 830,537,814 kilometers at an average fare of $0.014.

Direct Social Savings on First Class Passenger Services

It is assumed that all first class passengers actually carried by rail in 1910 would have chosen to travel an equal number of passenger kilometers by stagecoach had the railroads not been built. Table 3.4 lists stagecoach fares for fourteen major prerailway stagecoach routes in 1876. The average fare for the total of 6,002 route kilometers in the table is exactly $0.07, while the unweighted average passenger rate is $0.061. The lowest rate per passenger kilometer was charged for travel between Mexico City and Toluca. This low rate of $0.033 per passenger kilometer probably resulted from the fact that the run to Toluca and back could be made in a single day, thus reducing

TABLE 3.4

Passenger Travel Costs by Stagecoach, 1876

Route	Distance in Kilometers	Fare Charged	Rate per Passenger Kilometer
1. México–Veracruz(a)	577	$31.00	$0.054
2. México–Morelia	390	19.00	0.049
3. México–Querétaro	220	15.00	0.068
4. México–Irapuato	344(b)	22.00	0.064
5. México–Guanajuato	370	25.60	0.069
6. México–Guadalajara	835	45.00	0.054
7. México–San Miguel	284(b)	19.25	0.068
8. México–San Luis Potosí	465	32.00	0.069
9. México–Toluca	66	2.00	0.033
10. México–Cuernavaca	58	4.50	0.078
11. México–Amecameca	70(b)	3.00	0.043
12. México–Cuautla	122(b)	6.00	0.049
13. México–Monterrey	1,005(b)	69.00	0.069
14. México–Matamoros	1,196(b)	99.00	0.083

Notes: (a) The fare from Mexico City to Veracruz is that for the year 1864. Rail transport part of the way to Mexico City thereafter eliminated the full route for stagecoaches.

(b) These distances are approximate. They are calculated partly on the basis of contemporary estimates of distances by road (that is, to points part way to the indicated destination) and partly on the basis of distance by road in 1970. Since the difference, if any, involves a reduction in length (because modern roads are less circuitous) the resulting cost per passenger kilometer given here may be less than what actually obtained in 1876.

Source: Francisco Calderón, *La República Restaurada, La vida económica.* In Daniel Cosío Villegas, *Historia moderna de México* (Mexico: Editorial Hermes, 1955), pp. 604–6.

overhead costs. The same cost-reducing factor probably helped keep down the cost of stagecoach travel to two other nearby towns, Amecameca and Cuautla. On the other hand, improvements in the condition of the highways would have reduced most of the 1876 rates substantially. The cost of travel from Mexico City to nearby Cuernavaca, for example, was affected by the poor condition of that road. Assigned a low priority in the distribution of federal highway maintenance funds, the road lacked even a director until June 1877.[28] Improvements in that road would probably have reduced the passenger rate from nearly $0.08 to something near the average for trips to other nearby towns (under $0.05). Corresponding reductions in other fares would follow improvements to other highways. With this in mind, the stagecoach fare used in the social savings estimate is set at $0.05. In the United States, according to Boyd and Walton, average stagecoach fares were somewhat lower. These authors employ a rate of U.S. $0.06 per mile for 1890, or $0.04 per kilometer in pesos of 1877.[29]

The estimate of direct social savings due to transportation of first class passengers has two components. The first is a price differential estimate. It captures merely the difference in the fares paid by first class rail passengers in 1910 and the stagecoach fare for 1876. The second component is a measure of the value of the additional time that would have been lost if these passengers had been forced to rely on stagecoach conveyance instead of the more rapid railroad.

If all first class rail passengers who actually traveled by rail in 1910 had to be carried by stagecoach, a certain number of man hours of labor would have been lost, due to the difference in speed between the two modes of travel. Estimating the value of these lost hours is analogous to the estimation of savings due to inventory size reduction in the case of freight shipment, where the alternative—for example, canals in the United States—involved much slower shipment. Time

28. *MF, 1877–82* 2:438.
29. Boyd and Walton, "Social Savings," pp. 243–44, employ a rate of U.S. $0.06 per mile for their 1890 estimates, based on scattered nineteenth-century data which show rates from U.S. $0.05 to U.S. $0.135. At the 1890 exchange rate, U.S. $0.06 amounts to just over seven centavos, and about the same in pesos of 1877. This amounts to approximately $0.04 per passenger kilometer.

saved is a function of the difference in speed between railroad and stagecoach. With the exception of the Mexico City–Veracruz run, stagecoaches seldom traveled at night. Even the best of the federal highways were subject to hazards due to falling rock, landslides, washouts, and the like. Travel in the rainy season was especially risky. Frequent holdups were endemic on Mexican highways in the prerail era.[30] Nonetheless, stage travel could have been made easier by improved roads and an enlarged force of *rurales*. With road hazards and bandits removed, stagecoaches might have equaled the nighttime performance of the railroads. It is assumed that no more than 20 percent of all railroad passenger kilometers were traveled at night, and that better highway conditions would have made night travel equally possible by stagecoach. Stagecoach speed is assumed equal to the high estimate for the Mexico City–Veracruz line, or fifteen kilometers per hour. Using this speed not only omits time required for resting and changing horses, it also assumes a general improvement in road conditions in Mexico to at least the level of the best of them as well as an extension of the federal highway system required to provide stagecoach transportation between points not served by them in 1876. Average passenger train speed is estimated at forty kilometers per hour, a conservative figure for 1910.

The opportunity cost of the time lost in travel by first class passengers is then measured in ten-hour work days valued at twice the average daily wage for railroad workers in 1910. This valuation is inevitably arbitrary. It is based on contemporary estimates of the value of time spent on traveling by airline passengers in the United States. Gronau's study indicates that passengers using this form of transportation for business travel valued their time at approximately twice the U.S. hourly wage in manufacturing.[31] For Mexico, estimates of wage rates in industry are not available. The Colegio de México series are based on daily *minimum* rather than *average* wage rates.[32] In

30. Extended literary accounts of such incidents are contained in Payno, *Los bandidos del Río Frío*.

31. Reuben Gronau, *The Value of Time in Passenger Transportation: The Demand for Air Travel* (New York: National Bureau of Economic Research, Occasional Paper No. 109, 1970), and Boyd and Walton, "Social Savings," p. 236.

32. El Colegio de México, *Estadísticas: Fuerza de trabajo*, pp. 147–54.

1910, the average *minimum* daily wage reported for industrial workers was $0.59. In the mining industry, the Colegio reported an average daily minimum of $1.04. The corresponding minimum reported by the National Railways of Mexico for 1910 was $0.96, comparable to the Colegio's estimated minimum for mining.[33] The *average* wage paid on the National Railways, however, was $1.78 per day. Since the National Railways Company was a truly national firm, and employed more than half of all railroad workers in 1910, the average wage paid to its employees is used as the basis for estimating the opportunity cost of travel time. Twice the average railroad wage in 1910 ($3.56, or $2.15 in pesos of 1900) is thus used in the construction of the estimates reported in table 3.5.

It is possible, of course, given Mexico's highly skewed income distribution, that some first class rail passengers were income earners who actually enjoyed an average income well in excess of this figure. On the other hand, many of the men traveling in first class must have derived their incomes on some other basis than an hourly or daily wage. While the additional time required by stagecoach travel could well have involved much heavier costs than this procedure allows in some cases—especially in the case of businessmen of all kinds and certain professional men—many of the first class travelers must have been landlords, clerics, tourists, housewives, children, servants, and the like, for whom the opportunity cost of the additional time spent traveling was probably quite low. To take this into account, the time lost by using the stagecoach alternative is estimated by assuming that one half of all first class passengers were unproductive in gross national product terms.

Table 3.5 gives the results of the social savings estimate for first class passengers. Out of a total savings of about 12.5 million pesos of 1900, $0.82 million or only 6.6 percent is the estimated opportunity cost of the additional time required by stagecoach. Thus, even if all passengers were productive, and at wages several times higher than those used for constructing the estimate, the savings in time costs would still be very small. The remainder of the savings, or about $11.6 million, represents the difference between first class rail and stagecoach fares. These figures imply an average railroad fare plus

33. See the *Annual Report* for 1910 of the National Railways of Mexico, in *AHSCT* 10/2329-1.

TABLE 3.5
Estimate of Direct Social Savings on First Class Passenger Services, 1910

A. Time Cost

  1. Railroad passenger kilometers, 1910   229,906,677 kms.

  2. Daylight passenger kilometers
     (80 percent of 1.), 1910   183,925,341 kms.

  3. Daylight passenger kilometers by
     Income earners (50 percent of 2.)   91,962,671 kms.

  4. Daylight hours required by stagecoach
     (at 15 k.p.h.)   6,130,845 hrs.

  5. Daylight hours required by rail
     (at 40 k.p.h.)   2,299,067 hrs.

  6. Additional hours required by
     stagecoach (4. − 5.)   3,831,778 hrs.

  7. Value of additional time (in ten-hour
     days) required by stagecoach
     (estimated at twice the average
     railroad daily wage of \$2.15)   \$823,832

B. Price Differential

  8. Cost of traveling 229,906,677
     kilometers by stagecoach (1876 rate of
     \$0.05, equal to \$0.07278 in pesos
     of 1900)   \$16,732,608

  9. Actual first class passenger revenue
     total for Mexican railroads in 1910
     in pesos of 1900   \$ 5,101,554

10. Additional cost of traveling by
     stagecoach (8. − 9.)   \$11,631,054

C. Direct Savings (7. + 10.)   \$12,454,886

time cost of $0.040 per passenger kilometer (or $0.024 in pesos of 1900). The corresponding implied stagecoach fare plus time cost is $0.130 per passenger kilometer (or $0.079 in pesos of 1900). The total cost *per kilometer* of transporting 1910 first class rail passengers the same distance by stagecoach is more than three times greater than the railroad cost.

The estimated direct social savings due to first class passenger transport of $12.5 million amounts to approximately 1 percent (1.05) of Mexico's gross domestic product in 1910.[34] Since a large component of first class travel consisted of "comfort," as distinguished from basic transportation (available at the prevailing second class rates), this estimate probably represents a considerable exaggeration of the real benefits. The demand for luxury travel (as distinct from basic transportation) is believed to be highly elastic by contemporary students of transport economics.[35] If the direct social savings estimate calculated in table 3.5 were recalculated, assuming a unit price elasticity of demand, the social savings estimate would fall to just over one half of 1 percent of the gross domestic product, and for higher elasticities, the social savings rapidly decline to quite negligible amounts.

Direct Social Savings on Second Class Passenger Services

Estimation of direct social savings due to railroad second class passenger service is based on the assumption that foot travel was the appropriate alternative for such travelers. In this case, the cost of the alternative to rail transport depends entirely on the estimated time costs. Following recent studies of basic transport demand,[36] the opportunity cost of time spent traveling by second class passengers is

34. Mexican gross domestic product estimates in current pesos are taken from Leopoldo Solís, "La evolución," p. 12. The Solís estimates are deflated by using the Mexico City consumer price index in El Colegio de México, *Estadísticas: Fuerza de trabajo,* p. 172.

35. Fogel, "Comments," p. 3.

36. Gronau, *Value of Time;* Boyd and Walton, "Social Savings"; Arthur De Vany, "The Revealed Value of Time in Air Travel," *Review of Economics and*

valued at the average railroad daily wage in 1910, or $1.78 ($1.08 in pesos of 1900). Again, it is assumed that half of the passengers were productive in gross national product terms. The cost of traveling by foot is estimated by assuming that foot travelers would have averaged thirty kilometers a day. The savings estimate thus measures the cost to the economy of losing the output of the work days lost due to the slowness of foot travel.

The savings estimate is presented in table 3.6. The social savings attributable to second class passenger service is less than one third as large as the savings on first class services: $3.9 million or 0.33 percent of 1910 gross domestic product. While this result is extremely sensitive to the assumed opportunity cost of travel, the use of the average railroad wage rate as a proxy for this variable makes it more than likely that the result actually exaggerates the real benefits. More than half the Mexican labor force was employed in agriculture in 1910, while less than 15 percent of the U.S. labor force was similarly occupied when the contemporary studies of travel opportunity costs were made. If a lower wage, closer to the mean for the Mexican labor force were employed, the social savings estimate would decrease still further. Moreover, it is not unlikely that far more than the assumed 50 percent of all passengers were unproductive. We have not corrected for weekend travel, for the considerable qualitative evidence that large numbers of women and children accompanied migrants to the north, that the number of foreign tourists and special trains for religious pilgrimages increased markedly in the last years of the *Porfiriato*, or that seasonal unemployment in agriculture (or even intraseasonal migrations of agricultural laborers) reduced the opportunity costs of travel to near zero even for many potentially productive workers.

It is reasonable to conclude, therefore, that the direct contribution of railroad passenger services to Mexican economic growth in the *Porfiriato* was negligible. If the rich had switched back to stagecoach and the poor had continued to walk, the direct loss to the economy would have been very small.

Statistics 56 (1974):77–82; David A. Hensher and Williard E. Hotchkiss, "Choice of Mode and the Value of Travel Time Savings for the Journey to Work," *Economic Record* 50 (1974):94–112; John Kraft and Arthur Kraft, "Empirical Estimation of the Value of Travel Time Using Multi-Mode Choice Models," *Journal of Econometrics* 2 (1974):317–26.

TABLE 3.6

Estimate of Direct Social Savings on Second Class Passenger Services, 1910

1. Railroad passenger kilometers, 1910	830,537,814 kms.
2. Daylight passenger kilometers (80 percent of 1.)	664,430,251 kms.
3. Daylight passenger kilometers by income earners (50 percent of 2.)	332,215,126 kms.
4. Daylight hours required by railroads (at 40 k.p.h.)	8,305,378 hrs.
5. Ten-hour working days required by rail	830,538 days
6. Days required to walk 332,215,126 kms. at 30 kms. per day	11,073,837 days
7. Working days saved by rail travel (6. − 5.)	10,243,299 days
8. Value of additional time required to walk at average railroad daily wage of $1.08 (7. × $1.08)	$11,062,762
9. Railroad second class passenger revenue of 1910 in 1900 pesos	$ 7,178,726
10. Direct savings (8. − 9.)	$ 3,884,036

Railroads and Internal Migration

Some additional considerations call into question the conclusion reached on the basis of the social savings estimates alone. This is best illustrated by the issue of internal migration, an important factor in the rapid development of industry and agriculture in the northern states in the thirty years prior to 1910. Transport innovation may stimulate internal migration in a variety of ways. Even a relatively small direct savings to the economy from railroad passenger services could disguise a substantial stimulus to internal migration from reduced travel costs as well as other, unmeasured attributes of railway travel. A savings of $3.9 million on second class travel is small compared to Mexico's 1910 gross domestic product, but it implies a reduction of more than 30 percent in the average cost of an individual journey. In pesos of 1900, the time cost of traveling 332 million kilometers (at $1.08 per day) amounted to $11,959,743. Deflated railroad second class revenues in 1910 amounted to $7.2 million and the total time cost of rail travel in that year amounted to $896,981, or a total of $8,075,707. These figures imply a prerail travel cost of $0.036 per kilometer, and a rail fare plus time cost of $0.024. The cost of the average railroad journey in 1910 (67 kilometers) was $1.63 by rail and $2.41 on foot, a reduction of 32.4 percent in the cost of travel. For Mexico's poor, however, this probably did not represent an impressive individual savings. It is based on an assumed time cost of travel more than four times larger than the estimated minimum daily wage in agriculture ($0.26 in pesos of 1900). If this agricultural wage were used to calculate social savings, our estimate would fall from $3.9 million to minus $4.5 million. In fact, any assumed opportunity cost of $0.70 per day or less will yield a negative social savings estimate. Negative social savings would imply that the economy actually used more resources to transport second class passengers by rail than it would have lost had these passengers been removed from productive employment for as long as necessary to travel an equal distance on foot. At the individual level, the higher the traveler's wage, the more he could "save" by rail travel. The poorer the traveler, the less there was to gain from rail travel. For many, no doubt, the time cost of walking was less than the railroad fare. In 1910, the average rail journey of sixty-seven kilometers cost the equivalent of 6.3 days' work at the minimum daily wage in agriculture. Even for relatively well paid groups, like miners and bureaucrats, the average rail journey cost more than two days' wages.

These considerations indicate that the *economic* advantage of the railroad over foot travel was quite minimal, perhaps nonexistent. It is not unlikely that in narrow money-income terms, both the economy and the railroad's passengers would have been better off if everyone had walked.

But a pecuniary calculus is a poor estimator of human motivation. Rail travel may not have been cheap enough to reduce the economic costs of traveling, but its greater speed dramatically reduced the psychic costs of separation from home and family. A journey to distant opportunity, accomplished in a matter of hours by rail, would have required days of wearying travel on foot. The railroad made it possible to migrate without losing touch, without irrevocably breaking the ties which bound rural Mexicans to their land and their *pueblo*. To these intangible considerations must be added the greater comfort and safety of rail travel. Neither of these attributes of railroad passenger service is measured by the social savings estimate, but each must have played a role in reducing the costs of travel perceived by nineteenth-century Mexicans. It is therefore likely that social savings estimates which accurately reflect the insignificant direct stimulus of rail passenger services to economic growth underestimate to a significant degree the differences between rail and prerail conveyance from the standpoint of individual travelers. No matter how much the railroads encouraged people to travel, second class passenger savings (or costs) to the economy as a whole would be small, reflecting prevailing low wage rates. Yet the unmeasured benefits of rail travel to many thousands of Mexicans induced them to travel to distant places they had never gone before. The economy may have benefited significantly from this redistribution of the labor force, and from the greater mobility that railroads made a permanent part of Mexico's labor market.

The railroad also made a contribution to the diffusion of information about new opportunities. A large part of the nineteenth-century telegraph network, for example, was constructed by railroad companies as an obligation imposed by the terms of their concessions. Perhaps still more important, the railroads made rapid informal communication much easier. Railroad employees and their passengers passed along information on jobs and conditions by word of mouth from one end of the country to the other. The excitement of travel and the impact of new modes of consumption and life stimulated increased labor force participation along with greater mobility.

An additional range of railroad effects on migration are suggested by the indirect stimulus of railroad freight operations. By providing freight services to producers in areas previously isolated, the railroad caused sharp upward shifts in the demand for labor in sparsely populated regions, especially in the northern mining states. Higher wages in these newly developing areas certainly played a role in stimulating migration from areas of low labor productivity in the central and southern portions of the country.

In short, the small direct savings attributable to railroad passenger services does not diminish the importance of the railroad in stimulating the internal migration of the Porfirian era. The economy no doubt gained little in a direct sense from railroad transport of migrants. Had they walked, national income would not have been significantly reduced. But that is the point. Without the railroad, it is possible that neither the opportunities nor the knowledge of them nor perhaps even the desire to seize them would have developed so rapidly. The negligible direct contribution of railroad passenger service to the gross national product serves chiefly to indicate the importance of examining other aspects of the railroad's impact.

Chapter 4
Railroad Freight Services: Resource Savings and Economic Growth

The Problem

How much Mexico benefited from railroads depended on two factors: unit savings in transport costs and the volume of freight the railroads carried. Since geography made primitive overland transport the only alternative to railroads, unit savings should prove to have been large. The volume of freight the railroads carried depended in large part on two sets of factors: the level of economic activity prior to the railroads and the responsiveness of the economy to the transport cost reductions which the railroads made possible. Unlike more advanced countries, Mexico's backwardness in the 1870s and 1880s raised well-founded doubts among railroad promoters about the prospects for profitable operations. Much would depend, many of them said, on the railroad's unique ability to "create its own demand."[1] In the United States or Great Britain, these doubts were less compelling, for two reasons. First, both of these economies (and others in the North Atlantic) had already begun to industrialize before the construction of the railroads (in part, perhaps, because of the availability of cheap water transport). Railroad technology was a product of the industrial revolution, not its initiator. Both economies produced large quantities of transportable goods long before the iron horse. Second, both had already developed relatively efficient and competitive market structures which allowed entrepreneurs to take advantage of cost reductions, however small, and to translate them into increased production of transportable goods. In both cases, transport costs were already low, so unit savings were predict-

1. Bernard Moses, *The Railroad Revolution in Mexico* (San Francisco: Berkeley Press, 1895), p. 36.

ably small. Total savings were not negligible, however, because of the high volume of shipments.[2]

In backward regions like Mexico, where cheap water transport did not exist prior to the railroad, a different pattern occurred. While railroad construction usually followed prior geographic patterns of production and trade, the "developmental" impact of railroads often appeared as the most important benefit. In Mexico, this theme dominated early discussions about railroads and rallied support to public subsidies and other incentives for railroad enterprise. The promise and the reality came much closer together in this country than it did in many other backward areas of the world (including nineteenth-century Spain).[3] Nonetheless, significant obstacles had to be overcome. It is true that railroad construction, or just rumors of future construction, often led to increased activity along the new routes. By the time railroads actually arrived, lands had already changed hands, crops were planted, livestock bred, mines registered, wells dug, and houses built. The extent of these initial, and often haphazard, anticipatory activities was often limited, however, by existing property rights, by the lack of information (and experience) of appropriate markets or technology, or by high costs of exploration, discovery, and initiation of new enterprise. Even after the railroad arrived, these constraints still operated as did others, such as scarcities of capital for development and labor for the new jobs. Since large-scale production of transportables rarely preceded railroad construction, social savings had to depend largely on overcoming these obstacles. Where they were overcome (and this did not always happen), it was usually because railroad construction simultaneously created, or strengthened, the links between previously fragmented local markets, and between them and world markets. In this double process, the most important new links were those forged between regions rich in exploitable resources and the economies of the advanced countries of the North Atlantic. Mexican railroads created their own demand, but it was a demand derived from the expansion of the already industrializing nations.

2. See references to works by Fishlow, Fogel, and Hawke cited in chapter 1.

3. Gabriel Tortella Casares, *Orígenes del capitalismo en España* (Madrid: Editorial Tecnos, 1973).

The dynamics of the international flow of capital, the development of new primary product exporting economies, and the place of Mexico in this global process are already well known.[4] Foreign capital, the greater part of it from the United States, first entered Mexico on a massive scale to finance railroad construction and then moved chiefly into mining and large-scale plantation agriculture. It is to be expected, therefore, that railroad freight volume and total social savings were very large by 1910. Measuring social savings at the end of the *Porfiriato* will permit a test of this hypothesis and provide a cumulative measure of the railroad's impact. The purpose is to estimate the proportion of Mexico's economic growth in the Porfirian period that can be attributed to the direct benefits of railroad freight transportation. It should be kept in mind that while social savings estimates can reveal the approximate magnitude of the railroad's direct effects in a limited time period, they cannot tell us much about the structure of the growth process itself, nor do they resolve important issues that concern the development of Mexican society over the historical long run.

Unlike the savings estimates for passenger services, where arbitrary specification of critical variables (the opportunity cost of time and the proportion of "nonproductive" passengers) had to be made, the estimation of direct social savings on freight services is relatively straightforward and uncomplicated. Most of the necessary data are available either directly, from the publications of the relevant ministries and the annual reports of the railroad companies, or indirectly, by reconstruction with simple statistical manipulations of surviving quantitative information. Estimates of the relevant time series for freight services for a sample of fifteen major lines are presented first. Next, two estimates of social savings in 1910 are constructed by assuming a completely inelastic demand for transport and using cross-section data contained in the annual reports of the thirty-four companies that operated nearly all of Mexico's steam railroads in that year. The chapter concludes by estimating the price elasticity of de-

4. Fernando Rosenzweig H., "Las exportaciones mexicanas de 1877 a 1911," *TE* 27 (1960):537–69; Luis Nicolau d'Olwer, "Las inversiones extranjeras," in Cosío Villegas, ed., *Historia moderna de México: El Porfiriato, La vida económica*, vol. 2, pp. 973–1185.

mand for freight transportation in the Porfirian economy which makes it possible to calculate the direct contribution of railroads to the economic growth experienced in the period.

The Growth of Railroad Freight Services, 1873–1910

The period of most rapid expansion of railroad freight services began in 1884 with the completion of the Central's line from Mexico City to the U.S. border. As table 4.1 shows, the steady increase in tons carried by Mexican railroads was reversed in only two years between 1877 and 1908. The years 1886 and 1893 suffered declines of 8.6 and 9.0 percent respectively. Between 1873 and 1910, tons carried by Mexican railroads rose from 150,000 to 14 million. As the table indicates, however, the *rate* of increase diminished over the period. In the last decade of the *Porfiriato* the tonnage carried nearly doubled, but this pace contrasts unfavorably with the tenfold increase of the 1880s and the nearly 300 percent increase in the decade of the 1890s. Over the entire period, from 1873 to 1910, the number of tons carried increased at an average annual rate of 13.0 percent per year. The rates of increase per decade and quinquennium are indicated in table 4.1.

A more complete view of the railroad's freight services requires information about freight revenues and ton kilometers of freight moved. Neither the official yearbooks nor the summary volumes of railroad statistics contain such data.[5] Thus it has been necessary to examine the annual reports of most of the major lines. The annual reports of fifteen separate companies were examined in detail. They are listed in table 4.2. By the end of the Porfirian era, Mexicanization of some and mergers involving others had reduced the number of

5. For several years between 1900 and 1906, data on average length of haul and (less frequently) revenues earned per ton kilometer were reported in two summary volumes of railroad statistics published by the Secretaría de Comunicaciones y Obras Públicas: *Reseña histórica y estadística de los ferrocarriles de jurisdicción federal, 1900–1903* (Mexico, 1905) and *Reseña histórica y estadística de los ferrocarriles de jurisdicción federal, 1904–1906* (Mexico, 1907). Both volumes contain numerous misprints and should be used with caution.

TABLE 4.1

Tons Carried by Mexican Railroads, 1873–1910

Year	Metric Tons	Annual Variation (%)
1873	150,474	—
1874	122,234	−18.8
1875	136,853	12.0
1876	132,915	2.9
1877	158,884	19.5
1878	172,497	8.6
1879	199,012	15.4
1880	264,903	33.1
1881	397,637	50.1
1882	781,729	96.5
1883	851,916	9.0
1884	1,004,737	17.9
1885	1,161,466	15.6
1886	1,061,782	8.6
1887	1,467,572	38.2
1888	1,811,577	23.4
1889	2,106,839	16.2
1890	2,687,755	27.5
1891	3,199,805	19.0
1892	3,815,978	19.2
1893	3,470,118	9.0
1894	3,825,379	10.2
1895	4,361,316	14.0
1896	5,193,401	19.0
1897	5,830,407	12.2
1898	6,218,468	6.6
1899	7,277,303	17.1
1900	7,698,860	5.8
1901	7,843,266	1.9
1902	8,225,628	4.9
1903	9,585,512	16.4
1904	10,860,005	13.3
1905	11,424,253	5.2

TABLE 4.1 (*cont.*)

Year	Metric Tons	Annual Variation (%)
1906	12,398,603	8.5
1907	13,910,018	12.1
1908	14,223,296	2.3
1909	13,913,146	2.2
1910	14,072,457	1.1

Average Annual Increase by Decade and Quinquennium

Years	Annual Average Increase (%)
1873–1910	13.0
1873–1879	4.8
1880–1889	26.5
1890–1899	13.2
1900–1910	6.2
1873–1874	−18.8
1875–1879	9.8
1880–1884	38.7
1885–1889	15.9
1890–1894	12.7
1895–1899	13.7
1900–1904	8.4
1905–1909	5.1
(1906–1910)	4.3

Source: Appendix I.

TABLE 4.2

Railroad Lines Included in Sample

Company	Concession Number	Year Commencing Freight Services
1. Mexican	1	1854 (b)
2. Tehuantepec National	2	1895(c)
3. Sonora	6	1881
4. Interoceanic	9	1880 (d)
5. Mexican National	10	1874 (e)
6. Mexican Central	17	1881
7. Hidalgo and Northeastern	18	1881
8. Mérida–Progreso	23	1880
9. Mérida–Peto	28	1881
10. Peninsular	33	1883
11. Mérida–Valladolid	36	1883
12. Mexican International	40	1883
13. Mérida–Izamal	78	1883
14. Mexican Southern	82	1891
15. Mexican National Construction Company(a)	10	1887

(a) This company received two unconnected lines originally conceded to the Mexican National in a reorganization of the two companies arranged in 1886.

(b) The Mexico City–Veracruz line was not completed until 1873.

(c) Some freight services over scattered sections of line began earlier, but no records survive.

(d) The concessions for this line were originally granted to several separate companies, the first of which commenced freight service in 1880. The Interoceanic Railway of Mexico, Ltd., purchased the merged lines in 1888.

(e) This concession was originally granted to the Mexico–Toluca–Cuautitlán Railroad Company, which commenced freight services in 1874. The Mexican National Railroad Company took over the line in 1881.

TABLE 4.3
Tons Carried by Sample Lines As a Percentage of Total, 1873–1910

Year	Sample Line Tons Carried	Percent of Total
1873	150,474	100.0
1874	122,234	100.0
1875	136,853	100.0
1876	132,915	100.0
1877	158,884	100.0
1878	172,497	100.0
1879	199,012	100.0
1880	264,903	100.0
1881	397,637	100.0
1882	779,864	99.7
1883	848,003	99.5
1884	998,774	99.5
1885	1,155,171	99.5
1886	1,050,450	99.0
1887	1,440,554	98.2
1888	1,778,869	98.3
1889	2,067,796	98.3
1890	2,473,350	92.6
1891	2,865,161	89.2
1892	3,283,576	86.2
1893	2,872,092	82.3
1894	3,160,963	82.3
1895	5,022,891	86.1
1896	4,325,079	83.1
1897	4,880,315	83.4
1898	5,183,579	83.2
1899	6,104,319	83.6
1900	6,360,407	82.5
1901	6,183,668	78.7
1902	7,250,721	88.1
1903	8,169,284	85.2
1904	8,899,387	82.0
1905	9,358,984	81.9

TABLE 4.3 (cont.)

Year	Sample Line Tons Carried	Percent of Total
1906	9,946,451	80.2
1907	11,093,058	79.1
1908	11,544,862	81.2
1909	10,594,940	76.2
1910	10,966,585	77.1

Source: Appendices I and II.

companies to seven.[6] An indication of the importance of these lines is the proportion of total tons they carried. This information is contained in table 4.3. The sample lines, as the table indicates, carried between 76.2 and 100 percent of all tons shipped by steam railroad in Mexico between 1873 and 1910.

The best index of the volume of railroad freight services is a measure of the number of ton kilometers of freight actually moved. Most of the major companies examined began reporting these data in the late 1890s. With the establishment of the *Secretaría de Comunicaciones y Obras Públicas* in 1892, efforts were made to improve reporting techniques. Railroad companies were required to submit detailed financial and operating statistics to the ministry at the end of each year.[7] Marginal notes in the annual reports and letters exchanged between company and ministry officials indicate that the reports were more than mere formalities. Inconsistencies were reported to higher ministry officials, inspection of company facilities was undertaken by engineers employed in the ministry, and separate

6. The government-owned *Ferrocarriles Nacionales de México* had absorbed lines 4, 5, 6, 7, and 14 on the list while the five Yucatecan lines numbered 8, 9, 10, 11, and 13 were merged into the *Ferrocarriles Unidos de Yucatán* by 1910.

7. Even the earliest concessions required railroad companies to report regularly on their operations. The Ministry of Communications and Public Works issued new regulations, however, which required all companies to report more thoroughly on their operations and financing than most had been accustomed to doing, and officials of the ministry were more diligent than their predecessors in insisting upon compliance; Macedo, *Tres monografías*, p. 207.

reports were filed annually by the government representatives appointed to the boards of directors of nearly every company.

For the period from the early 1870s to the late 1890s, a variety of sources was used to derive the ton kilometer estimates. For years where the necessary data were unavailable, estimates were produced in several ways. The preferred technique was linear extrapolation of estimated revenues earned per ton kilometer. Ton kilometers were then calculated from freight earnings data. Where earnings per ton kilometer could not be estimated, investigation frequently confirmed grounds for a reasonable estimate of the average length of haul, or produced sufficient qualitative evidence to lend weight to guesses about it. In a few cases, early in the era, estimates were based on somewhat arbitrary decisions about the probable relationship between total length of the line and average length of the haul.[8] The resulting series then must be used with caution for the years prior to 1896, although the margin of error in the series data is probably quite small. After 1905, several lines converted from calendar to fiscal year reporting. In the last two years of the period, with most of the country's railroads in the hands of the government-controlled National Railways of Mexico, fiscal year reporting was the dominant practice. To convert from the fiscal to the calendar year, the series were adjusted by assigning 40 percent of the volume of traffic to the first semester of the fiscal year and 60 percent to the second.[9] Caution in the use of the series is therefore again required for the years 1906 to 1910.

It may be thought that the declining proportion of tons carried on the sample of major lines, especially in the last decade of the *Porfiriato,* imparts a downward bias to the estimates of ton kilometers, with the sample increasingly less representative of the railroad system as a whole. A high proportion of the new lines constructed after the early 1890s, however, served mainly as feeder connections to the major roads built earlier. Each time a ton of freight was transferred from one line to another, it entered the reported data as a "new" ton of freight. As the number of separate lines increased, especially in the late 1890s and early 1900s, the tonnage figures became increasingly inflated. This problem probably diminished somewhat with Mexican-

8. See Appendix II.
9. A similar procedure is adopted by Hawke, *Railways,* pp. 45–46.

ization of the major lines, but not by much. Mexicanization affected what amounted to major trunk lines that did not exchange much freight between them. Most of the feeder lines that accounted for the double counting remained outside the government-owned National Railways Company. The tonnage data in table 4.1 therefore suffer from an increasing upward bias, while the ton kilometer data from the sample lines in table 4.3 are a more reliable index of railroad output. Cross-section data for 1910 reveal that the sample lines actually accounted for 93.3 percent of all ton kilometers of freight carried, even though they carried only a little more than three fourths of all tons of freight tabulated by the separate companies.[10]

Estimates of the number of ton kilometers of freight carried by railroads in the sample are presented in table 4.4. While the general pattern of growth is similar to that indicated by the increase in the number of tons carried, the rate of increase is somewhat more rapid. The average annual increase for the entire period 1873 to 1910 is quite high: 15.6 percent. As in the case of the tonnage data, the rate of increase slows during the last decade of the *Porfiriato* down to an annual rate of 7.6 percent from a high of 32.7 percent during the 1880s.

To eliminate the effect of new railroad construction from the increase in freight carried, table 4.4 also shows the annual average rate of expansion of the railroad network. If it is assumed that each new kilometer of track constructed resulted in a proportional increase in the quantity of freight carried, the rate of expansion of the railroad network can be subtracted from the rate of increase in the number of ton kilometers of freight moved by rail. The result of such a manipulation of the data is to reduce the rate of increase from 15.6 to 5.6 percent for the entire period and to alter somewhat the pattern of declining growth rates noted above. During the great construction boom in the early 1880s, for example, the railroad network expanded so fast that even an annual average increase of 43.7 percent in the quantity of freight services produced could not keep up with the even faster rate of expansion of the railroad network. And in the 1890s, as might be expected, the quantity of freight shipped recovered from the depression of the middle of the decade much more

10. Compare the sample total of 3,258 million ton kilometers in table 4.4 with the total for all lines, 3,456 million in table 4.8 below.

TABLE 4.4

Ton Kilometers of Freight Carried by Sample Lines, 1873–1910

Year	Ton Kilometers
1873	15,047,380
1874	12,196,112
1875	13,665,128
1876	13,227,658
1877	15,856,716
1878	16,992,577
1879	30,066,554
1880	36,355,691
1881	56,160,448
1882	110,262,487
1883	203,241,172
1884	183,742,963
1885	221,879,931
1886	204,328,872
1887	269,792,330
1888	425,672,004
1889	510,147,635
1890	602,896,885
1891	730,176,264
1892	921,794,744
1893	794,350,896
1894	767,976,209
1895	886,362,458
1896	1,034,247,193
1897	1,164,262,613
1898	1,193,219,506
1899	1,448,677,901
1900	1,669,958,691
1901	1,717,283,322
1902	2,208,913,689
1903	2,423,065,828

TABLE 4.4 (*cont.*)

Year	Ton Kilometers
1904	2,571,488,964
1905	2,649,154,220
1906	2,821,503,707
1907	3,260,320,561
1908	3,057,758,882
1909	3,187,323,136
1910	3,248,885,261

Average Annual Increase by Decade and Quinquennium

Years	Ton Kilometers	Kilometers of Track Constructed	Difference
1873–1910	15.6	10.0	5.6
1873–1879	12.2	7.7	4.5
1880–1889	32.7	25.0	7.7
1890–1899	11.0	4.2	6.8
1900–1910	7.6	4.0	3.6
1873–1874	−18.9	2.4	21.3
1875–1879	19.8	8.8	11.0
1880–1884	43.7	45.1	−1.4
1885–1889	22.6	7.6	15.0
1890–1894	8.5	5.0	3.5
1895–1899	13.5	3.3	10.2
1900–1904	12.2	5.7	6.5
1905–1909	4.4	2.9	1.5
(1906–1910)	4.8	2.6	2.2

Source: Appendix II.

rapidly than did the rate of construction. Nonetheless, a marked slowdown is again observed toward the end of the period from rates well above the increase in national income to rates of growth in freight services of between 1.5 and 2.2 percent on average for the last years of the *Porfiriato*. These are the lowest adjusted growth rates encountered in the whole period (except for the early 1880s) and reflect slower growth rates in the industries that made most use of the railroads. Except for these last few years, however, the extremely high rates of growth in the production of railroad freight services indicate that this industry played a dynamic role in the economy of Mexico.

Railroad freight revenues usually appear in the government's statistical yearbooks and the published volumes of railroad data merged with income from other sources as "diverse" as telegraph, baggage and express, warehouse, insurance, lightering and other port facilities, supplemental stage and wagon lines, and tourist hotels. Fortunately, company annual reports almost invariably distinguish between revenues from freight services and income from these other activities. On the other hand, neither the published government statistics nor the annual reports of the companies distinguish revenue freight from company freight carried free, from ballast, or from construction freight usually carried "at cost" and charged to capital account. Larger companies in the earliest years, and all firms after the mid-1890s, clearly made these distinctions. Wherever possible, company freight has been excluded from the tonnage data reported in table 4.1 and from entering the estimates of ton kilometers in table 4.4. Construction freight and the charges reported against capital account for its carriage have been included in the data, but for most years the quantity was negligible. Since most concessions required Mexican railroad companies to carry "materials for other railroads" at very low rates, the inclusion of construction freight in the series does not appreciably alter the resulting shipping cost estimates. Freight revenues earned by the fifteen sample lines examined are reported in table 4.5.

Interpretation of the revenue series is complicated by the same difficulties that beset the presentation of total output estimates in Chapter 2. Again, data in current pesos are deflated first by employing the Colegio de México average wholesale price index for the

TABLE 4.5
Freight Revenues Earned by Sample Lines, 1873–1910

Year	1	2	3	4
1873	1,294,411			
1874	1,811,844			
1875	1,891,429			
1876	1,768,758			
1877	2,165,523			3,150,729
1878	2,346,628	3,445,856		
1879	2,714,788	3,968,989		
1880	3,196,280	4,666,103		
1881	4,660,682	6,754,611		
1882	7,025,467	10,094,062		
1883	8,843,016	12,815,966		
1884	6,895,471	10,155,333		
1885	6,563,597	9,218,534	8,106,676	
1886	7,334,189		9,854,814	9,425,774
1887	8,520,804		11,463,694	12,396,584
1888	11,949,387		14,645,162	14,576,519
1889	12,505,678		15,378,054	14,031,388
1890	13,356,225		15,670,878	15,607,508
1891	14,784,003		14,954,010	17,378,195
1892	16,253,087		14,527,485	16,583,087
1893	15,897,251		16,125,323	15,108,554
1894	16,794,136		17,817,148	17,855,447
1895	17,891,809		18,675,657	19,180,884
1896	19,535,868		19,661,039	19,112,888
1897	23,555,599		26,498,617	22,924,331
1898	25,214,962		30,116,860	28,506,014
1899	29,727,189		32,841,528	33,609,327
1900	32,090,235		32,113,306	32,113,306
1901	32,880,951		31,958,643	26,823,964
1902	37,443,608		34,149,806	30,924,792
1903	44,149,674		44,317,874	35,182,916
1904	47,248,226		43,329,589	44,101,036
1905	48,819,425		39,313,449	40,346,619
1906	52,145,658		41,447,889	38,231,375

TABLE 4.5 (*cont.*)

Year	1	2	3	4
1907	60,319,201		48,154,935	45,122,837
1908	55,961,250		42,594,581	42,502,848
1909	65,382,518			45,578,721
1910	71,272,668			42,755,330

(1) Current Pesos
(2) Adjusted by Export Price Index (1900–1901 = 100)
(3) Adjusted by Domestic Price Index 1 (1900 = 100)
(4) Adjusted by Domestic Price Index 2 (1900 = 100)
Source: Appendix II.

entire republic (Index 1) and then by using the Colegio's Mexico City consumer price index (Index 2). Neither of these indices is entirely appropriate for this purpose, and neither is complete for the entire period, from 1873 to 1910, covered by the data. The Mexico City index is again extrapolated between 1877 and 1886 by assuming that it moved in proportion to movements in the Colegio export price index lagged six months.[11]

Taken together, the ton kilometer and revenue series make it possible to estimate the revenues per ton kilometer earned by Mexican railroads in the sample for each year of the *Porfiriato*. This information, in current and deflated pesos, is reported in table 4.6. The sample average revenue per ton kilometer data make it possible to test some contemporary observations based on less reliable information.

First, it seems quite clear from the data that the Mexican Railway, heavily overcapitalized and enjoying a monopoly on nearly all freight originating in the foreign trade sector prior to 1884, charged extremely high rates.[12] The dramatic decline in revenues per ton

11. See discussion below in Appendix III.
12. Contemporary observers claimed that the Mexican Railway company was charging higher rates than had been charged by wagoners and muleteers prior to the construction of the railroad. Calderón rejected this charge (*La vida económica*, pp. 623–25, 637–41) after comparing wagon and railroad rates charged for transporting goods between Mexico City and Veracruz. The Mexican Railway was, indeed, less costly, but as Calderón observes, not very much less costly than the transport system it replaced. For contemporary commentary on the Mexican Railway's high rates see Matías Romero,

kilometer in the 1880s was due largely to the opening of the Mexican Central's competing route to the United States and the subsequent completion of additional lines with international connections.[13]

Second, it can be observed from the data that the decline which began in 1879 was halted in 1893. Thereafter, all three series show a marked tendency toward stability. After fluctuating about a mean of 2.05 *centavos* from 1892 to 1900, revenue per ton kilometer (deflated by Index 2) dropped quickly to less than one and a half *centavos* in 1902 and rose above that mark only twice in the next eight years. It seems clear, therefore, that the depreciation in Mexico's silver currency which accelerated during the 1890s did not result in compensating adjustments in railroad tariffs sufficient to raise revenues earned per ton kilometer.[14] In contrast to the rapid depreciation of the peso, railroad revenues per ton kilometer, in both current *and* deflated pesos, remained remarkably steady. With a major source of their inputs and most of their stockholders located abroad, chiefly in the United States and Great Britain, Mexican railroad companies had to meet rising foreign currency expenses out of constant peso earnings per unit of service. Most companies suffered significant pressures on their profit margins, which neither the diminishing sympathy of the government nor their own transitory pooling arrangements sufficed to abate. Not until after most of the major lines had been purchased by the government did the Monetary Reform of 1905 relieve these pressures by putting Mexico on the gold standard.

While the dramatic reduction in freight revenues per ton kilometer in the early 1880s was due mainly to increasing competition, the failure of the companies to increase rates after this period despite the depreciation of the peso and the consequent domestic inflation had other causes as well. First, competition continued to intensify during

Railways in Mexico: an article in answer to an article of the Hon. John Bigelow entitled "The Railway Invasion of Mexico," published in Harper's New Monthly Magazine for October, 1882 (Washington, 1882), pp. 8–11; *Railroad Gazette,* 18 February 1881, pp. 98–99; 8 June 1883, pp. 364–65; 31 August 1883, p. 579; 20 May 1892, p. 37; and *The Economist* 46 (5 May 1888):565.

13. On the effect of competition on the rates of the Mexican Railway, see *Railroad Gazette,* 14 December 1883, pp. 326–27; 4 June 1886, p. 384; 27 November 1891, pp. 884–85.

14. For a general discussion of government transport policy in this period, see above, chapter 2.

TABLE 4.6

Revenue Per Ton Kilometer of Freight, Sample Lines, 1873–1910

Year	1	2	3	4
1873	.086			
1874	.149			
1875	.138			
1876	.134			
1877	.137			.199
1878	.138	.203		
1879	.090	.132		
1880	.088	.128		
1881	.083	.120		
1882	.064	.092		
1883	.044	.063		
1884	.038	.055		
1885	.030	.042	.037	
1886	.036		.048	.046
1887	.032		.042	.045
1888	.028		.034	.034
1889	.024		.031	.027
1890	.023		.026	.026
1891	.020		.020	.024
1892	.018		.016	.018
1893	.020		.020	.019
1894	.022		.023	.023
1895	.020		.021	.022
1896	.019		.019	.018
1897	.020		.023	.020
1898	.021		.025	.024
1899	.021		.023	.023
1900	.019		.019	.019
1901	.019		.019	.016
1902	.017		.015	.014
1903	.018		.018	.015
1904	.018		.017	.017
1905	.018		.015	.015
1906	.018		.015	.014

TABLE 4.6 (*cont.*)

Year	1	2	3	4
1907	.019		.015	.014
1908	.018		.014	.014
1909	.021			.014
1910	.022			.013

(1) Current Pesos
(2) Adjusted by Export Price Index (1900–1901 = 100)
(3) Adjusted by Domestic Price Index 1 (1900 = 100)
(4) Adjusted by Domestic Price Index 2 (1900 = 100)
Source: Appendix III.

the 1890s with the construction of new lines from Veracruz to Mexico City and between points already served by rail throughout the Central Plateau.[15] In addition, conversion of the National's lines to standard gauge increased competition in the carriage of freight from the Central Plateau to the U.S. border.[16] Second, since wages throughout the Mexican economy lagged behind the rising price level after the mid-1890s and most railroad inputs produced in Mexico were labor intensive, a part of the squeeze on profit margins was relieved by passing the pressure along to employees and local suppliers. Evidence in the company annual reports, which occasionally contain wage and salary data, as well as the coincidence of rising labor agitation and strike activity in this decade, are eloquent testimony to this practice.[17] The railroads were not alone in reaping the distributional advantages of the *pax porfiriana,* but they did not fail to partake.

A further reason for the failure of earnings per ton kilometer to increase during the 1890s and after lies in the changing composition of railroad freight. While earnings per ton kilometer failed to in-

15. Calderón, "Los ferrocarriles," pp. 543–69.
16. The conversion of the National to standard gauge was begun in 1902 after four years of planning and efforts to secure adequate financing. Conversion to standard gauge was completed in 1903. See Powell, *Railroads of Mexico,* p. 135.
17. On railroad labor organization, see Moïsés González Navarro, *La vida social,* vol. 4 of the *Historia moderna de México: El Porfiriato,* ed. Daniel Cosío Villegas (Mexico: Editorial Hermes, 1957), pp. 299–300, 306–10.

crease, railroad tariff schedules did.[18] The reason for this paradox lies in the rapid increase in the proportion of export freight. Railroad tariffs were maintained at differentially low rates for mineral and agricultural export freight and the proportion of these types of freight in the total increased more rapidly than that of other types of freight.[19] The very process of export sector expansion which the railroads did so much to induce contributed importantly to reduce the profits from their operations.

Direct Social Savings on Freight Services, 1910

To construct savings estimates for railroad freight services, the cost of prerail freight transportation was examined. Three means of transporting freight were employed in the prerail era: Indian porters, mules and donkeys, and wagons. Although *commercial* wagon, mule and donkey service ceased entirely along routes now served by rail, Indian porters survived long into the railway era, along with the ubiquitous burros.[20] Railway second class baggage allowances were

18. The major companies did not undertake any major revisions of their freight classification systems until late in the decade. Major revisions proposed by the companies in 1897 were approved by the government in early 1898; Mexican Central Railroad Company, Ltd., *Annual Report, 1897* (New York, 1898), p. 23. The companies did, however, adjust their tariffs within the classification systems already in use. In addition, the pooling arrangements between the major international carriers permitted them to fix and maintain higher rates during the years 1892–1894 and 1897–1899. Reports in the press described rate increases as high as 100 percent on third class freight; *The Economist* 50 (13 August 1892):1033. The Mexico City Chamber of Commerce organized a vigorous protest against the new rates which continued for much of the decade; *Railroad Gazette*, 10 September 1892, p. 730. In addition to the international pools, some lines entered into local pooling arrangements for traffic between competing points: "Précis of Mr. Jackson's Report of condition of the Interoceanic Railway dated 1st. July 1894," *AHSCT* 9/65–7, pp. 33–34.

19. See below, chapter 5.

20. Moses, *Railroad Revolution*, p. 9. The railroad companies themselves took note of this competition for local traffic since short hauls were usually squeezed for higher rates. The Chairman of the Board of the Interoceanic Railway discussed the declining competition from mule and donkey carriage

TABLE 4.7
Wagon Freight Transportation Rates, 1878–1879

Route	Distance (kilometers)	Price Per Ton Kilometer
1. México–Toluca	79	$.221
2. México–San Luis Potosí	235	.231
3. Ciudad del Maíz–Tantoyoquito	161	.183
4. San Luis Potosí–Zacatecas	207	.132
5. México–Zacatecas	453	.119
6. Guadalajara–Zapotlanejo	38	.118
7. Guadalajara–Tepatitlán	80	.135
8. Guadalajara–Lagos	205	.106
9. Zacatecas–Lagos	225	.193
10. Zacatecas–Aguascalientes	122	.178
11. San Luis Potosí–Querétaro	243	.179
12. Tepatitlán–San Juan de los Lagos	79	.058
13. Linares–Matehuala	262	.111
14. Guadalajara–Santa Ana Acatlán	44	.163

Source: *Memoria de Fomento, 1877–82,* vol. 2.

usually fixed at 25 kilos, and some freight formerly carried by porters and donkeys probably shifted to the railroads. By 1910, nearly all of the competition had ended, although continued reliance on prerail modes of transport for short hauls apparently persisted. Trains of mules and donkeys competed with wagons in the prerail era over the federal highway network where wheeled traffic was possible. Between cities and towns not connected by vehicle road, mule trains alone were used. Wagon transport was less costly, but it was available only on improved roads. Table 4.7 presents wagon freight rates over major prerail federal highways reported by highway directors in their annual reports for the fiscal year ending 30 June 1879. The average of the fourteen rates reported is $0.16. This may be somewhat low;

at the annual stockholders meeting in 1893; *South American Journal,* 11 November 1893, p. 492 ff.

TABLE 4.8
Ton Kilometers of Freight and Freight Revenues of Mexican Railroads, 1910

Company	Ton Kilometers	Revenues
Mexican	175,127,279	$ 5,681,012
Tehuantepec National	207,560,072	5,470,135
Sonora	49,064,157	921,763
Interoceanic	209,203,914	6,882,223
National Railways	2,566,839,094	44,886,469
Mexican National Construction Company	2,308	289
Veracruz	2,449,421	176,166
United of Yucatán	23,207,370	1,475,056
Monte Alto – Tlalnepantla	919,974	59,692
Mexican Southern	15,431,646	5,955,722
Mexican Northern	13,347,410	534,960
Toluca – Tenango	847,308	42,058
Esperanza – El Xúchil	210,397	13,802
Coahuila and Zacatecas	24,794,640	910,395
Jalapa – Teocelo	415,362	52,409
Cazadero – Solís	1,266,570	43,207
San Juan – El Juile	36,634	2,008
San Marcos – Huajuapan de León	569,348	32,900
Occidental of Mexico	462,943	23,907
Ixtlahuaca, Mañi and Presa Grande	735,000	44,115
Torres – Minas Prietas	518,650	43,972
San Rafael – Atlixco	4,734,735	178,051
San Luis Potosí – Río Verde	5,094,572	188,100
Parral and Durango	2,283,714	221,270
Mineral of Chihuahua	1,295,995	74,215
Nacozari	19,051,883	1,094,644
Kansas City, Mexico and Oriente	4,068,383	195,763
Pan American	8,421,621	431,085
Tlalnepantla – Mexico	1,188,223	52,346
Inter-California	36,498	25,409

TABLE 4.8 (*cont.*)

Company	Ton Kilometers	Revenues
Tultenango–Yondesé	4,321,633	398,023
Zitácuaro–Joconusco	432,763	23,100
South Pacific of Mexico	62,966,747	1,789,598
Tenayuca–Cuautepec	6,997	410
Northwestern	48,625,938	1,556,684
Minatitlán	550,800	52,012
Totals	3,456,090,000	$79,532,972

Source: Appropriate files in the *AHSCT*.

nonetheless, the savings estimates below employ a still lower rate of $0.10 in order to approximate a best practice *minimum* rate for prerail freight carriage.[21]

Cross-section data for construction of the savings estimate for 1910 are presented in table 4.8. Data for sixteen small companies operating 4.4 percent of 1910 steam trackage are missing. Ton kilometers of freight shipped was calculated directly by multiplying total tons carried by average length of haul as reported in the annual report of each of the railroad companies. The revenue data was taken directly from the same reports. These data indicate that in 1910 Mexican railroads carried 14,072,457 tons of freight an average distance of 245.5 kilometers for a total of 3.456 billion ton kilometers. With total freight earnings of $79.5 million, the cost of railroad freight services amounted to $0.023 per ton kilometer.

Two estimates, "A" and "B," of 1910 social savings on freight services are constructed, each using a different method for adjusting current peso figures to pesos of 1900. The A estimate employs the Colegio de México consumer price index for Mexico City (Index 2 in

21. Every contemporary estimate encountered was higher than the $0.10 used here. A survey of prerail transport rates by a government civil engineer is contained in a document entitled "Ferrocarril de Huatusco al Camarón, Ingeniero de Comisión," in *MF, 1883–85* 2:903–14. This survey concludes that "$.21 per ton kilometer is the general [meaning, in context, the average] price of transportation before the railroads disturbed the old system," ibid., p. 906.

TABLE 4.9
Wagon and Railroad Cost Indices, 1877–1910

Year	Index of Real Wages (1900 = 100)	Index of Railroad Revenues Per Ton Kilometer (1900 = 100)
1877	95.7	709.9
1878	—	717.7
1879	—	753.4
1880	—	710.5
1881	—	709.4
1882	—	426.1
1883	—	256.3
1884	—	212.4
1885	85.6	164.8
1886	93.1	203.8
1887	94.3	179.7
1888	88.5	152.1
1889	96.5	132.3
1890	94.5	120.2
1891	84.8	104.2
1892	82.5	91.4
1893	97.6	104.5
1894	101.1	113.3
1895	102.4	104.8
1896	100.4	98.2
1897	107.9	105.3
1898	114.9	109.8
1899	110.1	106.8
1900	100.0	100.0
1901	101.9	99.7
1902	99.1	87.4
1903	114.1	94.9
1904	109.9	95.3
1905	102.9	96.0
1906	99.2	95.8
1907	100.8	96.4

TABLE 4.9 (*cont.*)

Year	Index of Real Wages (1900 = 100)	Index of Railroad Revenues Per Ton Kilometer (1900 = 100)
1908	97.5	95.4
1909	94.0	106.8
1910	84.7	113.9

Sources: El Colegio de México, *Estadísticas económicas del Porfiriato: Fuerza de trabajo y actividad por sectores* (México, n.d.), pp. 156, 172, and table 4.6.

tables 4.5 and 4.6) to adjust both the 1877 wagon rate and the 1910 rail cost per ton kilometer.[22] Using the consumer price index causes some exaggeration in the A estimate. This index rose from 68.7 in 1877 to 100 in 1900 and to 165.7 in 1910, while the cost of wagon transport rose more slowly between 1877 and 1900, and railroad costs increased substantially less in the final decade of the *Porfiriato*. In the case of wagon haulage, the price of the largest input, the real wages of labor, increased only 4.5 percent between 1877 and 1900. Railroad costs measured by an index of railroad revenues per ton kilometer in current pesos rose only 13.9 points from 1900 to 1910. These two series are presented in table 4.9. Using the Colegio index to inflate the 1877 wagon rate overstates the real cost of wagon shipment, while deflating 1910 railroad rates with the same index understates the rail costs. This combination of overstated wagon costs and understated rail costs biases the A estimate upwards. To eliminate the upward biases in the A estimate, the B estimate is calculated using real wages as a proxy for a wagon cost index to adjust the 1877 wagon rate to pesos of 1900, while the current (1910) railroad rate is deflated by using the index of railroad revenues per ton kilometer. Instead of an extremely volatile wholesale price index, which does not reflect the costs of producing transport services, the B estimate is calculated, in effect, with two indices of transport sector prices.

22. The Mexico City wholesale price index is found in El Colegio de México, *Estadísticas: Fuerza de trabajo*, p. 172.

The B estimate contains implicit *downward* biases, however, and thus may be considered a minimum estimate.[23] Labor accounted for less than 50 percent of the cost of wagon haulage and real wages were probably more stable than the cost of any other input.[24] The cost (in pesos of 1900) of feeding the approximately one million horses and mules that would have been required to transport the railroads' 3.456 billion ton kilometers of freight in 1910 would have reflected the 78 percent increase in the price of corn and the more than 100 percent increase in the price of barley in the years between 1877 and 1900.[25] Price series on the costs of other inputs are not available for the required length of time, but it is unlikely that the almost negligible increase in wages over the period could have been true for the prices of other inputs. Thus, the 4.5 percent increase in real wages between 1877 and 1900 *understates* the likely course of wagon transport costs over the period. At the same time, the government's monopoly of rail transport by 1910 may have kept rail rates above what they would have been had the industry remained competitive.[26] Thus, deflation of the railroad rate by the percentage increase in revenues per ton kilometer *understates* the reduction required for calculation of social savings by failing to remove monopoly rent from railroad revenues in 1910. For these reasons, it appears that the A and B estimates bracket the "true" social savings figure.

The A and B estimates are presented in table 4.10. The A estimate comes to $455.4 million or 38.5 percent of Mexico's 1910 gross

23. To be more precise, the estimate should be considered what Fogel calls a "least upper bound," since we are still assuming perfectly inelastic demand. Robert W. Fogel, "Railroads and American Economic Growth," in Robert W. Fogel and Stanley Engerman, eds., *The Reinterpretation of American Economic History* (New York: Harper and Row, 1971), p. 196 n.

24. The following discussion assumes a perfectly elastic supply of labor and other inputs at each observed price over thirty years. This assumption is obviously implausible, but any departure from it would merely strengthen the argument.

25. For price series on these commodities, see El Colegio de México, *Estadísticas: Fuerza de trabajo*, pp. 57–64. The estimated number of horses and mules assumes all railroad freight is transferred to wagons where each animal pulls an average of .4 tons 30 kilometers per day for 300 days in the year. Cf. Fishlow, *American Railroads*, p. 94.

26. As table 4.6 indicates, freight rates ceased to decline after 1902.

TABLE 4.10
Estimates of Direct Social Savings on Railroad Freight Services, 1910

A. *Estimate*

(a) Ton kilometers of freight moved, 1910	3,456,090,000 Ton kms.
(b) Cost of wagon shipment at $0.10 per ton kilometer (equal to $0.146 in pesos of 1900 deflated by Index 1)	$503,414,069
(c) Actual Railroad freight earnings in 1910 (deflated by Index 1)	$ 47,998,172

Estimate *A:* (b) − (c)
= $455,415,897

B. *Estimate*

(a) Ton kilometers of freight moved, 1910	3,456,090,000 Ton kms.
(b) Cost of wagon shipment at $0.10 per ton kilometer (equal to $0.104 in pesos of 1900 adjusted by Index of real wages)	$361,161,405
(c) Actual railroad freight earnings in 1910 (deflated by railroad cost index)	$ 69,827,016

Estimate *B:* (b) − (c)
= $291,334,389

104 : *Growth Against Development*

domestic product.[27] The B estimate is $291.3 million or 24.6 percent
of 1910 gross domestic product. These estimates bracket the probable cost, *ceteris paribus*, of shifting all ton kilometers of freight actually
conveyed by rail in 1910 from the railroad onto wagons. In order to
transport by wagon the freight actually carried by railroad in 1910,
Mexico would have had to sacrifice between 24.6 and 38.5 percent of
its 1910 gross domestic product, transferring resources from other
uses to the transport sector.

Fogel's estimates of railroad social savings in the United States in
1890 included a substantial allowance for "hidden costs" in the calculation of the disadvantages of wagon and water shipment. These
hidden costs included the cost of higher risk of loss or damage and
the probable losses due to the longer time required for shipment by
nonrail means and the closing of northern water routes in winter.[28]
In the case of Mexico, no such estimation of the hidden costs of
wagon transport has been included in the estimates. Information on
insurance rates in the prerail era are unavailable and even if they
were, higher prerail insurance costs could not easily be decomposed
to distinguish between the risks "embodied" in wagon transport and
those associated with a higher incidence of banditry in the pre-
Porfirian era. While wagons in Mexico were at least as slow as canal
and river boats in the United States, and the U.S. winter shutdown
has something of a parallel in Mexico's rainy season which made
many roads impassable or at least more treacherous from June
through September, no adjustment in the wagon rates has been made
to account for the cost of slower shipment and seasonality. The
wagon rates reported in table 4.7 and used as a basis for the savings
calculation are dry season rates. For routes where rainy season rates
were found, they varied from 16.6 to 50.0 percent above the dry
season rates.[29] Fogel's calculation of the hidden costs due to higher
risk, slowness, and seasonality amounts to more than the overt

27. Estimates of Mexico's gross domestic product at current prices are
found in Solís, "La evolución económica," pp. 3–5. Solis's estimates are converted to pesos of 1900 by using the Mexico City wholesale price index cited
above (n. 22).

28. Fogel, *Railroads,* pp. 41–48.

29. Calculated from wagon freight rate data in the reports of the federal
highway directors cited above.

charges collected for nonrail transport.[30] If the same relationship between hidden and overt charges were applied to Mexico, the savings estimates presented above would more than double.

The use of prerail dry season wagon rates to measure freight savings probably makes them a measure of railroad direct savings over a 1910 *technological* second best alternative. Most prerail freight traveled not in wagons but on mule or donkey back, and much of it traveled in the rainy months of the year. The social savings estimates therefore embody the assumption that in the absence of railroads Mexico would have invested in the extension of the wagon-passable federal highway system from approximately 4,400 kilometers in 1877 to somewhat more than 250,000 kilometers in 1910 in a way that would have improved rainy season road conditions markedly.[31]

Surviving data do not make it possible to calculate precisely the likely cost of such a highway extension program. So long as the total cost of all government subsidies to the railroad was equal to or less than the cost of constructing the hypothetical expanded highway network plus government highway maintenance costs in 1910, then the savings estimates above do not overestimate the benefits to Mexico from avoiding reliance on the technically feasible least cost alternative to the railroads. Government subsidies to railroads could not have exceeded $200,000,000 during the *Porfiriato*.[32] In the re-

30. This is true only for Fogel's interregional savings estimates. See Fogel, *Railroads*, pp. 210–14.

31. This crude estimate is based on figures cited by Fishlow which suggest a maximum "feasible" capacity of somewhat less than 20,000 tons of freight per route mile. Fishlow, *American Railroads*, p. 93. Applying this U.S. estimate to Mexico yields a required minimum of 167,000 route miles, or approximately 250,000 kilometers of highway to accommodate the 3.5 billion ton kilometers of freight shipped by rail in 1910.

32. In response to a request from Pablo Macedo, the Ministry of Communications and Public Works compiled an estimate of all subsidies paid by the federal government to railroad companies up to 30 June 1902. This estimate, $144,891,743.92, is far less certain than its apparent precision suggests. Allowing for subsidies paid after 30 June 1902 (the ministry published no summary records after that date) and for the omission of state and municipal subsidies, it is unlikely that direct subsidy payments exceeded $200,000,000 in pesos of 1900. For Macedo's data, see *Tres Monografías*, pp. 230–31.

ports of the *Secretaría de Fomento* in the 1870s, highway construction costs are reported to vary from a low of $2,000 to a high of more than $7,000 per kilometer.[33] Using only the lower figure, the cost of adding 245,000 kilometers of highway comes to $490,000,000. This figure must be viewed as a considerable underestimate of the costs which would have been encountered. That it is nearly 150 percent higher than the upper limit estimate of government railroad subsidies (and makes no allowance for 1910 highway maintenance costs) suggests that the 1910 savings estimates here have made ample allowance for technologically efficient adjustment to the absence of the railroad.

A wagon cost of $0.10, used for estimating railroad savings in this study, comes close to the lowest that prevailed in Mexico in 1877. But, except for the flat, dry regions in the extreme north and the best maintained of the federal highways elsewhere, wagon transportation was not characteristic of pre-Porfirian Mexico. Even on the best roads, traffic data reported by the directors of twenty-four federal highways between 1877 and 1882 indicate that the tonnage hauled by mule train or burro considerably exceeded the quantity of freight shipped by wagon on all but six of the twenty-four routes.[34] On only three of the highways did the proportion of tons carried by mule or burro drop below 20 percent. In two of the three cases, traffic was monitored at a point just outside a major city on a highly traveled

33. The chief of the section of the Fomento Ministry in charge of federal highways estimated in 1882 that "the construction of a paved road in good condition in terms of strength and durability through broken terrain such as ours could never be calculated at less than three to four thousand pesos per kilometer," *MF, 1877–82* 2:5. Other contemporary estimates run considerably higher. Mariano Barcena, a civil engineer employed by the Fomento Ministry in various capacities including highway director and railroad construction inspector, reviewed the low cost involved in the construction of a tramway between Tehuacán and La Esperanza and concluded that the tramway's cost of $5,893 per kilometer was an amount with which "a good highway could scarcely be constructed, for data exist in the Ministry of Fomento on the costs of highways in diverse locations, and in many a kilometer reaches a cost of $8,000"; *Los ferrocarriles mexicanos* (México, 1881), p. 25. Reports on the progress of construction and reconstruction are contained in the published reports of federal highway directors cited above.

34. Calculated from data in *MF, 1877–82*, vol. 2.

short stretch of road leading to what are today merely suburbs.[35] In the third case, that of the highway between Jalapa and San Marcos, the road was unusually well maintained because it met the Mexican Railway at San Marcos after passing through a region of intensive commercial agriculture.[36] In one case, that of the Mexico City– Cuernavaca highway, where human porters are reported explicitly (instead of included in the data as additional foot travelers), they competed with wagons and other beasts of burden for the carriage of freight. In addition to the 126,161 mules and donkeys counted at the checkpoint, the director's report listed "33,616 people on foot with freight."[37]

There are at least three plausible reasons for the observed preponderance of mule and donkey over wagon carriage. The first is suggested by the reputation of mule trains for reliability in the transport of particularly valuable freight. But the descriptions of the type of goods transported by mule and donkey that were submitted by some highway directors along with their traffic reports suggest that high value items did not form a significant portion of the freight carried by beasts of burden.

The second is suggested by the fact that the local roads that fed into the federal highways were almost entirely impassable for wheeled vehicles. Agricultural or artisan producers were more likely to hire mules or donkeys for the whole journey to market than pay the extra cost, suffer the inconvenience, and submit to the long delays and possible damage or destruction involved in transferring freight from animal packs to wagons on reaching the federal highway. The longer the contemplated wagon haul, of course, the greater the probability of transfer, but most frequently such transfers were effected after sale of the output to a middleman in the local market.

The third reason for mule and donkey competition with wagons, and the most difficult to assess, is the possibility that a considerable portion of this traffic consisted of shipments by noncommercial car-

35. The three highway sections with very low proportions of freight carried by pack animals were Jalapa–San Marcos, Zacatecas–El Refugio, and Guadalajara–Santa Ana Acatlán.

36. For a description of the Jalapa–San Marcos road, see *MF, 1877–82* 2:786–96.

37. *MF, 1877–82* 2:486.

TABLE 4.11
Average Length of Freight Haul, Sample Lines, 1873–1910
(kilometers)

1873	100.0
1874	99.8
1875	99.8
1876	99.5
1877	99.8
1878	98.5
1879	151.1
1880	137.2
1881	141.2
1882	141.4
1883	239.7
1884	184.0
1885	192.1
1886	194.5
1887	187.3
1888	239.3
1889	246.7
1890	243.8
1891	254.8
1892	280.7
1893	276.2
1894	243.0
1895	176.5
1896	239.1
1897	238.6
1898	230.2
1899	237.3
1900	262.6
1901	277.7
1902	304.6
1903	296.6
1904	288.9
1905	283.1
1906	283.7

TABLE 4.11 (*cont.*)

1907	293.9
1908	264.9
1909	300.8
1910	296.2

Source: Tables 4.3 and 4.4.

riers. If much freight was carried by farm or hacienda work animals attended by the producers themselves or their employees, the commercial freight rates used to construct the savings estimates do not reflect the real 1877 cost of nonrail freight transport. Fishlow has suggested that[38]

> if a crude, non-commercial method of carrying goods to market prevails, individuals may be sacrificing leisure for the essential task of transportation. When a more efficient distribution network is substituted, instead of an equivalent input of labor services into other activities, the result may be increased leisure.

There is no question that an important proportion of prerail freight consisted of a "crude, non-commercial method of carrying goods" in nineteenth-century Mexico. The railroad effectively eliminated the use of wagons and mule trains in long distance transport but did not immediately put an end to their use in short distance transport of agricultural and artisan output. It was precisely in competition with existing *commercial* carriers of long distance freight that the railroads had their greatest impact. The average length of haul for freight on Mexican railways in 1910 was 245.5 kilometers. Table 4.11 shows that the length of haul on the fifteen lines included in our sample was near 300 kilometers by 1910 and varied between 200 and 300 kilometers from the completion of the Central in 1884 to the end of the period. In short distance hauls from farm, hacienda, or rural sweatshop to local markets, the railroad did not eliminate (nor have modern highways even today) the prerail modes of conveyance. Only

38. Fishlow, *American Railroads*, p. 29.

a very small portion of the railroad's freight would have shifted to noncommercial carriers. Thus, the savings estimates that assumed commercial carriage as the appropriate counterfactual alternative are not biased by the assumption.

The Price Elasticity of Demand for Transportation

Beginning in 1886, and continuing for the next fourteen years, Gabriel Mancera, owner and manager of one of the few Mexican-owned railroad lines in the nation, took the occasion of his company's annual reports to the *Secretaría de Fomento* to comment on Porfirian transport policies.[39] Many of his comments were critical. In his first essay, in 1886, Mancera constructed social savings estimates on the freight and passenger services provided by his own railroad, the Hidalgo and Northeastern, from 1881 through 1886 and extrapolated his results to the entire Porfirian rail network. He estimated that for his line alone, "the quantity saved by the 259,461 passengers who from 1881 through 1886 inclusive have traveled on this railroad amounts to $224,274.64 and that the 153,165 tons of freight that have been transported provided the public a benefit of $1,159,225.64"[40] The total, $1,383,530.28, Mancera noted, was nearly double the total subsidy payments owed to his company by the federal government and the Hidalgo state government combined. For the nation as a whole, Mancera estimated railroad savings at approximately $43,000,000 in 1886, a sum in excess of the entire budget of the federal government.[41] From these calculations, and the then current difficulties encountered by federal and state governments in making promised subsidy payments to the railroad companies, Mancera concluded that

39. The annual reports of the Hidalgo and Northeastern Railway containing Mancera's comments are found in *AHSCT* 18/43–1, 18/43–2, 18/36, and 18/88.

40. *Informe anual de 1886, Ferrocarril de Hidalgo y Nordeste, AHSCT* 18/43–1, p. 14. The report is signed by Mancera and dated 28 February 1887.

41. Ibid., pp. 14–15. In pesos of 1900, Mancera's estimate comes to $55.2 million; using data from the fifteen lines included in the sample above, and the same estimating procedure, our estimate for 1885 lies between $21.0 million (A) and $17.7 million (B).

the federal government should modify the terms of railroad concessions by "prudently increasing the tariffs while at the same time reducing the rate of subsidies and assuring their payment."[42] Mancera had concluded, that is, that very large social savings implied a greater capacity to pay for transportation on the part of transport users than current tariff rates allowed the railroads to take.

In 1886, the *Secretaría* had not yet abandoned the policy of publishing the annual reports of major railroad companies as documents annexed to the ministry's *Memorias* to the Congress.[43] The files of the ministry contain a reply to Mancera's remarks, which is interesting not only for the thinly veiled sarcasm of its official author but because it implicitly attacks Mancera's estimates as exaggerated on the grounds that they embody the assumption of zero price elasticity of demand for transportation. Manual Velázquez de León, *Oficial Mayor* of the ministry, writing no doubt on instructions of the minister, General Carlos Pacheco, described Mancera's estimates as "very ingenious."[44] They "can be taken into consideration in making a study of the advantages brought to the country by the railroads, but not," he continued, "from the point of view of a savings which in reality has not been produced; for if there were no railroads there would not have been created that increase in traffic which can be measured by comparing the former [traffic] with the present. . . ." Railroads themselves had caused the increase in traffic "because transportation is made cheaper; and while the lower the price the more will traffic increase, the contrary happens if said price is increased."[45]

Mancera was not convinced. The Hidalgo and Northeastern annual reports contain social savings estimates, along with extended comments on various aspects of government policies, throughout the 1890s. Velázquez de León, exasperated by lengthy comments on the lack of a systematic concessions policy in the annual report for 1891, dispatched an official rebuke to Mancera informing him that "this

42. Ibid., p. 15.

43. The *Memoria* of the Fomento ministry covering the years 1883–1885 was not published until 1887. No further *Memoria* containing such documents were published until after the transport section of the ministry had been transferred to the new Ministry of Communications and Public Works.

44. *AHSCT* 18/43–1, pp. 16–17.

45. Ibid., p. 17.

type of reflections . . . ought not to be included in a document, which, by its very nature, must acquire the publicity accorded documents which contain . . . statistical points of importance."[46] Mancera continued, nonetheless, to include his comments, and his savings estimates, in his company's annual reports through 1900. The new *Secretaría de Comunicaciones y Obras Públicas,* organized in 1892, abandoned the practice of publishing such documents as railroad annual reports. No longer a source of public embarrassment to officials, Mancera's comments were thereafter simply ignored. By 1900, the last year Mancera personally wrote his company's annual report, his estimate of social savings from the operation of his own line had risen to $1,800,000 for the year 1900 alone, while his extrapolation to the nation as a whole yielded an estimate of $127,500,000, "more than all federal, state and local revenues combined."[47] For the Hidalgo and Northeastern, Mancera used his estimates to calculate a social rate of return on the government construction subsidies paid to his company. In round figures, he wrote, "the public, through its elected officials, has lent its money at a rate of 90 percent [interest] per year."[48]

Mancera never acknowledged the importance of his assumption of perfectly inelastic demand for transportation. Velázquez de León would therefore be pleased to notice that modern economists have confirmed his view that this assumption introduces an upward bias in estimates of direct social savings. Both of the 1910 estimates constructed above assume that in the absence of railroads, all freight actually conveyed by rail would have been carried by wagon between exactly the same points. This is precisely the assumption Mancera made, and it is wildly unrealistic. In the absence of the railroad, some economic activities would have ceased, some would have shifted location, and some would have continued to produce where they were. The quantities of transportables produced, the mix of output pro-

---

46. *Informe anual de 1891, Ferrocarril de Hidalgo y Nordeste, AHSCT* 18/43–1, p. 68; Velázquez's letter is in ibid., p. 72.

47. *Informe anual de 1900, Ferrocarril de Hidalgo y Nordeste, AHSCT* 18/43–2, pp. 6–8. For 1899, the year to which Mancera's estimates referred, our estimating procedure yields estimates between $177.4 million (A) and $123.6 million (B).

48. Ibid., p. 10.

TABLE 4.12

Direct Social Savings on Freight Services for Alternative Values of Price Elasticity of Demand for Transportation

Elasticity	"A" Estimate of Social Savings		"B" Estimate of Social Savings	
	MILLIONS OF 1900 PESOS	PERCENT OF 1910 GDP	MILLIONS OF 1900 PESOS	PERCENT OF 1910 GDP
0	$455.4	38.5	$294.5	24.9
.5	196.9	16.6	176.9	14.9
.75	135.8	11.5	127.6	10.8
1.0	95.6	8.1	112.2	9.5
1.5	53.2	4.5	75.9	6.4
2.0	33.8	2.9	54.2	4.6

duced by transportable goods firms, and the aggregate demand for transport under the nonrail system are unknown. Nevertheless, the effect of higher transport costs on the amount of transport services required may be estimated for alternative assumptions about the price elasticity of demand for transportation. For each assumed elasticity, the reduction in transport services demanded corresponds to a quantity of resources freed from the transport sector for other uses. Therefore, as the elasticity of demand increases, the quantity of freight services required of the nonrail economy declines. Because of this reduction in demand for transport, the social savings (and thus the percentage of the gross national product lost by eliminating the railroad) also decreases.

As table 4.12 illustrates, both of the 1910 estimates display considerable sensitivity to alternative assumptions about the elasticity of demand for freight transportation. Interpretation of these results is made problematical by the lack of sufficient information to specify a 1910 aggregate demand elasticity for the Mexican economy. Nevertheless, a crude estimate of the price elasticity of demand for transportation may be constructed using railroad price and output data together with national income and population estimates.

The elasticity estimate is based on the following relationship:

$$R = a + b_1K + b_2F + b_3Y + b_4P,$$

where

R = Demand for transportation, measured in ton kilometers of freight services produced;

K = Kilometers of track constructed and in operation;

F = Price, measured as average income per ton kilometer of freight carried;

Y = National income;

P = Population;

b_i = Corresponding elasticities when the equation is estimated in logarithmic form; and

a = A constant term.

Inclusion of the variable K, which is a measure of installed capacity, is useful because of the effect of extensions of the railroad network on aggregate demand. The equation thus distinguishes increases in demand due to changes in the price of railroad services. The equation further assumes that rising population and national income exert independent effects on the demand for transportation which also need to be separated from the effects of price changes.

The first three variables, R, K, and Y, are taken from the data found in tables 4.4, 2.3, and 4.6, respectively. Population is estimated by interpolation between census dates.[49] For the period of seventeen years, from 1878 to 1894, exports (Y_A) are used as a proxy for national income. For the period 1895–1910, a second estimate is made using the Solís gross domestic product estimates (Y_B).[50] The price elasticities estimated in both cases are quite close to each other: .558 and .428. While an elasticity in the range of .50 seems indicated by these results, it would be prudent to increase the estimate by 50 percent and accept .75 as a reasonable upper bound estimate.[51]

49. El Colegio de México, *Estadísticas: Fuerza de trabajo*, p. 25 and Clark Reynolds, *The Mexican Economy: Twentieth Century Structure and Growth* (New Haven: Yale University Press, 1970), p. 19.

50. El Colegio de México, *Estadísticas: Comercio exterior*, 133; Solís, "La evolución económica," pp. 3–5.

51. These equations may suffer from some degree of multicollinearity, impossible to eliminate completely. (Serial correlation is not high, however,

TABLE 4.13
Estimates of Price Elasticity of Demand for Transportation, 1878–1910

---

(1) Log R = −17.63

$$+ .634 \text{ Log K} - .558 \text{ Log F} + .047 \text{ Log Y}_A + 3.11 \text{ Log P}$$
$$(.11217) \qquad (.22046) \qquad (.72236) \qquad (3.36815)$$

R = .996. R^2 = .991

(2) Log R = −12.66

$$+ .877 \text{ Log K} - .428 \text{ Log F} + .473 \text{ Log Y}_B + 2.16 \text{ Log P}$$
$$(.98945) \qquad (.29875) \qquad (.34358) \qquad (2.92066)$$

R = .994. R^2 = .988

Contemporary work in developed economies suggests it is reasonable to reject demand elasticity figures higher than 0.75.[52] Demand is thought to be even more inelastic in less developed regions.[53] Use of a maximum elasticity estimate insures that the corresponding social savings figures may be accepted as minimal. (See table 4.13.)

with the Durbin-Watson test negative at the 95 percent level.) Various efforts were made to control for intercorrelation of the independent variables by changing the form of the equation (eliminating the population variable, adding a time trend, fixing parameters, and the like). The calculated price elasticity in each case remained below .75. The implicit assumption behind these estimates is that while the supply curve of transportation was shifting during this period, the demand curve was not, or, if it was, the slope of the separate demand curves did not vary more than 50 percent above the slope of the regression plane. This is a strong assumption, but for the purposes of this estimate, it is important only that the elasticity used to derive the final, lower bound estimate of social savings should not be underestimated.

52. George W. Wilson, "Notes on the Elasticity of Demand for Freight Transportation," *Transportation Journal* 17 (1978):11; Dean Worcester, Jr., "On Monopoly Welfare Losses: Comment," *American Economic Review* 65 (1975): 1016, table 1; Leonard W. Weiss, *Case Studies in American Industry* (New York: Wiley, 1980); and James Sloss, "The Demand for Intercity Motor Freight Transport: A Macroeconomic Analysis," *Journal of Business* 44 (1971):62–68.

53. See P. E. Stonham, "The Demand for Overseas Shipping in the Australian Export Trade," *Journal of Transport Economics and Policy* 3 (1969): 333–49.

The level of social savings implied by a price elasticity of demand equal to .75 is between $127.6 and $135.8 million, or 10.8 to 11.5 percent of Mexico's gross domestic product in 1910. This range may be considered a lower bound on the actual savings to the Mexican economy, for in addition to a possibly inflated estimate of the price elasticity of demand for transportation, a number of downward biases were built into the original estimates. These downward biases arose chiefly from (1) the assumption of constant marginal costs in prerail wagon transport over an enormous range of output, (2) the assumption that the highway network could have been expanded sixty times and improved to the recorded 1877 dry season level and then maintained for less than the actual outlay of public resources on railroad subsidies, and (3) the assumption that the hidden costs of wagon transport were negligibly greater than the hidden costs of rail transport per unit of freight service. Relaxing any one of these assumptions could substantially increase the savings estimates. Taking all three into account, it is not unlikely that railroad social savings were actually much closer to 20 than to 10.8 percent of Mexican national income.

Railroads and Porfirian Economic Growth

Between 1877 and 1910, Mexico's gross domestic product increased from roughly $435.5 million to an estimated $1,184.1 million, measured in constant pesos of 1900.[54] The total increase in output of the Mexican economy thus came to approximately $748.6 million. Only a part of this increase represented real gains in productivity, however. Population increased from 9.7 to 15.1 million over the same period, a rise of approximately 56 percent.[55] If the percentage rise in population is subtracted from the increase in output, the gain in productivity amounts to some $506 million. The direct savings attributable to

54. The 1877 figure is taken from estimates prepared by the author; data available on request. The 1910 figure is from Solís, "La evolución económica," pp. 3–5, deflated by Mexico City wholesale price index in El Colegio de México, *Estadísticas: Fuerza de Trabajo*, p. 155.

55. Population data are in El Colegio de México, *Estadísticas: Fuerza de trabajo*, p. 25.

railroad freight services accounts for 17.0 percent of the increase in total product and 25.2 percent of the productivity gains in the Mexican economy during the *Porfiriato.*

Railroad benefits were probably concentrated in the final two decades of the *Porfiriato.* Table 4.14 presents "least upper bound" (not corrected for price elasticity) estimates of freight savings between 1877 and 1910, based on data for the sample lines. During the 1870s, freight savings were low because of high freight rates charged by the Mexican Railway and the low volume of shipments. Our estimates show negative savings for 1877 and 1878, an indication of the downward biases built into the estimating procedure. The savings grew steadily in the 1880s, with the completion of the major trunk line construction projects. By the 1890s, when relatively complete national income estimates become available, direct freight savings (before adjustment for price elasticity) reached 10 percent or more of the gross domestic product. It is in the period from the mid-1890s to the end of the *Porfiriato* that railroad benefits were concentrated. Since it is likely that a large portion of the initial impact of the railroad involved reemployment of idle resources (rather than real productivity gains), it may be more appropriate to measure the railroad's benefits against economic growth in the last half of the *Porfiriato* alone than for the period as a whole. In this period, the gross domestic product increased from $746.5 in 1895 to $1,184.1 million in 1910.[56] In the same period, population increased from 12.6 to 15.1 million.[57] The total increase in the gross domestic product comes to some $437.6 million; adjusted for population growth, productivity gains totaled $350.1 million. Railroad freight savings come to 29.1 percent of the increase in total income, and 36.4 percent of the rise in productivity. Since the B estimate of $127.6 million in direct savings constitutes a downwardly biased minimum estimate, railroad direct benefits probably explain more than these figures suggest—as much as half of the economic growth of the Porfirian era.

In the dynamics of the period, this conclusion seems more than justified, for railroads did much more than provide cheaper transport. A very high proportion of the productivity gains in the Mexican

56. Solís estimates deflated as indicated in note 54 above.
57. El Colegio de México, *Estadísticas: Fuerza de trabajo,* p. 25.

TABLE 4.14
Direct Social Savings on Railroad Freight Services, Sample Lines,
1877–1910

Year	1	2	3	4
1877	−842,626	(−)0.26	−1,351,981	(−)0.42
1878	−972,417		−1,448,759	
1879	1,240,789		1,598,282	
1880	1,262,634		949,952	
1881	1,781,191		2,913,514	
1882	2,384,438		7,309,748	
1883	13,318,780		15,312,319	
1884	14,428,437		14,402,651	
1885	20,976,137		17,694,503	
1886	17,845,457		15,979,762	
1887	23,527,103		21,048,543	
1888	44,197,945		34,338,917	
1889	56,226,914		40,987,115	
1890	68,254,741		49,094,463	
1891	88,979,280		62,209,995	
1892	117,593,356		78,545,180	
1893	100,517,162		67,796,988	
1894	94,007,937		65,430,799	
1895	109,838,038	14.71	75,552,542	10.12
1896	131,432,133	18.10	88,184,873	12.15
1897	146,662,161	18.66	99,295,453	12.63
1898	145,298,339	15.04	101,747,888	10.53
1899	177,405,096	16.68	123,552,394	11.62
1900	210,965,882	19.81	142,420,448	13.37
1901	223,315,524	22.11	146,476,216	14.51
1902	290,825,576	29.47	187,989,824	19.05
1903	317,760,853	31.85	206,688,067	20.72
1904	330,462,047	25.17	219,142,186	16.69
1905	345,529,185	30.37	225,983,048	19.86
1906	372,748,945	34.00	240,415,344	21.93

TABLE 4.14 (*cont.*)

Year	1	2	3	4
1907	429,775,456	34.19	278,131,713	22.13
1908	402,890,310	33.30	260,876,212	21.56
1909	418,686,767	33.65	271,855,682	21.85
1910	430,477,297	36.35	276,677,771	23.37

(1) "A" Estimates
(2) Percent of GDP
(3) "B" Estimates
(4) Percent of GDP

economy, especially after the late 1880s, when they were largest, occurred because of the flow of foreign capital and technology into Mexican industry and agriculture. Railroads stimulated this flow, not only because they provided cheaper transport, but also because they helped to alter the traditional image of Mexico in foreign capital markets. The demonstration effect of public subsidies to the first major foreign private ventures in more than half a century in this formerly notorious land of high risks and bad government contributed to making Mexico a leading recipient of foreign investment flows in the short space of a decade and a half. Without the railroads, without foreign-owned railroads especially, Mexico's Porfirian modernization would have been far less rapid. Railroads were indispensable to economic growth in Porfirian Mexico.

Chapter 5
Linkage and Leakage:
The Structural Impact
of the Railroads

Introduction

The Porfirian growth process differed from that of the more advanced industrial nations in the nineteenth century. Like many backward areas, Mexico depended on foreign financing both for the creation of social overhead capital (including railroads) and for the development of new industries. Growth was most rapid in those industries that produced or processed primary products for export. The growth of industries producing for the domestic market, while not negligible, was dependent on both foreign financing and the prosperity of the export sector. Since the spillovers from the export sector were relatively weak, and demand for manufactured products was largely derivative, the Porfirian economy became highly vulnerable to external pressures and did not develop the capacity to sustain economic growth under less favorable international conditions.[1]

Had Mexico begun a process of modernization half a century earlier—not a very plausible counterfactual supposition, to be sure—the structure of its economy in the late nineteenth century would have more closely resembled that of the industrializing North Atlantic nations. With a much smaller supply of foreign capital and much weaker demand for primary products in the world market, Mexico would have had to base its growth on a much different mix of products and alter its institutional development correspondingly. Had railroad construction begun in earnest in the late 1830s, financed by a state development bank like Lucas Alamán's pioneering experiment

1. For an overview of economic growth during the *Porfiriato*, see Roberto Cortés Conde, *The First Stages of Modernization in Spanish America*, trans. Toby Talbot (New York: Harper and Row, 1974), chapter 5.

in that decade, construction would have proceeded more slowly and with a decidedly different geographic orientation.[2]

As it happened, Mexico joined most of the world's backward regions along a growth path characterized by dependence on external flows of capital and technology and by specialization in the production of export commodities for foreign markets. Railroads played a major role in fostering this kind of structural evolution. If railroad development had failed to induce massive foreign investment in export production, the rapid economic growth of the Porfirian period would not have occurred.

This chapter discusses three aspects of the railroad's impact on the structure of economic life in Porfirian Mexico. First, the sectoral distribution of the forward linkage effects of railroad development is analyzed to measure the extent of the railroads' differential stimulus to export production. Second, some evidence is examined on indirect benefits accruing to the economy through backward linkage effects. To what extent did the Mexican economy benefit from railroad demand for manufactured inputs and to what extent did this demand "leak" abroad? Third, the leakage of railroad demand for inputs suggests the need to measure the full extent of the foreign exchange costs of railroad financing and operation. In all of these areas, the railroad's impact differed markedly from the pattern of railroad development in the more advanced industrial countries.

Sectoral Distribution of Benefits

Analysis of the direct savings of the railroads would be incomplete without measuring the distribution of the benefits. The impact of the railroads on the structure of output is related directly to disproportions in this distribution. Cheaper transport costs may stimulate some kinds of production more than others; if the forward linkage effects of railroad construction are not evenly distributed, changes occur in the economy's product mix. Typically, transport linkages have their greatest effects on the production of commodities whose location is fixed by nature, but similar positive effects may also be observed in

2. Robert Potash, *El Banco de Avío de México* (Mexico: Fondo de Cultura Económica, 1959), chapters 4–10.

industries where significant economies of scale may be achieved from rising output in expanding markets. *Ex ante,* the analysis of these effects should focus on those aspects of railroad construction and operation that favored one or another sector. *Ex post,* the distribution of benefits may be analyzed by studying sectoral utilization rates. The *ex ante* approach confronts an important identification problem. To estimate the stimulus of transport innovation on a sector's output requires data sufficient to distinguish the railroad's effect from that of other forces working in the same direction. In the case of Mexico, changes in the structure of the economy's output were caused not only by the railroads but by a series of other factors which tended to reinforce the effects of transport innovation. On the supply side, technological changes in the mining industry, for example, caused an outward shift in the supply curve at the same time that the railroads were causing a similar shift in the same direction. On the other side, foreign demand for Mexican output was rising more rapidly than internal demand. Since all of these factors converged to produce a more rapid growth rate for the export sector, the differential effect of the railroads cannot be measured. The data on export sector growth demonstrate that its rate of growth was higher than that of the rest of the economy, but there are no data that indicate what part of this faster growth ought to be attributed to that part of the shift in the supply curve produced solely by cheaper transport. Nevertheless, even if it is not possible to isolate the impact of the railroad from that of other factors which stimulated the differential growth of the export sector, it is possible to describe the effect that the railroads had together with other factors in producing changes in the structure of output. By means of an examination of the changes that took place in the distribution of railroad services between sectors of the Mexican economy during the *Porfiriato,* it is possible to derive an idea of the skewed distribution of the social savings produced by cheaper transport.

Railroads in the *Porfiriato* charged lower rates for carrying export goods and intensified this discrimination by reducing their rates still further for large shippers. Thus the reduction in transport costs which railroads introduced for large export sector firms was greater than the reduction provided to most small-scale producers for the domestic market. While the highest rates were charged on imported goods, exports paid rates very much below those charged on goods destined for domestic consumption. This system of freight classification corresponded to the policy of the Mexican government whose objective was to stimulate export sector production. The policy of the railroad companies coincided because the sparsely populated northern part of the country, where the most important new mining sites were located, was the least profitable section of the large trunk lines, owing to the lack of traffic. The management of the Central and the other major north-south lines used low freight charges to stimulate the development of freight-producing export enterprises in the northernmost states of the republic. In the case of sisal, an export product second in importance only to minerals, railroad companies in Yucatán charged low freight rates not only to stimulate business, but also because the railroad companies themselves belonged to groups of sisal planters and merchants.[3]

The Mexican Railway, and the other railroad companies operating in the states of Veracruz and Puebla, adopted the same rate policies as the north-south trunk lines and the Yucatán lines in the sisal growing areas.[4] According to Arthur P. Schmidt's study,

> crops bound for export might pay 46 to 69 per cent less per kilometer traveled on the *Ferrocarril Mexicano* than those destined for the domestic market; savings ranged from 33 to 42 per cent two decades later. Export crops could be charged 40 to 76 per cent less per kilometer than items for the national market on the *Interoceánico* in 1893, and 44 to 50 per cent less in 1899.

To illustrate the degree of discrimination against products destined for internal consumption, Schmidt calculated freight rates as a percentage of final price on five important agricultural commodities shipped from Córdoba to markets in Veracruz and Mexico City. As table 5.1 shows, the freight rates of the Mexican Railway discrimi-

3. See discussion of freight rates in chapter 2.

4. Arthur P. Schmidt, Jr., "The Railroad and the Economy of Puebla and Veracruz, 1877–1911: A Look at Agriculture" (Paper delivered at the meeting of the Southwest Social Science Association, Dallas, Texas, mimeo, 1973), p. 12. I am indebted to the author for making this important paper available to me before its publication.

TABLE 5.1

Freight Charges Per Metric Ton, Mexican Railway Co., Ltd., 1893

Commodity	From Córdoba to:	Freight Charges (pesos)	Charges As % of Córdoba Retail Value
Corn	Mexico City	8.90	17.8
	Veracruz	2.96	5.9
Beans	Mexico City	8.90	10.6
	Veracruz	2.96	3.5
Sugar	Mexico City	8.90	4.6
	Veracruz	2.96	1.5
	Export	1.27	0.6
Coffee	Mexico City	14.95	2.6
	Veracruz	4.97	0.9
	Export	3.38	0.6
Tobacco	Mexico City	14.95	5.7
	Veracruz	4.97	1.9
	Export	3.38	1.3

Note: The distance from Córdoba to Mexico City is 318 kilometers, and to Veracruz 105.7 kilometers.
Source: Arthur P. Schmidt, Jr., "The Railroad and the Economy of Puebla and Veracruz, 1877–1911." Paper presented at the Southwest Social Science Association meeting, Dallas, Texas, mimeo, 1973, p. 12.

nated not only against products produced exclusively for the domestic market (such as corn and beans), but also against that part of the output of sugar, coffee, and tobacco that was dispatched to domestic markets rather than exported.[5] Without knowing more about the production functions of these products and about the elasticities of supply and demand for each one, it is impossible to estimate precisely the effect of this discrimination on production and consumption. Nevertheless, in the case of these agricultural products in two states which supplied an important part of the urban market in the center of the country, the discrimination was quite strong.

5. Ibid., p. 14.

Schmidt also calculated the degree of discrimination in this region in favor of large-scale producers.[6] According to him,

> railroads structured their cargo rates to favor the large producer who could ship a full car of produce long distances. For example, differential rate distance charges on the *Ferrocarril Mexicano* could save a farmer from 5 to 21 per cent on a shipment of crops for the domestic market in 1899, and up to 32 per cent on goods being sent abroad. Using the *Interoceánico* in 1899, producers filling an entire railroad car could save 25 per cent per kilometer traveled. Such a saving could be further amplified if a full load brought a change in rate classification downward, as sometimes happened on the *Interoceánico* and the *Mexicano del Sur*.

In their rate policies, therefore, the railroads not only favored export producers against producers supplying the domestic market, but enhanced the profitability of large-scale producers, the haciendas, at the cost of small- and medium-scale producers.

More than half of the savings to transport users were concentrated by 1910 in the export sector, while at the outset of the railroad era, domestic production constituted the major portion of railroad freight. Data on the changing composition of railroad freight shipments during the *Porfiriato* is available for the nation's two largest lines, the National and the Central. They are the only two companies to have compiled precise data on freight shipments by commodity early in the *Porfiriato*. Table 5.2 divides the freight shipments of the two companies into export and domestic freight in order to estimate the magnitude of the sectoral shift in railroad utilization.

In the case of the Central, the table compares freight composition in 1885, shortly after completion of the through line from Ciudad Juárez (El Paso) to Mexico City, with that of the fiscal year ending 30 June 1908, the last year for which Central data are reported independently. The comparison probably understates the magnitude of the shift from domestic to export freight. In 1885, for example, nearly 40 percent (38.6) of the mineral products transported was salt,

6. Ibid., p. 12.

nearly all of which was consumed domestically.[7] In 1907–1908, domestic sector output in the minerals freight was very small, with salt accounting for less than 2 percent of this class of freight.[8] A considerable portion of the freight classed as General Merchandise and Manufactured Goods consisted of imports produced abroad.[9] The Central reports do not make it possible to remove from freight classified as domestic, quantities of chicle, chick-peas, india rubber, and other commodities which were actually exported.[10] Some portion of the livestock carried by rail also found its way abroad.[11] An undetermined quantity of goods consumed domestically actually entered the export sector as inputs, including machinery and equipment manufactured abroad as well as consumption goods for wage earners.[12] Similar biases which suggest over-reporting of domestic sector freight are evident in the data from the National. In both cases, the percentages calculated in table 5.2 overestimate considerably the proportion of domestic sector freight carried by the two railroads.

As an index of the benefits received by the export sector, the distribution of freight includes an additional downward bias, because it does not take into account the lower freight charges that this sector

7. The 1885 data are found only in the Company's manuscript report to the Secretaría de Fomento, in *AHSCT* 10/31–75.

8. Mexican Central Railway Company, Ltd., *Annual Report, 1907–1908*, p. 21.

9. The 1908–1909 report lists such items as drugs and chemical products, explosives, machinery and iron castings, foreign wines and liquors, and the like in the General Merchandise and Manufactures category; ibid., pp. 21–22.

10. These agricultural products are classified as export products in El Colegio de México, *Estadísticas: Fuerza de trabajo*, pp. 75–82, indicating that most of the output was actually marketed abroad.

11. Mexico exported over 170,000 head of cattle and several thousand pigs and sheep in fiscal year 1910–1911; ibid., pp. 348–51.

12. Since wages were generally higher in mining than in the rest of the economy, and mining regions were generally food deficit areas, cheap rail transport of consumption goods may have been quite significant. In addition to imported capital goods and other inputs, substantial quantities of domestically produced coal were transported for use in ore smelting plants. Marvin Bernstein, *The Mexico Mining Industry, 1890–1950* (Albany, N.Y.: State University of New York Press, 1965), pp. 21–25, 31–34, 36.

TABLE 5.2
Composition of Freight, Mexican Central Railroad, 1885, 1907–1908

	1885		1907–1908	
	Tons	Percent	Tons	Percent
A. Domestic				
1. Forest Products	18,352	10.1	333,066	8.4
2. Agriculture (minus coffee and henequen)	79,078	43.7	791,979	20.0
3. Livestock	20,712	11.5	123,577	3.1
4. General Merchandise and Manufactured Goods	33,168	18.4	409,163	10.3
B. Export				
1. Minerals	28,117	15.6	2,281,358	57.6
2. Coffee and henequen	1,303	.7	21,403	.6
Totals	180,730	100.0	3,960,546	100.0

TABLE 5.2 (*cont.*)
Composition of Freight, Mexican National Railroad, 1887, 1907–1908

	1887		1907–1908	
	Tons	Percent	Tons	Percent
A. Domestic				
1. Forest Products	43,636	22.4	333,687	17.1
2. Agriculture (minus coffee and henequen)	88,275	45.3	379,426	19.4
3. Livestock	8,572	4.4	63,507	3.3
4. General Merchandise and Manufactured Goods	21,040	10.8	229,568	11.8
B. Export				
1. Minerals	33,125	17.0	923,574	47.4
2. Coffee and henequen	—	.1	19,548	1.0
Totals	194,648	100.0	1,949,310	100.0

Sources: Mexican Central Railroad Company, *Annual Report*, 1885, 1907–1908, and Mexican National Railroad Company, *Annual Report*, 1887, 1907–1908.

paid. To convert the data on freight into figures which would indicate the distribution of benefits, it would be necessary to reduce the percentage of benefits received by domestic sector producers, taking into account that their savings per unit of freight shipped were less than in the export sector. If we assume as a reasonable approximation that the export sector paid rates 50 percent lower than the domestic sector, the percentage of benefits going to the export sector in the case of the Central increases from the 58.3 percent indicated in table 5.2 to no less than 73.6 percent. In the case of the National, the benefits to the export sector rise from 48.6 to 64.6 percent. If we add to this the overestimation of domestic sector freight already built into the estimates in the table, it can be concluded that the export sector received by far the greatest benefits from the operation of railroads during the *Porfiriato.*

Although it is not possible to estimate precisely the differential stimulus of the railroads for the export sector, it is clear that its growth was closely linked to transport development. In the case of the Central, table 5.2 shows that the tonnage of export sector freight increased seventy-five times in only twenty-three years from 1885 to 1908, while domestic freight increased only a little more than ten times in the same period. Export sector freight increased almost sixty times on the National in the twenty years from 1887 to 1908, while domestic freight increased slightly more than six times. These data not only reflect the fact that export sector production grew more rapidly than output for domestic consumption, but also that exports were more dependent on railroad transport.

A still cruder, but more general test of the disproportion in benefits "earned" by the export sector may be constructed from data on the volume of output in selected export and domestic industries in 1907. This sectoral output data can then be compared with railroad statistics that show the tonnage of the same commodities shipped by rail in 1910. Table 5.3 summarizes the comparison. Unfortunately, mineral output is reported in tons of metal produced, and data on ore output are not available. The table thus reports both the volume of metals output and freight, omitting mineral ore, in column one and then, in column two uses reported railroad ore shipments as a proxy for the volume of ore output. Column two therefore may seem to understate the actual number of tons of ore produced. If that were so, the tons of ore produced as a percentage of total output might turn out to be much closer to the percentage of ore shipments in total railroad freight. In fact, the opposite is more likely the case. The tonnage of ore produced in 1907 was probably much smaller than the total freight tonnage reported by the railroad companies in 1910. Mineral output was higher in 1910 than in 1907, and railroad tonnage figures include an unknown quantity of transfer freight counted more than once.

Table 5.3 indicates that while export output accounted for just over 20 percent of the tonnage of transportables produced in Mexico in 1907, it utilized more than half of the nation's rail transport facilities in 1910. On the other hand, domestic sectors produced nearly 80 percent of the transportables, but used only 46.8 percent of the railroad's capacity.

The data in table 5.3 contain two biases that make the reported figures significant understatements of the extent to which the export sector dominated the nation's rail system. First, export products probably traveled longer distances. Comparing simple tonnage data understates the real differences in utilization of rail services. Second, the table attributes to the domestic sector all of the lumber and agricultural produce transported for consumption in mining and the other export industries. In addition to the savings on transport of mineral output, the mining industry also benefited from lower labor and physical input costs due to cheap rail transport.

Adopting the downwardly biased figures in column one, the percentage of total output that utilized rail transport may be underestimated exactly. Since the output data are available only for 1907 and the freight figures are taken from railroad shipments in 1910, the percentages reported in table 5.4 are too low, but the disparity between domestic and export sector utilization rates are no doubt close to the mark. Export products were at least three times as railroad intensive as domestic output.

Foreign Linkages

The distribution of indirect savings through backward linkages was no less skewed than that of direct benefits via forward linkage effects.

TABLE 5.3
Comparison of Tons of Transportables Produced and Tons of Freight Shipped on Mexican Railroads

Sector	Thousands of Tons Produced (ore excluded)	%	Thousands of Tons Produced (ore included)	%
A. Domestic				
1. Lumber	3,210.7	35.9	3,210.7	30.6
2. Domestic Agriculture	5,114.6	57.1	5,114.6	48.9
Total Domestic	8,325.3	93.0	8,325.3	79.5
B. Export				
1. Export Agriculture	352.6	3.9	352.6	3.4
2. Metals	276.0	3.1	276.0	2.6
3. Mineral Ore(a)	—	—	1,515.1	14.5
Total Export	628.6	7.0	2,143.7	20.5
Totals	8,953.9	100.0	10,469.0	100.0

TABLE 5.3 (*cont.*)

Sector	Thousands of Tons of Freight (ore excluded)	%	Thousands of Tons of Freight (ore included)	%
A. Domestic				
1. Lumber	536.0	24.3	536.0	14.4
2. Domestic Agriculture	1,203.1	54.7	1,203.1	32.4
Total Domestic	1,739.1	79.0	1,739.1	46.8
B. Export				
1. Export Agriculture	269.4	12.2	269.4	5.2
2. Metals	193.0	8.8	193.0	7.2
3. Mineral Ore(a)	—	—	1,515.6	40.8
Total Export	462.4	21.0	1,978.0	53.2
Totals	2,201.5	100.0	3,717.1	100.0

(a) Railroad tonnage used to estimate output volume.
Sources: Tons of output for 1907 are found in El Colegio de México, *Estadísticas: Fuerza de trabajo*, pp. 65–78. Only those products for which both volume data (1907) and freight shipments (1910) were available have been included. Thus, small quantities of minor agricultural products were excluded. Domestic agriculture includes rice, rye, corn (maíz), wheat, cotton, cacao, sugarcane, and tobacco. Export agriculture includes only coffee and sisal and ixtle fibers. Freight tonnage data were taken from the annual reports of thirteen railroad companies which carried 97.1 percent of the estimated total ton kilometers of freight in 1910. The annual reports are found in appropriate files in the *AHSCT*.

TABLE 5.4

Rail Shipments (1910) As a Percentage of Total Output by Volume (1907)

Sector	Percentage
A. Domestic	
1. Lumber	22.3
2. Domestic Agriculture	23.1
B. Export	
1. Export Agriculture	68.0
2. Metals	68.7

Source: Table 5.3.

Mexican railroads were constructed and operated with imported rails, supervisory and engineering personnel, locomotives and rolling stock, spare parts, and iron bridges. On occasion, even fuel (coal and wood), ties for laying track, and unskilled labor were imported. Paying in gold for most of these imported inputs, and earning their revenues in depreciating silver currency until the Monetary Reform of 1905, the railroad companies adopted every conceivable measure to reduce their consumption of imports.[13] Nonetheless, as table 5.5 indicates, not even the largest of the railroad companies succeeded in reducing its dependence on external supplies. During the fifteen and a half years in which the Central reported its foreign purchases, fully 37.64 percent of the company's operating expenses were spent on imports. Applying the Central's ratio of foreign to domestic expenditures to the railroad system as a whole implies an annual "leakage" of between $10 and $25 million per year during the last decade of the

13. This, in any event, was their perennial claim in reports to stockholders. "A constant effort has been made to curtail, as much as possible, the purchases of material in the United States and Europe and, wherever practicable, to make purchases in Mexico," the president of the Central reported as early as 1894 (Mexican Central Railway Company, Ltd., *Annual Report, 1894*, p. 10). President Raoul of the National reported a similar policy to his stockholders the year before (Mexican National Railroad Company, *Annual Report, 1893*, p. 8).

TABLE 5.5
U.S. Currency Expenses, Mexican Central Railroad, 1891–1906

Year	U.S. Currency Expenses (IN 1,000's OF PESOS)	U.S. Currency Expenses (IN 1,000's OF DOLLARS)	Average Rate of Exchange	Column One As a Percentage of Total Expenses
1891	1,997	1,550	128.83	42.67
1892	1,984	1,386	143.13	39.67
1893	1,942	1,213	160.04	37.80
1894	2,099	1,089	192.69	38.45
1895	1,757	930	188.94	31.38
1896	1,978	1,048	188.65	29.33
1897	3,031	1,448	209.39	34.33
1898	3,323	1,550	214.41	36.27
1899	4,458	2,158	206.57	42.85
1900	5,686	2,785	204.18	47.99
1901	5,650	2,708	208.64	45.17
1902	7,096	2,957	239.95	46.77
1903	7,664	3,237	236.80	40.46
1904(a)	3,340	1,512	220.82	33.36
1905(b)	4,421	2,133	207.31	25.12
1906(b)	6,401	3,203	199.83	32.31

(a) January to June only.
(b) Fiscal year ending 30 June.
Sources: Mexican Central Railroad Company, *Annual Reports*, 1891–1906.

Porfiriato.[14] This leakage included nearly all inputs with an industrial bias which the railroads required for their construction, maintenance, and operation. Mexican railroads could not have provided much stimulus to the already developed industrial economies of the United States, Great Britain, France, and Germany through their demand for these inputs. But what is more important, they provided hardly any stimulus at all to the industrial development of Mexico through their demand for industrial materials.

This fact is hardly surprising. The Mexican railway network in 1910 had scarcely reached the length of the U.S. system in the 1850s.[15] By 1859, the output of the U.S. railroads in passenger and freight ton miles was already higher than that of Mexico's railroads in 1910.[16] The backward linkage impact of Mexican railroads does not improve, however, even when the comparison is adjusted for differences in levels of railroad development. In the antebellum United States, railroads provided a significant contribution to the expansion of the iron and machinery industries in the 1850s.[17] U.S. railroads consumed nearly the entire output of Bessemer steel in the period immediately after the Civil War.[18] In Mexico, a single steel plant,

14. Estimated railroad gross revenues were $49.7 million in 1900 and $103.5 million in 1910. Operating costs are calculated in both years by assuming a coefficient of exploitation of 0.55. Applying the Mexican Central ratio of foreign currency expenses to operating costs yields $10.3 million ($49.7 × .207) for 1900. In 1910, the same procedure yields an estimate of $21.4 million. A check against this procedure indicated a conservative bias. The Mexican Central ratio applied to the operating costs of eight major lines with a coefficient of exploitation of 59.5 yielded an estimated $24.7 million in foreign currency expenses in 1910. Gross revenue (total output) data are reported in table 2.4.

15. Mexican steam railroad trackage under federal concession totaled 19,205 kilometers in 1910 (see table 2.3 above), or roughly 11,569 miles. U.S. total trackage came to 12,908 miles in 1852. By the outbreak of the Civil War, the U.S. system totaled 30,626 miles; Alfred Chandler, ed., *The Railroads: The Nation's First Big Business* (New York: Harcourt, Brace and World, 1965), p. 13.

16. Mexican data are reported in tables 3.2 and 4.4 above. Ton miles in 1910 came to roughly 1.8 billion, passenger miles to 637 million. Fishlow, in *American Railroads*, p. 337, estimates U.S. ton miles as 2.2 to 2.6 billion and passenger miles at 1.8 to 1.9 billion in 1859.

17. Fishlow, *American Railroads*, p. 160.

18. Fogel, *Railroads*, pp. 130–31.

constructed in 1903, produced small quantities of rails and steel plate in the last years of the decade, but imports accounted for the overwhelming bulk of these inputs until long after the *Porfiriato*.[19] It was precisely because the United States had already achieved a considerable industrial development *before* the introduction of the railroads that the industrial stimulus from their construction and operation could have been captured by domestic rather than foreign industries.

The single most important source of backward linkages from the railroads for the Mexican economy came from the consumption needs of railroad workers. For most railroad companies, wages accounted for between one fourth and one third of gross revenues (or 40 to 55 percent of operating expenses.) (See table 5.6.) In 1910, wages and salaries accounted for 32.3 percent of the gross revenues of the National Railways, and 53.8 percent of the company's operating costs.[20] The average daily wage received by National Railways' employees was $1.78. At the bottom of the pay scale were some 1,865 unskilled laborers earning an average of $0.96 per day. Of the company's 26,106 employees, 6,808, or 26.1 percent, earned less than an average of $1.25. At the other end of the scale, 1,338 employees (5.1 percent) earned more than $4.00 per day. Of this top 5.1 percent,

19. Steel output data are conveniently summarized in Frédéric Mauro, "Le développement économique de Monterrey (1890–1960)," *Caravelle*, no. 2 (1964):113–23. Imports of steel plate, rails, and other railroad materials are recorded in El Colegio de México, *Estadísticas: Comercio exterior*, p. 329. See also Fernando Rosenzweig, "La industria," in Cosío Villegas, ed., *Historia moderna de México: El Porfiriato, La vida económica*, vol. 1, pp. 234–37, 380–82. Monterrey production of such items, negligible until the Mexicanization of the major railway companies, still accounted for less than one third of total consumption in 1911, the year in which Monterrey output reached its highest point, both absolutely and relative to total demand; Rosenzweig, "La industria," pp. 381–82. Repair and construction facilities for railroad rolling stock were established by most of the large companies, but the spare parts and manufactured construction materials continued to be imported in their entirety; ibid., p. 387. Nevertheless, some authors have suggested that *potential* railroad demand provided part of the stimulus for the construction of the Monterrey steel works. For a cautious statement of this view, see William E. Cole, *Steel and Economic Growth in Mexico* (Austin: University of Texas Press, 1967), pp. 8–9.

20. Wage data, not published in the company's printed reports, were reported in detail to the Secretaría de Comunicaciones y Obras Públicas. The *Annual Report* to the Secretaría for 1910 is found in *AHSCT* 10/2329–1.

TABLE 5.6
Wages and Salaries As Percent of Gross Revenue, 1895–1910

Year	Mexican Railway	Tehuantepec National	Sonora	Mexican National	National Railways	Mérida–Peto	Hidalgo and North-western	Mexican International
1895			17.4					
1896								
1897								
1898								
1899								
1900							29.4	
1901	32.4		56.7	33.2				
1902				38.9				
1903	28.3		54.8	30.6				
1904			56.4	32.2				
1905	28.5		50.9	33.4		21.7	35.0	
1906	24.0			43.4				
1907	23.9	38.9		35.8				
1908	26.4			33.4				
1909	26.2				33.6			
1910	25.6	19.2	29.3		31.2			31.2

Source: Annual Reports of the indicated companies in appropriate files of the *AHSCT*.

670, or more than half, were foreigners. More than two thirds of the company's 1,074 foreign employees (4.1 percent of the total) were thus represented among the 5 percent best paid employees of the line. This pattern of wage and status discrimination by the government-owned railroad company merely reflected employment patterns throughout the industry.[21] The effect of such discrimination was probably to reduce the domestic final demand linkage effect of railroad expenditures by concentrating purchasing power in the hands of employees with a high propensity to consume imports. At the same time, the relatively low level of wages limited the consumption of most employees to the barest necessities. Table 5.7 shows that the real wages of railroad workers rose more slowly than prices during the last decade of the *Porfiriato*. Even nominal wages dropped back to 1900 levels on two of three lines that reported wage data throughout the decade. Assuming that the National Railways were typical of the railroad industry as a whole, approximately $33.3 million was paid in 1910 by railroad companies to their employees. Of this sum, nearly $5 million (14.7 percent for the National Railways) was paid to foreign employees. The average daily wage for foreign employees on the National Railways Company was $6.49, that of Mexicans $1.58.[22]

21. Data as detailed as that of the National Railways Company are scattered through the annual reports of most of the major lines at infrequent intervals in the unpublished versions submitted to the government. Data sufficiently detailed to reflect wage differentials between Mexicans and foreigners were found in reports of eleven different companies scattered over the years 1884 to 1910. In 1910, such data can be found in the reports of at least five railroad companies in addition to the National Railways. These are the Mexican Railway, the Sonora, the Tehuantepec National, the International, and the South Pacific. All indicate a high order of wage discrimination in favor of foreigners; *AHSCT* 1/326–4, 2/785–1, 6/41–2, 40/154–1, 288/87–3. Exceptions to this rule were rare and occurred only in cases where foreigners were not employed at all. Aside from two of the Yucatecan lines in the 1880s, only the Hidalgo and Northeastern, owned entirely by Mexican industrialist Gabriel Mancera, employed no foreigners.

22. Calculated from data in the *Annual Report, 1909–1910,* in *AHSCT* 10/2329–1.

TABLE 5.7

Average Daily Wage, Railroad Employees, 1900–1910
(Current Pesos)

Year	Mexican	Sonora	Mexican National	National Railways	Mexico City Wholesale Price Index
1900	1.53				100.0
1901			1.79		122.8
1902		2.71	2.08		120.8
1903		2.71	1.98		125.7
1904		3.31	1.96		106.8
1905	1.91	3.34	1.67		121.3
1906	2.09	3.25			135.9
1907	2.05	3.46	1.90		133.9
1908	1.94	3.82	1.93		131.9
1909	1.96	3.42		1.91	143.6
1910	1.65	3.52		1.78	165.7

Source: Annual Reports of the indicated companies in appropriate files of the *AHSCT*. The Mexico City Wholesale Price Index is from El Colegio de México, *Estadísticas: Fuerza de trabajo*, p. 172.

The Leakage of Indirect Benefits to Foreign Countries

In 1910, the total output of the railroad industry in Mexico was estimated above at $103.5 million while direct social savings (assuming a price elasticity of demand equal to 0.75) was calculated to lie between $127.6 and $135.8 million. To approximate a measure of the foreign exchange costs of the railroads (and the extent to which the stimulus of railroad development leaked abroad), estimates have been made to account for purchases of foreign inputs and the propensity of foreign employees to consume imports. To these estimates, two components have been added. The first is an estimate of railroad profit and interest remittances to foreign owners and creditors. The second is an estimate of the interest payments required on that portion of the external public debt originally contracted to meet railroad subsidy payments.

The first two components of the leakage may be estimated on the basis of evidence already discussed. Payments for foreign inputs for the entire railroad system are estimated on the basis of the Central's ratio for 1891–1906. This ratio (37.64 percent of operating costs) yields an estimated $21.4 million in 1910. The leakage due to the import consumption of foreign personnel is estimated by assuming that the National Railways was typical of the entire industry in its percentage of foreign personnel and degree of wage discrimination in their favor. An average propensity to consume imports of 0.5 was then assigned to the estimated $5.0 million in total wages paid to foreigners.

Profits and interest payments were remitted by railroad companies to their foreign shareholders and creditors throughout the *Porfiriato*. While railroad profit remittances in the form of dividend payments were usually quite small, reflecting the low paper profits of railroad investment in Mexico, interest payments on bonded debt were usually quite high.[23] The preferred method for raising capital was bond issuance, usually at a discount and frequently with a varying quantity of shares provided free as a bonus to capitalists willing to take the bonds.[24] Unfortunately, precise estimates of the flow of profit and interest payments cannot be made because the railroad companies did not report directly on the nationality of their creditors and stock-

23. There exists a considerable literature that details the low profitability of Mexican railroad companies in the Porfirian era. In addition to the annual reports of the companies themselves, see, for example, Eugène Viollet, *Le problème de l'argent et l'étalon d'or au Mexique* (Paris: V. Giard and E. Brière, 1907), pp. 77–83, where the problem of profitability is related to the fall in the price of Mexico's silver currency.

24. The National, for example, offered investors in its first subscription circular U.S. $1,000 worth of first mortgage 6 percent bonds plus another U.S. $1,000 in common stock for a payment of only $1,050 in 1880; *Railroad Gazette* (31 December 1880), p. 703. In the case of the Central, the first subscription circular offered forty shares of stock at par value of U.S. $100 per share, plus U.S. $1,000 in income bonds and U.S. $5,000 in first mortgage bonds (a total value at par of U.S. $10,000) for U.S. $4,250. Later circulars offered new subscriptions at the same par value for between U.S. $4,250 and U.S. $4,750. The subscriptions were taken during the course of the lines' construction between 1800 and 1884; *Railroad Gazette* (11 March 1881), p. 137, (14 April 1882), p. 232, (9 March 1883), p. 148, (16 January 1885), p. 47.

holders nor distinguish in their reports the sums paid to foreign as opposed to domestic investors. Most companies paid both dividends and interest in foreign currency whatever the nationality of their stockholders or creditors. In 1910, six major companies, which accounted for more than 85 percent of all railroad revenues, spent exactly one third of their combined gross revenues making service payments on their bonded debt and dividend payments to stockholders.[25] For the National Railways, 35.2 percent of gross revenues of $52 million were spent for such purposes.[26] The national government, which owned a majority of the voting stock in the enterprise, received a negligible return, because $16.7 million of the total of $18.6 million in payments went to pay interest on the bonded debt. The government owned a negligible quantity of National Railways' bonds. A modest dividend of 3 percent was paid on first preferred shares by the company, but the government's holdings were concentrated in second preferred and common stock. The government therefore received interest and dividend payments totaling only $1.4 million. The railroad's creditors and first preferred shareholders received $17.2 million.[27] On the assumption that 95 percent of all dividend and interest payments (after subtracting the $1.4 million received by the government) were made to foreigners, the leakage due to such payments was estimated by applying the ratio of service payments to gross revenues calculated from the annual reports of the nation's six major lines, or 33.3 percent. Profit remittances and dividend payments then are estimated at $34.5 million in 1910.

It is not possible to estimate precisely the proportion of Mexico's

25. The six companies were the Mexican, the Tehuantepec National, the National Railways of Mexico, the Sonora, the Interoceanic, and the United of Yucatán. Dividends and interest payments are reported in the published *Annual Report* of each of these firms for 1910.

26. National Railways of Mexico, *Annual Report, 1909–1910*, p. 9.

27. Calculation of the government's share in the dividends and interest payments made in 1910 required information on (1) the quantity and type of the company's total funded debt, and (2) the quantity and distribution of the government's holdings. The first is reported in the *Mexican Year Book: A Statistical, Financial, and Economic Annual, compiled from Official and other Returns, 1911* (New York: McCorquodale, 1912), p. 167. The second is reported by Nicolau d'Olwer, "Las inversiones extranjeras," pp. 1074–76.

external public debt in 1910 that had been contracted to meet subsidy payments owed to railroad construction companies during the *Porfiriato*. According to data supplied to Pablo Macedo by the *Secretaría de Comunicaciones y Obras Públicas*, Mexican railroads had received a total of $144.9 million in subsidies up to 20 June 1902.[28] Of this amount, $69.2 million had been paid through issues of public debt directly to the construction companies, while the remaining $75.7 million had been paid in cash, or in customs certificates redeemable at specified customshouses out of tariff receipts. In addition to the $69.2 million paid directly in bonds, a substantial portion of the cash payments had been financed by sales of public debt abroad.[29] Bazant has calculated that the rate of interest on new issues of the Mexican external debt ranged from 9.87 to 4.41 percent in the Díaz period.[30] Most of the outstanding external debt in 1910 consisted of bonds issued at nominal rates of interest between 4 and 5 percent. The flow of interest payments on bonds of face value $100 million is estimated conservatively at $4.5 million. This figure represents the interest payments made in 1910 on that portion of the external debt that was used to subsidize railroad construction during the *Porfiriato*.

Under the admittedly crude assumptions required for the construction of the leakage measure, table 5.8 indicates that $58.4 million, or fully 56 percent of total railroad gross revenues in 1910, were spent abroad. If the railroad subsidy portion of the external debt is added, the total leakage is estimated at nearly $63 million. In pesos of 1900, this amount reduces to $38 million, or between 28 and 30 percent of direct social savings in 1910.[31] Mexican railroads provided direct savings estimated above at between 10.8 and 11.5 percent of 1910 gross domestic product. The estimated direct leakage of railroad revenues and public interest payments related to railroads amounted to between 3.2 and 3.8 percent of gross domestic product

28. Pablo Macedo, *Tres monografías*, pp. 230–31.

29. Ibid., p. 232.

30. Jan Bazant, *Historia de la deuda exterior de México (1823–1946)* (Mexico: El Colegio de México, 1968), pp. 157–72.

31. The leakage estimate is deflated here by the Mexico City Wholesale Price Index found in El Colegio de México, *Estadísticas: Fuerza de Trabajo*, p. 172. It is compared to our "A" estimate of direct social savings, which was deflated by the same index. See above, table 4.12.

TABLE 5.8
Estimated Leakage Abroad of Railroad Revenues and Subsidy Debt Service, 1910
(Millions of Current Pesos)

1. Purchase of Foreign Inputs	$21.4
2. Imports Consumed by Foreign Personnel	2.5
3. Profit Remittance and Interest Payments	34.5
Total Leakage of Railroad Revenues	$58.4
4. Interest on Railroad Subsidy Portion of External Public Debt	4.5
Total Leakage	$62.9

Source: See text.

in the same year.[32] It would be appropriate to subtract this leakage from the social savings estimates only on the assumption that equal benefits would have been produced by a railroad system financed internally without reducing the supply of capital available to finance productive responses to cheaper transport. For the nineteenth or early twentieth centuries, the realism of such a counterfactual assumption is open to doubt. On the other hand, it is important in evaluating the railroad's impact to note that one of its effects was to intensify the existing comparative advantage of the advanced nations in the production of capital goods for transportation. The long run consequences of this effect were negative for Mexico. At the same time, foreign financing and equipping of Mexico's railroads imposed a long term foreign exchange burden of considerable magnitude. In 1910, the leakage estimated above at $63 million amounted to 23.7 percent of Mexico's total export earnings.

While no directly comparable leakage measure has been constructed for other countries, a survey of the relevant literature suggests that Mexico's economy received a much smaller stimulus to growth *per unit of transport savings* than did any of the more developed

32. The gross domestic product estimate is that of Solís, "La evolución económica," pp. 3–5.

North Atlantic nations. Great Britain, of course, became an exporter of railroad capital and technology by the mid-nineteenth century. The United States had assimilated the technology and virtually liquidated a much smaller foreign interest in its railroad network at the time its capitalists were embarking on Mexican projects. Most of the European continental systems, which like the United States had imported substantial quantities of British capital and technology, quickly eliminated foreign participation and its attendant leakages. In the Mexican case, where public "control" has been cited as evidence of a growing nationalism, Mexicanization served chiefly to stabilize the predominant foreign interest in the rail system and the leakage of a substantial part of the railroad's potential stimulus to economic growth.

Conclusions

Mexico was transformed during the Porfirian era from an economically backward nation into one which by 1910 displayed all the characteristics typical of modern underdevelopment. The railroads played a significant role in this process. Mexico was almost the only country in Latin America (with the possible exceptions of Argentina and Uruguay) where railroad construction resulted in communicating all of the nation's most important regions. In the majority of cases, railroad development was undertaken solely to connect centers of export production with the nearest ports (as in Brazil, Chile, Bolivia, the countries of Central America, and the sugar islands of the Caribbean). By contrast, in Mexico the railroads ran across a large part of the country in which the production of export products was negligible. Even so, the export sector dominated the railroad network, not only in terms of freight shipped, but also in terms of the benefits of "social" savings, which cheap transport brought to Mexico. While it is not possible to estimate with precision the proportion of the higher growth experienced by the export sector that can be attributed directly to the railroads, differentiating it from the effect of other factors working in the same direction, it is clear that the railroads had a far more stimulating effect on this sector through charging lower freight rates and other kinds of discrimination in its favor. In addition to the policies of the railroad companies, and the government's support of this discrimination, it is evident that the export sector made much more intensive use of railroad transport than did the industries and agricultural producers that supplied the domestic market. Railroads stimulated the growth of exports far more than production for the domestic market.

The impact of the railroads on the domestic sector of the economy may be compared with the effect that would have been produced by the installation of a series of artisan workshops. No less than 56 percent of the *gross* revenues of all Mexican railroads in 1910 leaked out of the country in the form of inputs purchased abroad, remission of dividends and interest to foreign creditors and stockholders, and the import consumption of foreign employees. Of the 44 percent of gross revenues that did not leave the country, more than half were spent on the wages and salaries of railroad employees. The vast majority of railroad employees were unskilled workers (*jornaleros*), paid less than one and a half pesos a day in the case of the National Railways.

The Mexicanization of the railroads did not reduce the burden of interest and dividend remissions to foreign capitalists because such a reduction did not even appear among the government's goals. On the contrary, the Mexican government contracted foreign loans at 5 percent interest in order to buy railroad stock which never managed to pay even half the return which the government had to pay for the right to "own" the National Railways. In fact, the government's purchase of a controlling share of the voting stock of the major lines placed the public credit at the disposition of the railroads' creditors, who exchanged somewhat risky interest-bearing bonds of the old companies for the government-backed certificates of the new enterprise. Instead of reducing the leakage of interest and profits abroad, Mexicanization of the railroads by the Porfirian regime guaranteed that it would continue by committing all the resources of the government, in the last instance, to the uninterrupted payment of the debts of the old companies.

Mexico would have had to pay more, at least in the short run, for the capital necessary to construct its railroad network if foreign capital had not been available or its participation deliberately excluded. But it is important to point out that the international market, which offered its capital to Mexico, could not offer, and did not offer, a faster route toward the development of a modern economic structure.

Chapter 6
Railroads and the New Concentration of Land Ownership

Introduction

Railroad construction initiated, and railroad operations intensified, important changes in the Mexican land tenure system during the Porfirian era. Because the transport savings introduced by the railroads were so large, both production possibilities and land values rose dramatically. The close connection between nineteenth century railroad construction (and other forms of social overhead capital investment) in underdeveloped countries and increasing land values has been recognized by economists, but the regressive distributional effects on land ownership have often passed unnoticed. According to one economist,[1]

> It may be, in fact, that the causal sequence *foreign loans — investment in infrastructure — increasing land prices* gives us the main key to understanding the magnitude and the direction of international capital flows towards the end of the nineteenth century.

From the point of view of peasant populations in the underdeveloped countries, Professor Gould's causal sequence is incomplete. To *increasing land prices* ought to be added: *increasing concentration of landholding*.

The railroad's impact on economic growth and structure has been analyzed in earlier chapters. The present chapter adds a partial analysis of the railroad's impact on the distribution of wealth and income in Porfirian Mexico by looking at the effects of rapid railroad construction in the early *Porfiriato* (1877–1884) on land tenure.[2]

1. J. D. Gould, *Economic Growth in History: Survey and Analysis* (London: Methuen, 1972), p. 186.
2. Portions of this chapter were published in John H. Coatsworth, "Rail-

Historians and contemporary observers agree that ownership of land in Mexico came to be much more highly concentrated during the regime of Porfirio Díaz than ever before.[3] Two general explanations have been formulated to account for this phenomenon. The most general, and the most common, explanation links the new concentration in landownership to the Porfirian political and social elite.[4] A tyrannical regime ruled the country on behalf of its great landowners who enhanced their wealth by means of official connivance and a rigid suppression of opposing political and social movements. So long as civil and international warfare prevailed, Mexican governments had to devote most of their energies to defending themselves against foreign and domestic enemies. The elite invested its resources in factional squabbles over political power and access to public funds. Not until the Díaz regime did the country enjoy a prolonged period of domestic political peace, and not until the *pax porfiriana* did the Mexican elite cease fighting among itself long enough to undertake a general assault against the rest of the population.

As a general formulation, this explanation is well founded. Political peace did free the landowning elite for an assault on the property rights and political liberties of the underlying rural population, but the assault began at the very outset of the Porfirian era and did not wait for a period of prolonged peace. Long before effective threats to the Porfirian regime had ended, and even before state and federal *rurales* had firmly established a monopoly on the use of violence in

---

roads, Landholding, and Agrarian Protest in the Early *Porfiriato*," *HAHR* 54 (1974):48–71.

3. For a survey of the evidence, see González Navarro, *La vida social*, pp. 187–239.

4. Manuel López Gallo, *Economía y política en la historia de México* (Mexico: Editorial Grijalbo, 1967), pp. 249–67; Oficina Internacional de Trabajo, *Poblaciones indígenas (Estudios y Documentos)*, no. 23 (Geneva, 1953), pp. 322–23; Raymond Vernon, *The Dilemma of Mexico's Development: The Roles of the Private and Public Sectors* (Cambridge, Mass.: Harvard University Press, 1965), pp. 51–53; George M. McBride, *The Land Systems of Mexico* (New York: American Geographical Society, 1923), p. 72; José Valadés, *El porfirismo: historia de un régimen: el nacimiento (1877–1884)* (Mexico: José Porrúa e Hijos, 1941), pp. 237–38.

the countryside, a crescendo of usurpations of ancient rural property rights had begun.[5]

A second explanation of the increased concentration of land-ownership during the *Porfiriato* has placed major responsibility on Benito Juárez and the Liberal movement, while reserving for the Porfirian regime a merely administrative or police function.[6] Naively idealistic in its approach to Mexico's social and economic backwardness, the Liberal party promulgated an unworkable constitution which deprived Indian communities (as well as the Church) of their property rights. Implementation of these constitutional provisions resulted in a redistribution of both Church and Indian communal property to already wealthy landlords and merchants. To raise money for its military campaigns against Conservative armies and the French expeditionary forces, the Juárez government also resorted to sales of so-called "vacant" public lands. What Juárez did only to meet an emergency, the Porfirian regime revived and expanded without any wartime necessity in a way that encouraged enormous additional concentrations of landed wealth. The Porfirian regime thus merely implemented Liberal constitutional provisions and Liberal public lands policies with greater efficiency and zeal.

This interpretation is also well founded in some respects, but it attributes the Liberal failure to imported European dogmas enshrined in the Constitution of 1857, and to European intervention which forced the sales of public lands, when the real causes of the Liberal failure were circumstantial rather than ideological or military. The Juárez regime was necessarily shortsighted because of its need to attract popular support and to raise funds to prosecute the war against conservatism and the Maximilianist regime, but the Reform Laws and the sales of vacant public lands in the Juárez era took place in an economy incapable of stimulating the large scale land seizures that characterized the Porfirian era later on. Liberalism did not err by

5. Valadés, *El porfirismo*, pp. 237–60.
6. Manuel Germán Parra and Wigberto Jiménez Moreno, *Bibliografía indigenista de México y Centroamérica, 1850–1950* (Mexico: Instituto Nacional Indigenista, 1954), p. lxxxiii; Roger D. Hansen, *The Politics of Mexican Development* (Baltimore: Johns Hopkins University Press, 1971), chapter 1; Vernon, *Dilemma*, pp. 36–38; Valadés, *El porfirismo*, p. 242; McBride, *Land Systems*, pp. 133–36.

failing to perceive the greed of the nation's *hacendado* elite. Nor did it fail through dogmatic adherence to European doctrines which envisioned a natural harmony between profit maximization and social progress. Liberal ideologues knew full well that men of wealth, whatever their political philosophy, could be counted upon to pursue their interests above all else, and they fought in large part to remove inherited colonial restraints on such behavior. What they did not know and could not predict were the effects of a rapid commercialization of agriculture *before* rather than *after* the full implementation of the Reform.[7]

Liberals fervently desired the development of national factor and product markets to end the isolation of regional and local producers. They fought to eliminate traditional obstacles to this development even when the task required forceful action by a powerful national government. Leading Liberal theorists and politicians demanded legislation to promote development of a national market through elimination of the *alcabalas,* through laws to promote immigration and stimulate invention, through lower tariffs, through the ending of debt peonage, and through confiscation and alienation of Church and Indian communal property.[8] Most of these aspects of the Liberal program seemed to require a great deal of time to bear fruit. Only the expropriation and distribution of church property was accomplished with dispatch.[9] Alienation and distribution of Indian communal property was regarded as only a first step in the development of a national land market and the transformation of Indian producers from primitive cultivators to capitalist farmers. Given time, this measure, complemented by other steps toward the creation of a national market, would induce the rise of a substantial class of small farmers, maximizing their money incomes by adopting new crops to

7. Jan Bazant, *The Alienation of Church Wealth in Mexico: Social and Economic Aspects of the Liberal Revolution* (Cambridge: Cambridge University Press, 1971).

8. On liberal economic conceptions and programs, see Jesús Silva Herzog, *El pensamiento económico en México* (Mexico: Fondo de Cultura Económica, 1947), pp. 62 ff; Charles A. Hale, *Mexican Liberalism in the Age of Mora, 1821–1853* (New Haven: Yale University Press, 1968), pp. 248–89; Alonso Aguilar Monteverde, *Dialéctica de la economía mexicana del colonialismo al imperialismo* (Mexico: Editorial Nuestro Tiempo, 1968), pp. 110–74.

9. Bazant, *Alienation.*

meet new demands and introducing new techniques to increase their efficiency.[10]

It would be difficult to prove that liberal visions of an agrarian system similar to that of the United States would have triumphed without railroads. The task of the historian is simply to indicate what forces foreclosed this possibility entirely. To attribute an important role to the railroads, and to the kind of modernization they promoted, is not to ignore the weight of the country's colonial heritage of social inequality, ethnic and cultural divisions, creole-European political monopoly, or the hegemony of the great landowners. It is rather to call attention to other aspects of this legacy which strongly suggest that without the intervention of some exogenous factor, the latifundist system would not have revived with such a vengeance in the Porfirian period. A number of studies, for example, have pointed to the weakness of the hacienda system in the colonial period and the first decades after independence: the low profitability of rural property, the tendency towards breaking up of a number of important haciendas, the low level of commercialization of many of the haciendas, the sale of haciendas each two or three generations burdened with heavy debts to the Church or to private money lenders, the instability of the labor force, the effects of civil and international warfare, and the like.[11] In spite of those aspects of Mexican *social* or *political* structure, which make concentration of property seem so "natural" during the *Porfiriato,* the economic aspects of the question suggest that the new concentration of land in this period took place on a scale that was greater than anyone could have anticipated.

Mexico's social history prepared the country well for the Porfirian reaction. Nevertheless, the critical variable is to be found neither in legal and constitutional changes (important as they were), nor in the political and social peace imposed by the Porfirian regime. The critical variable, which precipitated a new and intense movement toward concentration, was the new commercialization of agriculture that the railroads made possible.

10. Jesús Silva Herzog, *El agrarismo mexicano y la Reforma Agraria: Exposición y crítica* (Mexico: Fondo de Cultura Económica, 1959), chapters 2 and 3; Hale, *Mexican Liberalism,* pp. 178–82; Hansen, *Politics,* pp. 25–26.

11. See the works cited in Coatsworth, "Railroads, Landholding, and Agrarian Protest," pp. 53–55.

In the first years of the *Porfiriato,* the historian sees the end of one era and the beginning of a new one. The end of the earlier era is visible in the crescendo of aggressive agrarian movements (frequently linked to social banditry) which disturbed the country with greater and greater intensity during the long years of political instability beginning in 1830.[12] The beginning of the new era can be seen in the usurpations of Indian lands as a result of the stimulus to agricultural enterprise introduced by the construction of railroads. In the first years of the *Porfiriato,* these two eras came together violently in the last of the rebellions of the earlier period and the first wave of usurpations linked to the new commercialization. The new era stands out most sharply in the alienation and sale of vast quantities of public lands in the north of the country, almost without any opposition, upon the arrival of the railroads.

Available data on the sales of public lands are sufficient to illustrate the nexus between concentration of land and the arrival of the railroads. In the case of usurpations of village lands by *hacendados,* a phenomenon which increased rapidly during the same years, the data are extremely dispersed and in many cases have been lost. Almost the only records of this aristocratic landgrabbing which have come down to the present are those that have been left by its victims in the form of protests, petitions, manifestos, and rebellions which reached notice in the newspapers of the period. Unfortunately, these data have not come down in a form that makes it possible for the historians to make very fine distinctions between those incidents that arose as products of ancient injustices and those that were provoked by new usurpations. In reality, the two were often inseparably jumbled in the protests themselves, in which *hacendados* are frequently accused of traditional abuses recently committed.[13]

Both forms of the new concentration (usurpation and purchase of public lands) during the *Porfiriato* took on considerable importance in the early years of the new regime, between 1877 and 1884. While the sales of public lands continued after the depression of 1884–1886,

---

12. Jean Meyer, *Problemas campesinas y revueltas agrarias (1821–1910)* (Mexico: Sep Setentas, no. 80, 1973), pp. 8–32; and Leticia Reina, *Las rebeliones campesinas en México, 1819–1906* (Mexico: Siglo XXI, 1980).

13. Coatsworth, "Railroads, Landholding, and Agrarian Protest," p. 53.

the agrarian disturbances subsided.[14] By the inauguration of the second Díaz administration in 1884, usurpation of village lands had become an integral part of normal social progress, achieved almost without open protest from the victims, except in the case of the Yaqui Indians of Sonora and the Mayas of Yucatán. By 1884, violence had once again been isolated at the two extreme ends of the country. By that time, other economic factors came into play which gave further impulse to the commercialization and concentration of land but in a slower and more regular way. From the mid-1880s on, the data on usurpations (that is, the protests which reached the press) disappear, and the usurpations themselves, along with the sales of public lands, are no longer produced by the abrupt intervention of an essentially exogenous factor as the railroads had been, but instead by factors now integrated into the "normal" functioning of the economy: internal inflation, increasing world market prices for Mexican agricultural products, the entry of foreign capital into the land market, speculation in mineral lands, and the like. For these reasons, the analysis of the impact of the railroad on land tenure focuses on the first years of the *Porfiriato* when the impact of the railroad can be seen clearly in the evidence of usurpations and public land sales and when other factors that tended to the same result had not yet reached their later importance.

Railroads and the Usurpation of Indian Village Lands

From the point of view of Mexico's *hacendados,* railroads presented unique opportunities. The connection between transport facilities and land values was well known. As railroads reached productive areas formerly isolated or poorly connected to external markets, land values increased markedly.[15] To maximize their appropriation of

14. But the agitation against the sale of "vacant" lands in the populous states in the center of the country continued until the end of the decade, according to González Navarro, *La vida social,* pp. 187–99, 239–44.

15. On the connection between railroads and land values, opinion is unanimous although systematic data are lacking. See Viollet, *Le problème de l'argent,* pp. 62–63; González Roa, *El problema ferrocarrilero,* pp. 75–88; Silva Herzog, *El agrarismo,* pp. 125–26. McBride was the only author to recognize

these external benefits, *hacendados* had to anticipate railroad construction and move quickly to secure additional property in the path of the new lines. To be fully profitable, this expansion of the haciendas required that new properties become available at something near the prevailing prerailroad prices. Two methods were in fact employed by *hacendados* to appropriate additional lands. The first method involved enforcement of the Reform Laws, which required alienation of Indian communal landholdings and the distribution of such lands in individual parcels. Once the formerly inalienable property had been distributed, the individual holdings were acquired at relatively low cost through artful combinations of legal sale and illegal expropriation.[16] The second method involved purchase of "vacant" public lands from the government at low prices fixed by decree. Both of these methods required the sympathetic intervention of public authorities, but neither can be explained on legal or political grounds without analyzing the economic context of the process.

Long before the arrival of the iron horse, of course, Mexico's European conquerors set about expropriating tribute and then land from the mass of Indian cultivators.[17] Laws decreeing the distribution of communal lands—passed in a number of states long before the Reform—had already supported efforts by *hacendados* to encroach on communal property rights.[18] Liberal politicians and theorists supported such legislation from the earliest days of the nation's independent life partly because of its presumed importance for the creation of an economic and social regime more conducive to individual initiative and thus to economic growth.[19] Until the 1857 Constitution, however, the legal basis for overthrowing the colonial system of communal land grants to Indian villages remained insecure, and state laws encouraging or even requiring distribution of

the link between railroad construction, land prices, and usurpation of village lands, in *Land Systems*, p. 72.

16. González Navarro, *La vida social*, pp. 187–216.

17. For data on communal landholding and its destruction, see ibid., pp. 199–212.

18. Luis González y González, "El subsuelo indígena," in Daniel Cosío Villegas, ed., *Historia moderna de México: La República Restaurada, La vida social* (Mexico: Editorial Hermes, 1956), pp. 314–20.

19. Silva Herzog, *El agrarismo*, p. 40 ff. Conservatives frequently held similar views; González y González, "El subsuelo," pp. 316–17.

communal lands went generally unenforced.[20] Even in the case of the Reform, it is difficult to find the evidence of widespread usurpation and destruction of Indian communal landholdings which many historians have suggested. One recent work on the impact of the Reform in the center of the country, which could not be accused of excessive sympathy for the Liberal movement, cites only a few isolated cases of usurpation among a series of protests against prohibitions on religious processions, against the payment of new taxes, and the like.[21] Another recent study of the Reform in Oaxaca concludes that prospective buyers of disamortized properties were discouraged by the prevailing political and economic insecurity of the period, and that Indian villagers sold their land freely in the few cases that occurred.[22] These observations are confirmed by the most exhaustive study yet published of nineteenth-century peasant rebellions. Leticio Reina's work provides documentation of all known major and minor disturbances from 1819 to 1906. Only a very small number of pre-1856 cases provide evidence of actual recent usurpations, and none of the rebellions between 1856 and 1877 involved protests against usurpation or division of lands produced by the Laws of the Reform.[23] The great majority of agrarian movements before the *Porfiriato* were either (1) reactions against political changes such as official anticlericalism inspired by religious causes (for example, prohibition on religious processions), the appointment of new local officials, new taxes, and the like, or (2) "aggressions" or invasions of hacienda lands carried out by Indians (at opportune moments of political instability), and not protests against recent usurpations by *hacendados*.

In any case, a thorough investigation of the Mexico City press

20. González y González mentions such efforts in the states of Chihuahua and Zacatecas (1825), Puebla and Occidente (1828), Michoacán (1829), and Mexico (1833). The governor of Veracruz is cited by González y González claiming efforts to force distribution of communal lands in 1826; ibid., pp. 314–15, 319.

21. T. G. Powell, *Liberalismo y el campesinado en el centro de México (1850–1876)* (Mexico: Sep Setentas, no. 122, 1974), chapters 2–5.

22. Charles Berry, "The Fiction and Fact of the Reform: The Case of the Central District of Oaxaca, 1856–67," *Americas* 26 (1970):281–83.

23. Reina, *Las rebeliones campesinas*, pp. 45–433. See also William B. Taylor, *Drinking, Homicide and Rebellion in Colonial Mexican Villages* (Stanford: Stanford University Press, 1979), pp. 146–51.

during the Restored Republic (1867–1877) failed to turn up more than a few well-known cases of agrarian protest. The few cases encountered were the ones that the existing secondary literature had already mentioned. On the other hand, beginning in 1877, a crescendo of reports on agrarian movements, protests, manifestos, petitions, and rebellions appear in the newspapers of the capital.[24] The examination of these newspapers, and a variety of secondary sources, yielded information on a total of fifty-five serious conflicts between Indian villagers and neighboring haciendas between 1877 and 1884. Most of the incidents involved alleged illegal usurpations by *hacendados*. Nearly all involved some form of active resistance by the villagers — prolonged litigation, petitions to officials, violent protests, or armed rebellion. In a series of maps (figures 6.1 to 6.4), the locations of these incidents have been plotted against the actual and projected railroad network.[25] The result is striking. Of the fifty-five incidents recorded, only five (9.1 percent) took place more than a day's walk (forty kilometers) from a railway or the route of a railroad for which the federal government had issued a still active concession. Nearly 60 percent (thirty-two of the fifty-five) of the incidents took place within twenty kilometers of an actual or projected rail line.[26]

Despite obstacles to easy communication, there is no question that news of railroad concessions and even of the exact routes ran far ahead of actual construction. Landowners could read the texts of each concession in the *Diario Oficial*. Newspapers in the capital as well as those in the provinces reported fully on every detail of progress in construction and financing. State governors in 1876 and 1877 applied for local concessions and attempted to form private companies based on provincial as well as national and foreign capital to build newly authorized lines.[27] In San Luis Potosí, the state government issued new paper currency in 1878 in denominations of one centavo

24. A complete list of the incidents is found in Appendix III. This appendix also contains information on the nature of each incident and the sources used.

25. See Appendix III for a complete list of the railroads — projected, under construction, or completed — which appear in each of the maps.

26. Appendix III provides data on the distance of each incident from the nearest rail line.

27. Calderón, "Los ferrocarriles," pp. 491–502.

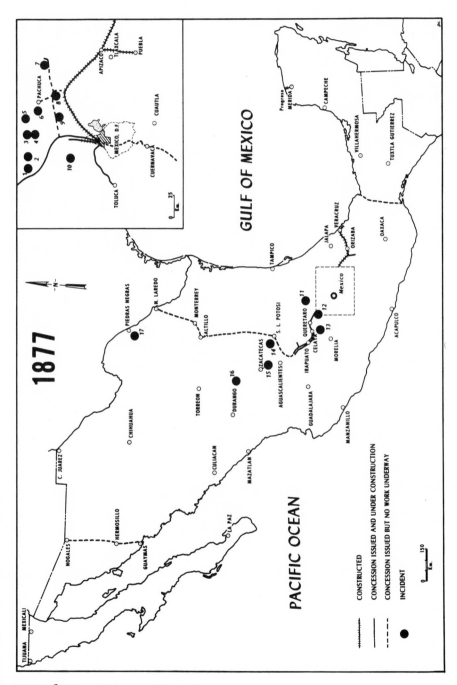

MAP 6.1
Railroads and Agrarian Conflicts, 1877

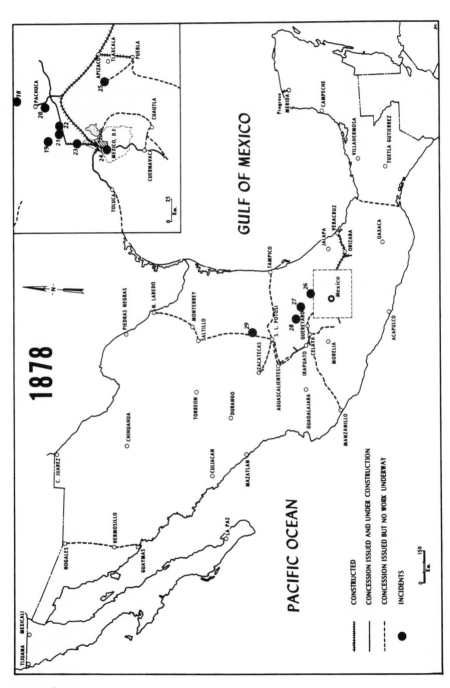

MAP 6.2
Railroads and Agrarian Conflicts, 1878

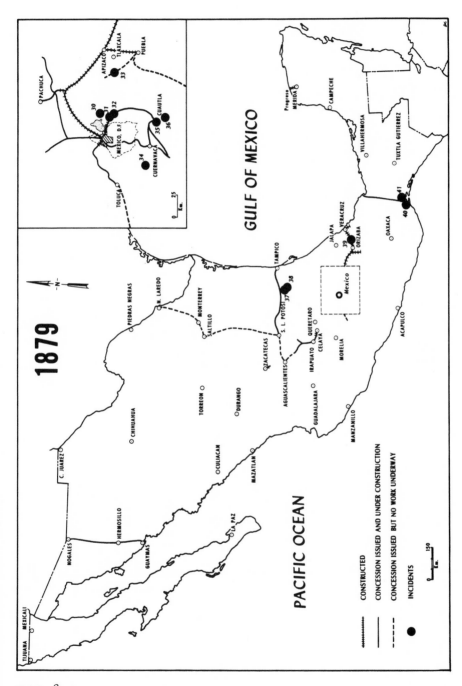

MAP 6.3
Railroads and Agrarian Conflicts, 1879

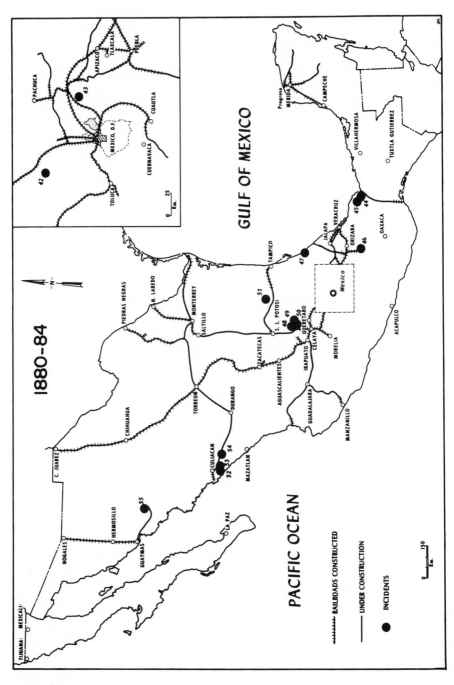

MAP 6.4
Railroads and Agrarian Conflicts, 1880–84

to five pesos which had to be used for payment of a special ten percent capitation tax surcharge imposed on all male citizens. New issues of the currency were printed in 1879 and 1880. The purpose of the tax was inscribed on each note: *"Ferrocarril de San Luis a Tampico."*[28]

Several cases came to the attention of the newspapers when village leaders or lawyers representing villagers were assassinated, imprisoned, or harassed.[29] Four incidents involving prolonged litigation resulted in return of some lands to the protesting villagers. Two of the four cases were among the five located more than forty kilometers from a rail line.[30]

At least nine of the incidents apparently owed their origins to alienations of communal lands under the Juárez regime and its successors.[31] Forced alienation to third parties in accord with the Reform Laws could be ordered by the courts if the Indian villagers refused to distribute communal property in private lots to individual members.[32] Whether *hacendados* had only begun to exercise their property rights effectively, or the Indians had been incited to disputes by the demagoguery of the rebelling Díaz and the subsequent displacement of Lerdista state and municipal officials is unknown. In any case, it appears that some *hacendados* had acquired legal title to communal properties which, before the construction of the railroads, they had not occupied effectively. In these nine cases of alienation, the Indians continued in physical possession of the lands until 1877 or after-

28. Antonio Kalixto Espinosa, "Emisión de billetes del Ferrocarril San Luis Potosí–Tampico, Años 1878–1880," *Archivos de Historia Potosina* 1 (1970): 219–23.

29. Harrassment was general. The worst case involved the assassination of four men representing a number of villages in legal proceedings at Actopán, Hidalgo, in February 1878.

30. Settlements involving the return of lands were reached in the case of the villages of San Pedro Tolimán and Santa María Peñamiller, both in the state of Querétaro in 1878. The governor of the state appointed mediators to resolve the disputes. *El Hijo de Trabajo* 3, no. 121 (17 November 1878):3.

31. See Appendix III.

32. Manuel Aguilera Gómez, *La reforma agraria en el desarrollo económico de México* (Mexico: Instituto Mexicano de Investigaciones Económicas, 1969), pp. 51–54.

wards, even in the case of the five villages whose lands had been legally expropriated years before, during the Juárez administration.[33]

Sales by the federal government of "vacant" public lands (discussed below) were probably involved in an unknown number of the fifty-five incidents. Many of the free villages, unable to produce colonial documents proving ownership of the lands they occupied, were acquired by *hacendados* at extremely low prices.

Of the fifty-five incidents reported, most took place some time before the actual construction of the nearby railroad line. Of the fifty incidents within forty kilometers of a rail line, twelve were reported after a concession had been issued but before any construction had begun, while thirty-two occurred after construction had begun but before the line had reached the immediate area. Two occurred in places where the projected line was never built.

Seven of the incidents that took place in 1877 occurred along the route of a projected Mexico City to León railroad line, the concession for which had been issued in 1874 and revoked two years later. In this case, the concession was canceled only after an initial survey for the route had been completed and a considerable sum of money had been spent on construction and preparation of the roadway. While the incidents reported here took place after the revocation of the concession, the government had already indicated that it assigned a high priority to finding a new concessionaire, and Mexico City newspapers had expressed optimism concerning the government's effort. A number of promoters were reportedly seeking the concession, which was finally issued to the Mexican National Construction Company as part of its line from Mexico City to the northern border in late 1880.[34] Because of the special circumstances surrounding this line, the map for 1877 includes the Mexico City–León line, despite the revocation of its concession the previous year.

The most serious agrarian disturbances in this period took place in the states of Sonora, Hidalgo, and San Luis Potosí. In Sonora, the construction of a rail line from Guaymas to Nogales, and concessions

33. See Appendix III.

34. Matías Romero, *Report of the Secretary of Finance of the United States of Mexico . . . Rectifying the Report of the Hon. John W. Foster . . . to Mr. Carlisle Mason* (New York: G. Putnam, 1880), pp. 54–62; Pletcher, *Rails, Mines and Progress,* pp. 35–105.

for a line from Guaymas to the coal fields on the Río Yaqui and for a railroad down the Pacific coast coincided with efforts by local land-owners and officials to adjudicate and seize lands long occupied by Indian cultivators. The Yaqui War, which lasted for more than two decades, was renewed as a direct consequence of these land seizures.[35]

In Hidalgo, violence erupted soon after the restoration of the Republic in 1867. Four of the fourteen incidents recorded in the late 1870s took place in the part of the state that had experienced a bloody rebellion led by Francisco Islas and Manuel Domínguez beginning in December 1869.[36] Between the suppression of this rebellion and 1877, local authorities complained repeatedly of recurring bandit attacks.[37] By 1877, however, reports from Hidalgo had changed; in this year, the Indians complained of attacks, not the haciendas. In November, "a force of cavalry under the command of one Barreiro" passed through two towns in the Actopán district and carried off a number of villagers as prisoners. Whatever the official reason for the arrests, the reports in *El Hijo de Trabajo* and *El Socialista* charged that the assault had been arranged by the Hacienda de la Concepción in order to eliminate resistance to its seizure of lands belonging to the villages of Santiago Tlapacoya and Jilenautla. In Tornacustla, also in the Actopán district, "soldiers" from the same hacienda were employed to drive villagers off their lands.[38]

Construction of the San Luis Potosí railroad began, with much fanfare, at the state capital in late 1878.[39] Complaints about usurpation of village lands are first reported in the press in early 1879. Violent seizures of hacienda lands began after Juan Santiago and a delegation of Indians returned from Mexico City where they claimed to have found titles to their lands in the *Archivo General de la Nación.*[40]

35. González Navarro, *La vida social,* pp. 249–53; Nathan L. Whetton, *Rural Mexico* (Chicago: University of Chicago Press, 1948), pp. 88–89; *MF, 1883–85* 3:553–73.

36. Silva Herzog, *El agrarismo,* pp. 97–98; Powell, *Liberalismo,* pp. 137–40; John Hart, "Agrarian Precursors of the Mexican Revolution: The Development of an Ideology," *Americas* 29 (1972):139.

37. Powell, *Liberalismo,* p. 139.

38. *El Hijo de Trabajo* 2, no. 70 (25 November 1878):4.

39. Calderón, "Los ferrocarriles," p. 500.

40. Valadés, *El porfirismo,* p. 253; Reina, *Las rebeliones campesinas,* pp. 271–75.

Santiago informed the villagers that President Díaz had authorized village leaders to make war on the *hacendados* of the district. A second center of rebellion developed shortly afterwards at Tancanhuitz. From 1879 until 1882, much of the Huasteca region was in turmoil.[41] A new uprising broke out in 1883. Centered at Ciudad del Maíz, it was led by the parish priest Fr. Mauricio Zavala who had apparently visited Santiago at his headquarters in the mountains at least once during the initial revolt at Tamazunchale.[42] Smaller outbreaks and protests involving several villages occurred in districts scattered through the states of Mexico, Morelos, Puebla, and Veracruz.[43]

In addition to the conflicts between individual villages and neighboring haciendas enumerated above, a number of more generalized forms of protest also occurred. In the spring of 1878 and again in 1879, Mexico City newspapers carried stories of meetings, and even a Congress of village representatives from states throughout the central plateau at which speeches were made demanding the return of usurped communal lands.[44] A project for a *ley agraria* circulated in several states acquiring the signature of thousands of *campesinos*.[45] In May 1879, approximately eighty *pueblos unidos* formed a *Coalición*, and named commissioners to petition the government for return of lands taken from them.[46] Occasionally, villages acted together through sympathetic lawyers who represented them in litigation as well as through petitions directed to government officials. In 1879, Fernando Castro and his associates were reported to be representing approximately forty-five *pueblos* in the states of Michoacán and Guanajuato. In June 1879, *El Hijo de Trabajo* reported "this gentleman has just sent a petition to Don Porfirio Díaz asking him to support the rights of the *pueblos* and to enact a *ley agraria,* or at least to insure that

41. Reina, *Las rebeliones campesinas,* p. 275; Meyer, *Problemas,* p. 22.

42. Rafael Montejano y Aguinaga, *El Valle de Maíz, S.L.P.* (Ciudad del Maíz, San Luis Potosí, 1967), pp. 311–21; Reina, *Las rebeliones campesinas,* pp. 279–80.

43. See Appendix III.

44. *El Hijo de Trabajo* 3, no. 101 (30 June 1878):4; 4, no. 137 (3 March 1879):3; 4, no. 138 (16 March 1879):3; 4, no. 149 (1 June 1879):1–2.

45. Ibid., 3, no. 118 (27 October 1878):2; 3, no. 124 (8 December 1878):2.

46. Ibid., 4, no. 146 (11 May 1879):3.

the courts make proper decisions under existing law without interference from political authorities."[47] Unfortunately, the exact location of many of the villages represented at these meetings and congresses and that of the villages which united to employ attorneys like Fernando Castro have not been preserved.

Not all of the conflicts over property rights along railroad routes involved *hacendados* pitted against Indian villagers. In several cases, not included in the fifty-five surveyed above, villages were reportedly fighting among themselves over land, and in one case two traditional rivals nearly came to open warfare in a conflict over which should be the site of a projected railway station.[48] Conflict also arose between railroad companies and villagers over the companies' practice of taking land for right-of-way without proper compensation.[49] Occasionally such conflicts broke out between *hacendados* and the railroad companies, but more frequently these larger landowners actively sought railroad lines and even donated the lands required for the roadbed.[50]

While the pattern and timing of the incidents illustrated in figures 6.1 to 6.4 clearly indicate the importance of the railroad in the process of usurpation, a number of the incidents occurred in areas that had previously experienced conflict. The early concentration of events in the state of Hidalgo, for example, suggests that the railroads merely rekindled an old struggle. The rebellion led by Francisco Islas and Manuel Domínguez, and the other still earlier (although less intense), conflicts in this region were apparently unrelated to transport development.[51] The series of incidents reported in the vicinity of Mixquiahuala to the west were linked not only to earlier patterns of conflict and violence in the state of Hidalgo, but also to the intervention of the Juárez regime. In 1867, the federal government had dis-

47. Ibid., 4, no. 150 (8 June 1879):3.

48. "Controversia entre el Gobierno de Tlaxcala y la Empresa (del Ferrocarril Mexicano) para el establecimiento de la estación en Santa Ana Chiautempán," *AHSCT* 1/7–1.

49. *El Hijo de Trabajo* 4, no. 161 (24 August 1879):4; 4, no. 178 (20 December 1879):3; 5, no. 184 (1 February 1880):3.

50. Repeated references to such donations may be found in the documents relating to railroad construction appended to *Memorias* of the Secretaría de Fomento from 1877 to 1885.

51. See Silva Herzog, *El agrarismo,* pp. 97–98.

tributed a quantity of public lands in the vicinity of Mixquiahuala in unusually small plots to local peasants in exchange for minimal payments.[52] The coming of the railroad then inspired an ultimately successful effort by several large *hacendados* in the area to dispossess the recipients of these lands.

Railroads and Public Land Sales

At least as important a means for acquiring land as illegal or semilegal seizure was the government program for distribution of vacant public lands. The first law permitting cash sales of vacant public lands was an 1863 wartime measure adopted by the Juárez government. In four years, the embattled republican regime distributed titles to 1.7 million hectares at a price averaging $0.06 per hectare.[53] Much of this land was acquired by merchants and traders willing to accept titles to public lands in payment of debts owed them by the Liberal government. A considerable element of compulsion existed at both ends of such transactions. Loans to the Liberal cause in wartime frequently amounted to virtual confiscations. Public debt issues printed to cover such forced loans circulated at enormous discounts. In such circumstances, public land titles were no doubt frequently preferred to Liberal government bonds for a variety of reasons. They represented a claim, however tenuous and speculative, to tangible assets. Recognition of such titles in case of Liberal defeat was not highly probable, of course, but recognition of Liberal government bonds by a victorious Conservative or Imperial regime could be ruled out with certainty. Conservative governments and the Maximilianist regime had not restored Church lands. The possibility, however faint, of retaining titles to public lands granted by Juárez made such instruments preferable to debt issues under conditions of forced lending.[54]

The sale and distribution of vacant public lands slowed considerably after the Liberal victory in 1867. With regular sources of

52. González y González, "El subsuelo," p. 25.
53. *MF, 1868*, p. 64.
54. A financial history of the Juárez government during the Reform and the French Intervention has yet to be written.

revenue restored, Liberal governments were reluctant to resort to methods which might undermine public confidence and slow economic recovery. Juárez, under attack in Congress from a number of opposition factions, was reluctant to continue large-scale alienations of the national patrimony. He also opposed further sales because of a desire to prevent further concentration of landholding.[55] Immediately after the restoration of the republic in 1867, Juárez issued a new decree making all titles to vacant public lands conditional on the absence of injury to third parties.[56] The prices fixed by the government for sales of public lands were raised by decree to an average nearly four times higher per hectare than the wartime levels.[57] Thus, in addition to changed conditions, in which titles to vacant public lands were no longer sought as a less onerous alternative to public debt issues, the government itself adopted policies which further reduced the attractiveness of public lands as a speculative investment. Sales declined dramatically. In the first two full years of the restored republic, the *Fomento* ministry reported sales aggregating only 161,212 hectares at an average price of $0.23 per hectare.[58] Sales remained low through the decade before the Porfirian coup d'etat.[59]

Toward the end of 1877, according to Francisco Maza, head of the new Department of Vacant Lands in the Ministry of *Fomento*, the

55. McBride, *Land Systems,* pp. 94–95; Whetton, *Rural Mexico,* p. 86; Calderón, *La vida económica,* pp. 63–64.

56. Calderón, *La vida económica,* pp. 63–64.

57. The average wartime price had been $0.06 per hectare (see note 53). The average price paid in 1868–1869 was $0.23 per hectare; *MF, 1868–69,* pp. 69–70.

58. Ibid.

59. In the year ending 30 November 1877, only 110,325 hectares of vacant public lands were sold; *MF, 1876–77,* p. 448. In 1878, sales rose to 380,345 hectares at an average price of $0.21; *MF, 1877–82* 1:42. By 1884, the sales had reached 5,635,901 hectares at an average price of only $0.07; *MF, 1883–85* 1:237. The fall in the price, it should be noted, was due to increasing sales of lands in the northern states as the railroad advanced. The schedule of prices fixed by decree of the president actually rose between 1877 and 1884. The highest prices were fixed for public lands in the Federal District and adjacent states; the official price in this area was ten to twenty times higher than the prices fixed for public lands in the Territory of Lower California and the states of Chihuahua, Coahuila, Durango, Nuevo León, Sonora, and Tamaulipas; ibid., 1:246–47, 255.

number of claims for such lands began to increase dramatically.[60] The new regime had issued an unprecedented number of railroad concessions beginning late in that year. Maza attributed the rising interest in vacant lands to the inauguration of the Porfirian regime which, he said, "presaged an era of conciliation, peace and protection for the social conventions . . . [and] re-animated the spirit of enterprise and with it the desire to acquire lands. . . ."[61]

> In the aid of this desire [he continued] came the projects and
> the construction of easy means of communication as well as
> the decided success of the government in preserving the
> public order, and because of this, the desire was converted
> into a plausible reality and the claims for vacant lands
> increased repeatedly day by day.

Railroads and public order appeared, to the official most directly involved, intimately related to land-grabbing and the spirit of enterprise.

The largest claim for *terrenos baldíos* in this period were made in the northern states of Sonora, Coahuila, and Chihuahua.[62] The Sonoran claims rose from slightly over 2,000 hectares in 1875 to nearly a quarter of a million in 1886 and 1888. These sales of *terrenos baldíos* in Sonora faithfully mirror the history of the Sonora Railroad. The first concession was issued in mid-1875.[63] Sales jumped from 2,126 hectares in that year to 29,255 in 1876 and 30,639 in 1877. The first construction company failed to make the progress stipulated in its concession, and the government canceled the contract in June 1877 and reissued it to a new company. Lands sold in 1878 jumped to 42,973 hectares. When construction failed to begin as quickly as anticipated, sales declined to 28,507 hectares in 1879. Late that year, construction began in earnest, and in 1880 the number of hectares sold rose sharply to 99,377 and, as construction progressed, increased to peaks of 245,782 and 244,797 in 1886 and 1888, respec-

60. Maza's report is in *MF, 1883–85* 3:234–36.
61. Ibid., 3:234.
62. Dirección General de Estadística, *Anuario estadístico de la República Mexicana, 1894* (Mexico: Oficina Tip. de la Secretaría de Fomento, 1895), pp. 499–504.
63. *MF, 1877–82* 3:553–55.

tively. The Coahuila land sales clustered in two years, 1884 and 1888. In the earlier year the Mexican Central Railroad completed its line from Mexico City through Torreón to the U.S. border at El Paso.[64] In the later year, the National finally completed its trunk line through the state to Laredo on the Rio Grande.[65] In Chihuahua, sales of *baldíos* reached a peak in 1884 and 1885 with the completion of the Central.[66]

In Yucatán, the Caste War between Mexican authorities and the Mayan Indians had begun in the 1840s simultaneously with the expansion of large-scale plantation agriculture.[67] Railroad construction was limited to non-Mayan-dominated areas until the 1890s.[68] With scarcely thirty miles of track laid from Mérida along the route to Peto (over a hundred miles away), near the Mayan frontier, the Mérida–Peto Railroad Company predicted, in its annual report for 1886, that "the Caste War of Yucatán will end without doubt when this railroad arrives at its last station."[69] In the next annual report, the company repeated its claim that the railroad held the key to ending the Caste War, adding that the end of the war would make a large expanse of *terrenos baldíos* available for exploitation.[70]

In the early 1890s, railroad construction quickened. Two small lines, under construction from the coast of Quintana Roo (one inland from Puerto Morelos, the other from Ascensión Bay) encountered Indian resistance.[71] As the Ferrocarril Peninsular pushed construction of its line from both ends (Mérida and Campeche), land-grab-

64. Ibid., 3:374–77.
65. Ibid., 3:448–55.
66. Ibid., 3:374–77.
67. Nelson Reed, *The Caste War of Yucatán* (Stanford: Stanford University Press, 1964), pp. 7–8; Howard F. Kline, "The Sugar Episode in Yucatán, 1825–50," *Inter-American Economic Affairs* 1 (1948):79–100, and "The Aurora Yucateca and the Spirit of Enterprise in Yucatán, 1821–1847," *HAHR* 27 (1947):30–60.
68. The line from Mérida to Valladolid reached a point very close to the frontier, but far to the north of the principal Mayan concentrations.
69. Ferrocarril de Mérida a Peto, *Informe Anual de 1886, AHSCT* 23/261–1, p. 4.
70. Ferrocarril de Mérida a Peto, *Informe Anual de 1887, AHSCT* 23/261–1, pp. 4–6.
71. Reed, *Caste War*, p. 235.

bing along the route sparked a violent uprising among the heretofore pacified Mayas at Maxcanu in 1891.[72] As the Mérida–Peto line moved slowly forward, similar symptomatic incidents occurred. In 1892, Indians in the Peto district rose up against a series of usurpations, apparently inspired by the approaching iron horse.[73] Difficulties in finance and in obtaining adequate labor slowed construction during the mid-1890s. The Peninsular was not completed until 1898. The Mérida–Peto line was inaugurated on 15 September 1899 at ceremonies presided over by State Governor Francisco Canton, whose family controlled the railroad company.[74] After Governor Canton hammered the last spike in the line, General Nicolás Bravo, just sent by federal authorities to take charge of the new campaign against the Mayas, "took the sledge hammer and drove the first spike of the projected *Ferrocarriles Sudorientales de Yucatán,* to be driven straight through the Cruzob jungle to Ascensión Bay."[75]

In the case of Yucatán, then, the extension of the railroad network beyond the older sisal-growing areas in the 1890s is linked not only to sales of public domain and usurpation of village lands but to the intensification of the Caste War in its last phase.

Conclusions

The social and political implications of this process of concentration of landownership have been treated extensively in histories of the *Porfiriato*. Failure to recognize the critical role of transport development in the process has led to excessively personalistic or voluntarist interpretations of *Porfirismo* and the development of the state apparatus during this period. Porfirian officials at every level encouraged and defended the new concentration of landownership. The legislative history of the process can be traced to liberalism and the Reform movement. But the timing and intensity of the process are

72. Moïsés González Navarro, *Raza y tierra: La guerra de castas y el henequén* (Mexico: El Colegio de México, 1970), p. 192.

73. Ibid.

74. The concession for the Mérida–Peto Railroad was acquired by the Cantón family in 1880. Echánove, *Enciclopedia* 3:552.

75. Reed, *Caste War*, pp. 238–39.

intimately connected to the constellation of events and conditions that determined the pace and pattern of railroad development.

The process of usurpation and concentration of landowning was more widespread and continuous than the incidents of protest or the land sales data reveal. The peaceful transformation of Naranja, a Tarascan Indian village near Pátzcuaro, illustrates this quite well. In Paul Friedrich's account, the transformation began when surveyors arrived in 1881 and discovered beneath the Zacapu swamp "a black soil of rare fertility."[76] In 1883, "two Spanish brothers named Noriega . . . managed to acquire the ancient legal titles through collusion with the mestizos of the village, notably the mayor. . . ." In 1886, the Noriegas "formed a commercial company with eight other Spanish and mestizo parties . . ." to drain the swamp. The Naranjeños did not resist the usurpation of their swamplands "mainly because they lacked competent leaders." By 1900, five haciendas, including the Zacapu *Hacienda de Cantabria,* surrounded the village, encroaching on its lands. "Thus," concludes Friedrich, "did the villagers pass through a classic sequence. . . . Naranja had become a village of hired men and migrant plantation hands, a sort of rural semi-proletariat."[77] The history of Naranja in this period can be read as a testimony to the greed and influence of Spanish outsiders and mestizo collaborators. But it can also be read as a response to North American investment in Mexican railroads.

The surveyors arrived in Naranja less than a year after the Mexican government granted a railroad concession to the Mexican National Construction Company for a line through Pátzcuaro to Uruapan.[78]

76. Paul Friedrich, *Agrarian Revolt in a Mexican Village* (Englewood Cliffs, N.J.: Prentice-Hall, 1970), pp. 43–44.

77. Ibid., p. 46.

78. The concession was authorized by Congress on 1 June and issued by the Secretaría de Fomento to the company on 13 September 1880. The concession specified the construction of a narrow-gauge line from Mexico City to Nuevo Laredo on the northern border with the United States. The company was also authorized to construct a line from a point between Maravatío and Morelia to Manzanillo on the Pacific coast, passing through Zamora and La Piedad. On 15 July 1880, the company received another concession, originally issued to the government of the state of Michoacán in 1877, for a branch line to Pátzcuaro and Uruapan from Morelia and Salamanca. *MF, 1877–82* 3:348–49.

The Noriegas acquired title to the swamp in 1883, just after the National's line reached Acámbaro and work on the branch to Uruapan had begun.[79] The commercial company was formed in 1886 just as the railroad reached Pátzcuaro.[80] By the time the swamp was drained, a small private railroad linked the Zacapu with Irapuato on the Central's main line to the north.[81] Until much more research is done, it will be impossible to know how many leaderless villages peacefully lost their lands to greedy outsiders seizing properties in anticipation of railroad construction. It is conceivable that Naranja's experience was repeated in countless local dramas throughout the Porfirian railroad era.

If the results of this study may be extended somewhat, they suggest that foreign enterprise in the form of major railroad construction projects significantly altered the shape and balance of Mexico's agrarian system in the last quarter of the nineteenth century. The *Porfiriato* saw a considerable expansion and consolidation of the hacienda at the expense of competing rural institutions, notably the Indian free village. Until further research brings new evidence to light, the full dimensions of this process are difficult to specify. Regional variations, consistent with variations in natural conditions, local agrarian institutions, and the penetration of new transport and industrial technologies may prove to have been quite complex. It does seem possible to conclude, however, that Mexico's developing international economic connections will provide a list of variables quite critical to explaining the evolution of agrarian institutions during the *Porfiriato*.

In a brilliant chapter, in his study of railroad development in the United States, entitled "The Dynamics of Railway Extension into the West,"[82] Albert Fishlow traced the process of anticipatory settlement by family farmers whose courage and hard work the railroad followed quickly to reward. The Mexican analog to this process of anticipatory family settlement was a process of anticipatory usurpation of Indian communal lands and of public domain by the nation's latifundist, and increasingly entrepreneurial, ruling class.

79. The report on the construction of the branch line toward Pátzcuaro from Acámbaro is found in *MF, 1883–85* 3:276.
80. Ibid.
81. Friedrich, *Agrarian Revolt,* p. 44.
82. Fishlow, *American Railroads,* chapter 4.

Chapter 7
Conclusions and Comments

Mexico entered the last quarter of the nineteenth century as a backward, war-scarred, wreck of a nation. Among the most serious obstacles to modernization, which her rulers acknowledged, was a primitive transport system. Next to political and social stability, the country's elite viewed transport improvements in general and railroads in particular as the most important prerequisite to progress.[1]

Every Mexican government, from the 1850s on, actively sought to encourage railroad development with offers of generous subsidies and privileges to any group, domestic or foreign, which held out reasonable promise of accomplishment.[2] Success in these efforts awaited the first government to hold out a reasonable hope of paying the subsidies and honoring the privileges. The development of the railroad network during the thirty-four-year *pax porfiriana* proceeded rapidly under the aegis of foreign, predominantly United States, capital.

Contemporary observers, including Porfirian officials, viewed railroads as the principal engine of the nation's export-oriented economic growth. Increasing government regulation in the 1890s, and the Mexicanization of the bulk of the country's rail lines between 1902 and 1910, reflected the commitment of the regime to insure that the new transport system continued to play this role. The chief beneficiaries of the Mexicanization were foreigners: the foreign owners of Mexican railway bonds and the mainly foreign-owned export sector of the Mexican economy. Foreign bondholders benefited because the Mexican government now guaranteed payment of the bonded debt of railroad companies, which in some cases had been teetering on the edge of bankruptcy. More importantly, entrepreneurs who used the railroads benefited from the government's commitment to rationalize service and maintain low tariffs. Since most of

1. On contemporary opinion, see Calderón, *La vida económica*, pp. 698–732.
2. Ibid.; and David Pletcher, "México, campo de inversiones norteamericanas, 1867–1880," *HM* 2 (1953):564–74.

the railroads' freight came from the export sector, and most of the large enterprises producing for export were foreign owned, especially mining concerns, the benefits of Mexicanization went chiefly to them. Foreign mine owners avoided the costs and disruptions of service which, in the United States, had accompanied the manipulation of railroad corporations by various groups of North American financiers. North American capitalists knew best what benefits they gained from Limantour's successful efforts to keep the Mexican railroad system from falling into the hands of a North American monopoly.[3]

It is perhaps ironic, but by no means accidental, that Mexican railroads serving the needs of an export sector dominated by *foreign* entrepreneurs offer one of the few examples of a relatively successful state regulation and control of transport in nineteenth-century Latin America. Brazil and Argentina, where the productive resources of the export sector (coffee, sugar, wheat, and cattle lands) were owned by *nationals,* granted concessions, subsidies, and privileges to foreign-owned railroad companies which frequently subverted efficiency and good service.[4] In the case of Mexico, efficiency and good service were exacted by the needs of foreign capitalists as well as domestic entrepreneurs, and government policy was notably more successful in providing it.

The most severe critic of Porfirian transport policy in the revolutionary period, Fernando González Roa, aimed his harshest criticisms against Limantour's policy of reducing official incentives to further expansion of the railroad network.[5] He criticized both the 1899 Railroad Law and the Mexicanization program because they tended to discourage, rather than stimulate, still more rapid construction. Implicitly, González Roa argued in favor of policies more like those of Brazil and Argentina in order to secure an expansion of the railroad system into areas of the country that held no interest for foreign

3. A small number of Mexican capitalists who made use of the railroads' services or who had purchased bonds of the old companies also profited.

4. González Roa, *El problema,* p. 22; John H. Coatsworth, "Brazilian Railroads in the Nineteenth Century: Some Hypotheses," (Chicago, mimeo, 1972); Horacio Juan Cuccorese, *Historia de los ferrocarriles en la Argentina* (Buenos Aires: Ediciones Macchi, 1969), chapter 6.

5. González Roa, *El problema,* pp. 39–40.

capitalists. Thus both Porfiristas and Revolutionaries believed that railroads were indispensable for economic growth.[6] This study confirms that view.

An analysis of the direct social savings attributable to railroad *passenger* services does not, however, establish a significant *direct* contribution. If all of Mexico's 4.6 million first class passengers in 1910 had traveled by stagecoach, and all of the 11.2 million second class passengers had walked to their destinations, the cost to the economy would not have amounted to more than $14.6 million, or 1.3 percent of gross domestic product. Moreover, it seems likely that the demand for passenger travel was very elastic; without the railroads, many fewer people would have traveled, thus reducing still further the direct savings. But this is, of course, just the point. Highly elastic demand for passenger travel suggests that from the point of view of the individual traveler, the railroad made a big difference. The economy would not have suffered much had people traveled by stagecoach or on foot, but it is very likely that without the railroad, many would not have traveled at all.

For many Mexicans, the expense of a second class railroad journey was so high that such travel was avoided except in cases where long distances made walking dangerous or impractical. In 1898, Mexican authorities attempted to prevent the spread of yellow fever from Veracruz by imposing a quarantine and controlling railroad passenger traffic. William Newbold, president of the Mexican Railway, remarked to his stockholders the following year that this measure was not protecting Orizaba from the disease because "all roads to that place are open, and the natives of the lower class coming from the hot country can easily reach Orizaba on foot, and as a matter of fact, these people generally go by foot."[7] The high cost of rail travel probably explains why the output of passenger services in Mexico remained far below that of the United States at a comparable level of railroad development.[8]

---

6. Ibid., pp. 41–43; Macedo, *Tres monografías*, p. 234; Jaime Gurza, *La política ferrocarrilera del gobierno* (Mexico: Oficina Impresara de Estampillas, 1911), p. 15.

7. Cited in Schmidt, "The Railroad and the Economy," pp. 11–12.

8. See note 16 of chapter 5.

Despite their high tariffs in relation to the low levels of income prevailing in Porfirian Mexico, the railroads probably did play a significant role in stimulating the large-scale internal migration of the period. The "psychic" costs of travel in the prerailroad era are not included in our social savings estimates, because their elimination did not result in a measurable increase in national income. These costs included the discomfort and risk involved in prerailroad travel. They also included the anguish of permanent separation which, in the prerailroad era, confronted the villager who set out to seek his fortune in a distant place. The railroad made long distance travel far more comfortable than even the old luxury *diligencia,* while substantial diseconomies of scale made train robbery far less common than the traditional stagecoach holdup or highway mugging. Village migrants easily returned from unheard-of distances to attend local fiestas, to choose their brides, and to settle old feuds long into the twentieth century. The railroad's speed made the decision to leave home a far less serious affair than it had ever been. Mexicans traveled less by railroad than their North American counterparts, but the average distance each passenger traveled was nearly twice as long.[9]

The railroads made additional *indirect* contributions to the flow of migrants from village to town and from south to north. The widespread usurpation of free village lands in the center of the country helped to push people off the land. At the same time, the railroads continually marginalized large numbers of agricultural workers and peasants by redistributing comparative advantage away from some localities and occupations to others. *Pulque* producers in the Federal District and the state of Mexico, for example, were instantly marginalized as soon as the Mexican Railway reached Mexico City in 1873. The company began immediately to dispatch a daily *pulque* express down the mountains to Apizaco, in the state of Puebla, where lower cost producers profited from their new access to the Mexico

9. While the average journey of Mexican rail passengers in 1910 was 67 kilometers, that of North American passengers at a comparable stage of railroad development (the decade of the 1880s and 1890s) was 25 miles, or scarcely 40 kilometers. In 1910, the average journey was 33.5 miles, or 56 kilometers. Thor Hultgren, *American Transportation in Prosperity and Depression* (New York: National Bureau of Economic Research, 1948), p. 61.

City market.[10] The opening of major lines to the U.S. frontier made the Laguna the nation's foremost cotton region, displacing producers in the traditional cotton areas in the state of Veracruz (and reducing Mexico's dependence on cotton imports as well).[11] Major prerail commercial and industrial centers like Querétaro and León lost their importance, and with it many of their inhabitants, while miniscule villages like Torreón grew into major railheads and urban centers.[12]

Railroads helped to pull as well as to push. Indeed, the nearly simultaneous incidence of both railroad effects is important for explaining the railroad's stimulus to population movements. Railroads provided the single most important vehicle for long distance word-of-mouth communication in an era of almost universal illiteracy. Word of the demand for labor in the new cities and mining centers of the north flashed back instantly to the unemployed in towns like Querétaro and León. The *indirect* effect on migration of the railroad's direct impact on export sector growth and the location of economic activity was probably its most important contribution to the redistribution of population in the Porfirian period. The regional and sectoral wage differentials which inspired much of Mexico's long distance internal migration were due mainly to the skewed geographic impact of the direct social savings from railroad freight services on economic activity.[13] And while railroad-induced investment in labor-scarce regions created a demand for labor where none had existed before, railroads provided the workers in numbers sufficient to prevent wage rates from rising high enough to choke off the new development.

In contrast to the railroad's passenger services, freight transportation involved very high direct savings to the economy. Direct social savings due to railroad freight services amounted to a *minimum* of between $126.7 and $135.8 million, or 10.8 to 11.5 percent of gross domestic product in 1910. These minimum estimates are more than

10. Calderón, *La vida económica*, pp. 663–65.

11. Dawn Keremitsis, *La industria textil mexicana en el siglo XIX* (Mexico: Sep Setentas, no. 67, 1973), p. 160.

12. Alejandra Morena Toscano, "Cambios en los patrones de urbanización en México, 1810–1910," *HM* 22 (1972):179–87.

13. See the "minimum daily" wage rates reported in El Colegio de México, *Estadísticas: Fuerza de trabajo*, pp. 147–54.

twice as large as the *maximum* estimates of railroad social savings in the United States, England and Wales, and Tsarist Russia.[14] In fact, the estimate that is more comparable to these other cases is much higher. In the three earlier case studies, the authors deliberately assumed that in the absence of railroads, the same quantities of freight would have been shipped the same distances. (This is an entirely legitimate procedure if the objective is to construct a deliberately exaggerated or *maximum* estimate.) In the case of Mexico, had all freight shipments actually transported by rail in 1910 been transferred to wagons to be shipped the same distances, between 24.9 and 38.5 percent of Mexico's gross domestic product would have had to have been diverted from other productive activities to provide the necessary transportation. This contrasts with estimates of approximately 5 percent in the three other cases mentioned. A realistic *minimum* estimate for Mexico, which allows for a substantial reduction in the use of transport services in the absence of the railroad, suggests that perhaps as much as one half of the increase in per capita national income between 1880 and 1910 may be attributed to the construction and operation of Mexico's railroads.

It is perhaps ironic that in the single case where railroads have as yet proved to be really indispensable, they were constructed in a backward, largely agrarian economy long before the real beginning of that nation's industrial age. Indeed, the railroad contributed little to the industrial growth of Mexico during the Porfirian era, apart from the stimulus of low transport costs to the growth of modern export production (mainly mining and smelting) and the expansion of some traditional import substituting activities (notably textiles). Most of the freight on Mexico's railroads in this period is accounted for by the output of primary products for export. And nearly all of the railroad's backward linkages to industrial suppliers ran across the border to the United States (or over the ocean to Western Europe).[15] Mexican railroads certainly played a critical role in the growth of the Porfirian economy, but the growth they induced was as skewed as the composition of the freight they carried. The direct benefits of rail-

14. Fogel, *Railroads*, pp. 75–84; Fishlow, *American Railroads*, pp. 74–90; Hawke, *Railways*, pp. 405–8; Metzer, "Economic Aspects," part 2.

15. See chapter 5 above.

road development were appropriated mainly by the foreign owners of Mexico's mining industry. If the freight originating in the mining industry is added to other export freight as well as imports, more than two thirds of all railroad freight services are accounted for.[16]

If foreign entrepreneurs supplied much of the capital and foreign industry the bulk of the manufactured inputs for the rail system, foreign capitalists earned most of the net revenues. Taking together all the sums spent abroad by Mexico's railway companies for inputs, for the import consumption of foreign employees, for profit remittances and interest payments, more than half of the gross revenues of the nation's railway companies left the country in 1910, at a time when two thirds of the rail network had been Mexicanized by the Porfirian regime. If interest payments on the railroad subsidy portion of Mexico's external debt are added to these direct "leakages," the total flow of resources abroad as a direct result of railroad construction and operation sums to more than $60 million (nearly a quarter of total export earnings) in 1910 alone.[17]

Railroads had diverse effects on Mexico's social and political life. Many of the positive institutional externalities associated with railroad development in the industrial nations did not take effect in Mexico. Perhaps the most important social consequence of railroad construction lay in the impetus to greater concentration of land ownership. The usurpation of free village lands, together with the initial stimulus to sales of vacant public lands in the early years of the Porfirian regime, was intimately linked to the construction of railroads.[18] The new transportation system revived the great estate and made it a profitable enterprise after more than a half century of progressive disintegration. In this, as in other aspects of its effects on social life, the railroad facilitated the survival of traditional, even archaic, institutions.

By reviving the great estates and stimulating the flow of foreign capital to large-scale enterprise, the railroads contributed to a significant regressive redistribution of wealth and income in Mexico. The economy grew, but the ownership of productive resources and claims

16. Ibid.
17. Ibid.
18. See chapter 6 above.

to the benefits of economic activity came to be far more concentrated. The question of equity became an issue in the revolutionary upheaval that ended the Porfirian era. Growing inequality also had long term consequences for economic growth, because it discouraged investment in human capital. The positive economic effects of railroad construction came mainly from large-scale enterprise with little need for local skills and expertise. The estates remained labor intensive at relatively low levels of technology, while the modern factories and mines found it possible to import both the equipment and the specialized human resources they required. Pressure for public education and other forms of investment in human capital increased very little during the *Porfiriato* and may even have diminished in comparison with earlier periods. Despite the rhetorical support expressed by public officials, especially for educational advancement, the Porfirian government assigned a low priority to such efforts.[19]

The lack of social policies of the Porfirian regime was not merely the result of such a short term rational calculus. Social investment conflicted with other, more important objectives. Investment in infrastructure (including railroads) drew resources to other uses. External financing for both private and public projects required a propitious climate for private investment, and this requirement further constrained public initiatives. The social strata most likely to benefit from and to pressure for increased commitments to human capital formation suffered a loss of political influence that corresponded to their declining share of income and wealth. Finally, the evolution of the fiscal system and the state apparatus toward increasing centralization removed decision making further than ever before from the influence of such groups.[20]

Despite its lack of social policies, the Porfirian regime enjoyed a period of stability and calm unprecedented in Mexico's independent history. The railroads contributed to suppressing political and social conflict and therefore helped to stabilize the regime. The impact of

19. Coatsworth, "Railroads, Landholding, and Agrarian Protest," pp. 53 – 54, 70 – 71.

20. Paul Baran, *The Political Economy of Growth* (New York: Monthly Review Press, 1956), chapter 5; Fernando Henrique Cardoso and Enzo Faletto, *Dependencia y desarrollo en América Latina: ensayo de interpretación sociológica* (Mexico: Siglo XXI, 1969), pp. 17–22, and chapter 2.

the new transport system on elite behavior is difficult to measure, but some tentative observations can be made. Of all the effects that received attention from contemporaries, the speedy transport of troops is mentioned most often.[21] Until the very last years of the Porfirian regime, however, the railroads transported relatively small numbers of troops.[22] Political and social conflict was inhibited not by transporting troops, but by the credibility of railroads as potential transporters. If deterrent credibility is hard to measure in the atomic age, it is yet more difficult to assess retrospectively in the case of Porfirian Mexico.

Intra-elite political conflicts were diverted to more peaceful channels than Mexico had been accustomed to expect, and railroads were important to this diversion. The change was due as much to the railroads' impact on economic life as to their troop-carrying capacity. Distributional struggles within elites are frequently the product of hard times, which political instability makes worse. Each group or sector attempts to use government as a means of shifting limited resources away from competing interests. The railroads served landowners' interests in an impersonal way, bringing a kind of prosperity that cut across old political, personal, and regional divisions. Intense politicking often erupted over the selection of routes, but the Porfirian regime left so much latitude to foreign companies in this aspect that it escaped blame for the results. Moreover, political stability was quickly recognized as the *sine qua non* for more of the same. In much of Latin America, railroads helped to push intra-elite conflict down below the level of central governments not only because they cut transport costs or transported troops rapidly, but because they brought benefits which political instability might easily subvert. In Mexico, the benefits which accrued to local interests included not only the railroads themselves but the influx of foreign capital which the railroads helped to attract to productive enterprise at the local level.

Railroads played another, largely unmeasurable, role in Mexican social development. They speeded communication among regional

21. Foreigners were equally impressed. See Moses, *Railway Revolution*, chapter 1.

22. Nearly all of the railroad companies reported the number of "military" or "official" passengers separately in their annual reports to the government. The reports are found in *AHSCT*.

elites and between them and the political and economic center of the republic. It is true that the telegraph, and later the telephone, would probably have had the same effect. But in a society where face-to-face dealing kept, and still keeps, its traditional importance in political as well as economic enterprise, it would be difficult to argue that a different cause could have produced the same effect, at least not until the era of the automobile and the airplane. The railroad's stimulus to cohesive behavior within the elite (and the added effects of other types of foreign enterprise) makes it possible, for the first time since the colonial era, to identify a *national* elite, not readily separated into familial and regional groupings. Local and regional interests did not lose their importance, but for the first time since the Bourbon bureaucracy (with the possible exception of a brief period during the Maximilianist interlude), government ministries developed professional cadres, extended their relatively autonomous activities to every part of the country, and formulated policies based on perceptions of the national interest that did not merely aggregate narrow sectional concerns.

The railroads also stimulated, but in an important way also inhibited, the internationalization of Mexico's elite. Mexico did not attract large-scale foreign immigration in the late nineteenth century, in part because the development of mining as the country's chief growth industry required fewer hands and held out no promise of cheap land to Europe's peasants. The small immigration that did occur was largely confined to skilled workers and commercial adventurers. Of the foreign entrepreneurs in Mexico, Europeans (especially the French and the Germans) tended to settle and achieve a degree of integration into local society. North Americans, who brought with them the largest quantities of capital, had relatively little direct impact on the elite because they traveled to their properties like tourists on passenger trains, which made their investments accessible without the need to settle permanently in the country. North American managers, engineers, and skilled workers in the northern mining centers often received their wages and salaries in dollars, consumed a high proportion of North American imports with their earnings, and returned after their tour of service to their native land without learning more than a few words of Spanish, leaving behind very few Mexican acquaintances they could call friends. To the seacoast enclaves, familiar for centuries, the railroads added a new possibility—that of living as foreigners deep within the country.

Much has been written about the impact of railroad development on entrepreneurship and business organization in the United States and elsewhere to suggest the importance of the railroads as pioneer big businesses.[23] Their principal effects are said to have fallen in two areas: the efficiency of capital markets and the development of modern management techniques. In the case of the United States, however, Douglass North and others have cogently argued that both these effects of the railroads would have developed, with only slight delay, had some other industry been forced to pioneer.[24] In the case of Mexico, where industrial enterprise still remains largely dependent on foreign capital markets, railroads had little effect in any case. Mexican commercial banks did service the short term demand of foreign companies, including the railroads, but short term commercial lending institutions preceded the railroad boom of the 1880s. Entrepreneurship and business organization were affected, but not in ways that might have been predicted from the North American or European experience. Railroad enterprise had its chief impact on Mexican business organization not through the experiences of private entrepreneurs, but through the bureaucratic development of official agencies. Railroads had an important, and positive, effect on what political scientists have frequently called political "development." The promotion of such giant projects required that the state apparatus assume new functions and acquire new skills, particularly in the areas of financing and regulation. These new demands became especially pressing by the 1890s when the dependence of the country's new prosperity on the iron horse moved the government to intervene more and more in the industry.

The new skills and functions had little to do with corporate management in the private sector or with day-to-day operational problems, as in the United States. The most prominent of Mexican railroad entrepreneurs in the Porfirian period was Gabriel Mancera,

23. See Alfred Chandler, Jr., *The Visible Hand: The Managerial Revolution in American Business* (Cambridge, Mass.: Harvard University Press, 1977), chapters 3–6.

24. Douglass North, *Growth and Welfare in the American Past: A New Economic History* (Englewood Cliffs, N.J.: Prentice-Hall, 1966), pp. 114–15.

owner of the Hidalgo and Northeastern Railway. As early as 1890, more than a decade before Mexicanization of the railway system, this Mexican capitalist urged the government to take over the railroad system with arguments very similar to those employed by Limantour more than a decade later.[25] When the government set up the new *Ferrocarriles Nacionales de México* in 1908 to operate the lines it had acquired from North American and British companies, Mancera sold his railroad to the new company and became a member of its board of directors. Mancera's experience as owner-manager was of little use to the new government company. Operational management of the new system remained in the hands of North American experts who had managed the old foreign companies.[26] *Científicos,* technicians of state finance, provided the skills required to give direction to the new company's affairs.

The railroads did not contribute to the development of Mexican private entrepreneurship, but they did stimulate efforts of political technicians who sought to establish the requisite bureaucratic capacities within the public sector. These efforts were limited by constraints on government income and expenditure imposed largely by the desire of the country's leadership to remain attractive to foreign capitalists. Nonetheless, the need to finance state subsidies for railroad construction and for the Mexicanization program and the exigencies created by foreign as well as domestic demands for more efficient public administration made a major contribution to the development of an initial cadre of bureaucratic technicians in the public sector. If railroads did not stimulate the development of managerial talent and new forms of private sector organization, they did inspire a marked increase in competence within the state apparatus.

The development of the state did not occur independently of changes in Mexican society. The economic growth induced by the railroads cemented an historic compromise between Mexico's weak and fragmented bourgeoisie and its politically heterogeneous but increasingly powerful landowners. During the period of the Restored

25. See chapter 4 above. It is to be noted that Mancera sold his railroad to the government company after the failure of negotiations with a group of foreign capitalists who were unable to secure funding for the purchase. *Mexican Herald,* 28 March 1906, p. 1.

26. González Roa, *El problema,* pp. 138–39.

Republic, Liberal regimes made their peace with Conservatives who had fought until 1867 to restore the old precapitalist political order. The process began at the local and state levels as Liberal authorities replaced Conservative officials associated with the short-lived empire of Maximilian Hapsburg. The Liberals confiscated the properties of a few notorious collaborators, but left the land and other assets of most Conservatives alone. In part, this was due to the seizure of Church wealth that gave Liberal governments a source of rewards to their adherents without attacking the properties of their political enemies. In part it reflected an ideological commitment to respect for private property and a desire to consolidate the new order by promoting harmony. In the early years of the Porfirian regime, railroad construction helped to consolidate and strengthen the landowning class by blurring the differences that had once divided landowners along regional and ideological lines with opportunities for revival and expansion of their estates. The landed interest was further strengthened by the destruction of competing agrarian institutions, especially the free villages. New landowners with political ties to the Porfirian regime were created in the usurpations of village lands and the sales of public domain. These new landowners quickly discovered common interests with the older families and merged with them even when they represented Conservative political networks from the earlier era. In a short time, Mexico's *hacendados* acquired ownership over a much larger share of the nation's resources than ever before.

This strengthening of the landowning class did depend on the foreign resources that built the railroads and on the demand for agricultural products in the export sector and abroad, but it did not involve a significant penetration of foreign capital into directly productive activity. Foreign ownership of land increased during the *Porfiriato*, especially in the northern states near the border with the United States, but foreigners never represented more than a small minority of the landowning class of the country. Urban industry and commerce, on the other hand, developed in much closer association with foreign capital. The large-scale mining and metallurgical installations were mainly foreign owned, while even light industry and banking were closely tied to foreign finance. The urban bourgeoisie of the Porfirian era enjoyed an unprecedented prosperity, but only as junior partners of foreign interests. The new urban entrepreneurs thus formed the weaker sector of the Porfirian elite. Their weakness was reflected in the insensitivity of the regime to urban social problems, its willingness to pursue a policy of balancing foreign pressures in pursuit of national policy objectives, and, ultimately, in its increasingly authoritarian character.

The peculiar constellation of social and economic forces unleashed by the development of railroads in Mexico resembled what contemporary macrosociologists have come to identify as typical of the early development of modern authoritarian regimes. A strong landowning class, a relatively weak bourgeoisie, a defeated and demoralized peasantry, and, finally, the development of working class trade union and political organizations at an early point in the industrialization process—all characteristic of Porfirian Mexico—fit the prescription for a process of "modernization from above" that culminated in the Fascist regimes of the 1920s and 1930s in a number of developed countries. The principal difference between the case of Mexico and the cases explored by Barrington Moore and his successors lies in the crucial role played by external resources. The authoritarianism of the Porfirian regime and the alliance of social classes that stood behind it proved more fragile than their counterparts in Europe and Asia. The Mexican Revolution broke through the fragility of the Porfirian system and permitted a new set of political actors and social classes to define the nation's future. The authoritarian legacy of the Porfirian era remained, however, to be strengthened rather than undermined by the substitution of the national state and its network of rural clients for the agrarian oligarchy of the previous period. The result of this process was the creation of a modern "bureaucratic authoritarianism" under civilian, rather than military, rule by the middle of the twentieth century while other Latin American nations were still experimenting with more competitive, parliamentary regimes.[27]

The contradictory impact of the railroad in Mexico defies easy measurement. In narrowly economic terms, the railroad's positive effect on economic activity is no longer subject to question. Measured in 1910 in comparison with an economy forced to do without the new

27. See John H. Coatsworth, "Orígenes del autoritarismo moderno en México," *Foro Internacional* 16 (1975):205–32.

transport technology, Mexico derived more benefits than any other developed or underdeveloped country for which social savings estimates have yet been constructed. If the stimulus to industrialization through backward linkages was small or the foreign exchange costs of foreign financing and inputs were high, it may be concluded that there is little to add to the benefits already captured in the social savings estimates. If, however, the 1910 Mexican economy is permitted railroads, but constraints are imposed on the use of foreign capital and inputs, a different measure could result. On the one hand, the abrupt and massively regressive land tenure effects would be reduced or even eliminated and the nature of institutional and political development altered as a result. On the other hand, there is little doubt that these constraints would have slowed the development of the rail network, reduced the flow of foreign capital to productive enterprise in other sectors, and retarded the growth of national product. The consequence of a more nationalistic set of economic policies, even conceding their plausibility, would have been a 1910 gross domestic product well below the level actually achieved. In the historical long run, however, the short run costs of slower initial growth might have paid high dividends. Export-led growth, which the railroads promoted and sustained, revitalized old barriers and created wholly new obstacles to development: low levels of investment in human resources, overcommitment of private and public capital to export sector investment, public agencies and private activities highly specialized in channeling foreign capital rather than capturing domestic savings, information and communications systems structured to facilitate international transactions rather than local market activity, extreme concentration of wealth and income, and authoritarian rule.

If the broader issues of Mexican development are posed from the vantage point of today, a different, broader set of issues may be raised. What were the costs and benefits, over the historical long run, of the growth path on which Mexico embarked in the late 1870s? This question makes the impact of the railroads subordinate to more general issues. The appropriate counterfactual in this case is a contemporary Mexican economy displaying the cumulative effects of a different structural and institutional trajectory. The unique contribution of the railroads in moving the economy onto the path actually taken was no doubt related to the magnitude of the social savings they produced. If the counterfactual economy would have eventually achieved greater growth and higher levels of welfare along a different trajectory, then the contribution of the railroads would be negative in the same degree. Precisely because savings were high in the first period, railroads may be seen as foreclosing other possibilities with very large effects over the longer period.

It is not possible, given the current state of theory and methods, to select, specify, and measure an appropriate counterfactual trajectory against which to compare the actual course of the Mexican economy after 1880. While comparison with other countries can provide empirical data to discipline historical insight, the larger issues stand at the frontier between scientific discourse and ideological struggle. Even though the short run contribution of the railroads to economic growth was large, an evaluation of the long run impact of this innovation would have to take into account its indirect effects on a long list of variables which combined to create the underdeveloped country Mexico has become.

The issues raised by this study of the economic impact of railroads are relevant today. The current debate over petroleum policy, for example, poses questions not unlike those posed in this retrospective analysis of railroad development. The short run economic gains from a rapid expansion of crude oil production and export are weighed by policy makers and citizens against contradictory, if not entirely negative, judgments about the structural and institutional consequences of such a trajectory. The fact that such a debate is taking place at all demonstrates the profound changes that have occurred in Mexico since the Porfirian era. In the 1870s, virtually the only objection to the Díaz policy of rapid, willy-nilly issuance of railroad concessions came from individuals worried about the nation's territorial integrity. A century later, the debate over petroleum raises issues that scarcely occurred to Mexicans in the Díaz era. In the end, petroleum, like railroads, may make Mexico's economy more vulnerable to external pressures, increase disparities in income and wealth, reinforce the nation's historic failure to invest adequately in its own human resources, strengthen the autonomy of the state in the face of popular needs, and intensify the repressive aspects of succeeding regimes. The alternatives to such consequences, however, are now more powerfully represented in society and even within the state itself than a century ago. To reduce external dependence and growing inequality against the pull of market forces and marshall resources for developing the nation's human resources and industrial potential while encouraging popular participation in government and public administration may be beyond the capacity of current social and political organization. It is no longer, however, outside the range of historical options nor beyond the grasp of Mexico's people.

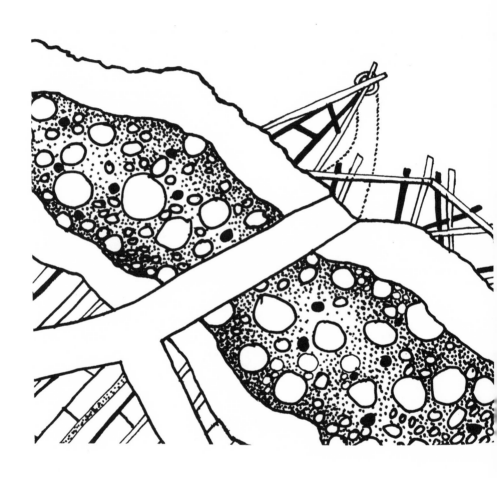

Methodological Appendix

Introduction

This methodological appendix has two purposes. The first is to introduce the theoretical concepts employed mainly in chapters 3 and 4, and especially the concept of "social savings" as it is currently used by economic historians. The second is to discuss some of the analytical issues involved in the use of these concepts to measure the economic impact of railroads in the case of Mexico.

Definition of Social Savings

The concept of "social savings" is briefly defined in chapter 1. The concept may be illustrated graphically, as in figure 1. The figure shows two economies, both using a fixed amount of transport services. The economy without railroads must pay a price of OP_1, for each unit of transport services it needs. The economy with railroad pays only OP_2 per unit. If both economies use the same amount of transportation, the economy without railroads will have to spend OP_1AC on transportation, while the economy with railroads will spend only OP_2BC. The difference between the two expenditures is equal to the shaded area in the figure. Because the railroad economy does not have to spend this extra amount, P_2P_1AB, for transportation, it can spend it on other things. Economists call this amount the "social savings" or, more precisely, the "direct social savings."[1]

---

1. An excellent review of the literature is contained in Colin M. White, "The Concept of Social Savings in Theory and Practice," *EHR*, 2d ser. 29 (1976):82–101. See also Robert W. Fogel, "Notes on the Social Savings Controversy," *JEH* 39 (1979):1–54; Patrick O'Brien, *The New Economic History of the Railways* (London: Croom Helm, 1977); Metzer, "Some Economic Aspects," pp. 26–77; Paul David, "Transport Innovation and Economic Growth: Professor Fogel On and Off the Rails," *EHR*, 2d ser. 22 (1969): 506–25; Peter D. McClelland, "Railroads, American Growth and the New Economic History: A Critique," *JEH* 28 (1968):471–88.

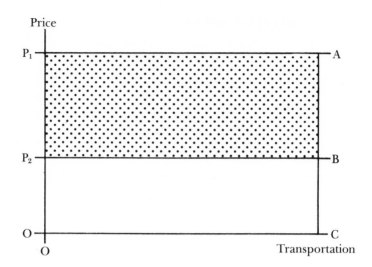

FIGURE MA.1
Direct Social Savings

The Counterfactual Method

To measure the economic impact of railroads in the real world, the economist or historian faces two problems immediately. First, the social scientist cannot conduct his experiment under strict controls. Mexico had nearly 20,000 kilometers of railroad in 1910. The historian cannot create another Mexico exactly similar to the first, except for the absence of railroads. Instead, he must use methods that are indirect and somewhat arbitrary to imagine what Mexico's 1910 economy would have been like without the railroads. Then he must measure, but very imperfectly, the difference between the gross national product of the imaginary Mexico without railroads and the gross national product of the real Mexico with them. This has been called the "counterfactual" method because it involves the "creation" of a situation or condition contrary to fact in order to test causal propositions about the real world.[2]

2. See J. A. Dowie, "As If or Not As If: The Economic Historian as Hamlet," *Australian Economic History Review* 7 (1967):69–85.

Even when the historian's imagination is brilliantly lucid, a second problem arises because the method of comparison between factual and counterfactual conditions is essentially a static method, the method of "comparative statics." Comparing two 1910 economies, one real and one imaginary, is not the same as comparing the real 1910 economy with the 1910 economy that would have existed if railroads had never been built. According to some writers, if railroads had never been built, Mexico might not have achieved thirty years of political stability during the *Porfiriato*.[3] To imagine a 1910 hypothetical economy without railroads is one thing. To imagine a 1910 counterfactual economy without Porfirio Díaz, foreign capital, and the infamous rural police is something else again. There is no way to solve this second problem within the limitations of available theory and data.

This second problem is not peculiar to studies of railroads, or to economic history. Nearly every generalization about historical processes involves a selection, by the historian, of the variables he wishes to isolate and the corresponding assumption that other variables are *constant*. Economists are unique in the use of a Latin phrase, *ceteris paribus*, to specify the limitations of their inquiries, but they are not alone in using the concept. To isolate and measure the economic impact of railroads, it is thus necessary to use a procedure similar to that employed in physical and natural sciences, where the properties of organisms or physical bodies are first measured, *ceteris paribus*, before the effects of environmental change or resistance are observed. The discussion that follows will focus on problems that arise in specifying an appropriate counterfactual Mexican economy for 1910. Nothing is permitted to change except the transport system.

Historical and Technological Alternatives

The first question that must be answered before constructing a counterfactual economy is "what kind of transportation system would Mexico have had in 1910 if no railroads had been built?" In part, this question is addressed in the text of this book. Analytically, there are

3. Macedo, *Tres monografías*, p. 234; González Roa, *El problema*, p. 42.

two choices. Should the direct social savings of the railroads be measured by comparing railroad transport costs with real transport costs from the prerail era, or should the economy be permitted to improve the efficiency of its nonrail transportation system before measuring? In the case of the United States, two important books have been written that give contrary answers to this question.[4] Robert Fogel's study uses reports of the United States Army Corps of Engineers on the feasibility of improving water transport and various studies on highway construction possibilities from the period to construct a counterfactual 1890 economy with 5,000 additional miles of canals and an improved system of land and river transportation. Albert Fishlow studied each railroad route of 1859 to determine what transport services were actually available in that year to absorb the railroads' freight and passengers. Fogel's counterfactual economy used the technologically most efficient alternative to the railroads. Fishlow's counterfactual economy used the historically available alternative. As figure 2 illustrates, these two measures will yield different results. A measure of social savings à la Fishlow will always be higher than that of Fogel (except where the most efficient alternative is immediately available). In figure 2, P_f is the railroad cost per unit of transportation, P_t is the cost of the technologically most efficient alternative, and P_h is the cost of the historically available alternative. For Fogel, social savings equal only the area P_fP_tBB', while for Fishlow, social savings include this area plus the rectangle above it, or the whole area of P_fP_hAB'.

The hypothetical economy in this study uses a technological alternative, similar to Fogel. It is thus assumed that without railroads Mexico's highways would have been improved and extended to permit year round transportation of freight at rates equal to those that prevailed in the dry season on the best roads for wagon transport before the construction of the railroads. For this reason, the estimates of direct social savings due to freight transportation in chapter 4 do not exaggerate the railroads' impact; instead, the estimates are probably too low, as is argued in the text.

4. See the works of Robert W. Fogel and Albert Fishlow cited above.

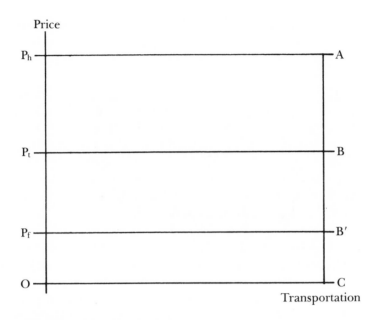

FIGURE MA.2
Historical or Technological Alternative

Biases Upward and Downward

A. PRERAILROAD RATES

As figure 2 illustrates, the cost of transporting goods and passengers in the counterfactual nonrail economy is the principal variable in the estimation of direct social savings. The railroad price is a historical fact; the counterfactual price has to be specified by the investigator. In his study of North American railroads in 1890, Fogel compared railroad rates with tariffs charged for shipment between the same points by canal in the same year.[5] This procedure was erroneous, because the canals still operating in 1890 were competing directly with railroads. These canals obviously enjoyed substantial cost advantages over canals that had ceased to operate and canals that were

5. Fogel, *Railroads*, chapter 2.

planned but never constructed. The application of rates from only those canals that survived therefore exaggerates the efficiency of the prerail transport system and results in an underestimate of the direct social savings of the railroads.

Fogel's use of water rates which competed with the railroad in 1890 suggests another more general criticism. By using such rates, Fogel built his conclusion into his test. It would be expected that the canals which survived to 1890 would charge, in a competitive economy, rates exactly equal to the railroads, taking into account hidden costs and the more indirect routes which the canals followed. Thus, the use of canal rates of 1890 for the counterfactual transport system does not result in a measure of the superiority of the railroad. Instead, it measures the degree to which the transport industry departed from perfectly competitive conditions in 1890 and the extent to which railroads and canals offered services which were not completely interchangeable.[6] Hawke, using canal rates from the period 1837–1846, and without intending a precise measure, estimated direct social savings on interregional agricultural freight for the United States in 1890 at approximately ten times Fogel's figure.[7] Thus, it is not appropriate to compare railroad transport costs with the cost of shipment by carriers in competition with railroads.

At the same time, the use of noncompetitive tariffs, charged by inefficient alternative carriers, as in the case of Fishlow, introduces the assumption that no improvement would be made in the nonrail transport system in the absence of the railroads.[8] For Fishlow's purpose, this assumption was appropriate, because he sought to construct a maximum estimate of the railroad's impact. To construct an estimate that is not a maximum, however, it is necessary to use rates from the *prerailroad* era which reflect an *efficient* use of nonrail technology. This is the procedure used in this study.

Such a procedure is not adequate when the construction of railroads is accompanied by significant changes in nonrail transport

6. Meghbad Desai, "Some Issues in Econometric History," *EHR*, 2d ser. 21 (1968):10.

7. Hawke, *Railways*, p. 22. Hawke's result is exaggerated, not intended by its author to be taken literally.

8. Fishlow, *American Railroads*, chapter 2.

technology. The use of wagon freight rates (even those that represented the most efficient use of these vehicles) would not be appropriate after the invention and diffusion of the internal combustion engine. For then the most efficient alternative to the railroads would be the motor truck—not widely used in Mexico until after 1910. (It is an altogether different problem to estimate the relative costs and benefits that Mexico might have paid, or gained, had the country waited four or five decades to improve its transport system with trucks rather than railroads. No attempt is made to assess this possibility here.)

B. DISTORTIONS IN THE TRANSPORT MARKET

The estimates of direct social savings measure the amount of resources saved by the economy only when prices are equal to marginal social costs for all transport carriers, real as well as imaginary.[9] Any distortion of prices could lead to more or less serious overestimation or underestimation of the real savings. The social savings can be exaggerated if railroad tariffs are less than marginal costs, or if the rates of the alternative carriers are greater than marginal costs. Railroad tariffs may be less than marginal costs when the government subsidizes construction or guarantees the debts contracted to finance construction. The same result may be produced by government regulation designed to maintain low rail rates, or under certain conditions, by the manipulation of rates to eliminate competition. The prices charged by alternative means of transport may exceed marginal costs when monopoly or oligopoly price fixing occurs to a significant degree. In such a case, the social savings estimate does not measure real resource savings alone, but erroneously includes monopoly rents redistributed to transport users when the railroad enters into competition.

Direct savings may be underestimated, on the other hand, if railroad rates are above and alternative rates below marginal social costs. Railroad tariffs, for example, may reflect the monopoly or oligopoly position of some railroad companies, especially over short lines

9. David, "Transport Innovation," pp. 513–14; McClelland, "Railroads," p. 114.

where competing railroads or water transport is not available. The marginal costs of the alternatives to the railroad may be higher than the prices they charge wherever railroad competition has forced a reduction in rates to the point where the competitor can no longer cover both fixed and variable costs. It is clear that these departures from perfect competition are entirely possible, even in the case of economies as notoriously competitive and free of restrictions as were those of nineteenth-century United States and England.[10]

The use of any railroad or nonrail rate can only be justified by a careful examination of the conditions that produced it. In chapter 2 of this study, and in appropriate sections of chapters 3 and 4, we have examined railroad and prerailroad tariffs in order to eliminate, at the least, the principal sources of *upward* bias in our estimates of direct social savings produced by conditions which may have involved departures from marginal cost pricing in railroad and prerailroad systems. The reader must judge for himself whether this effort, necessarily imprecise in any such study, has been successful.

C. CONSTANT COSTS OF THE PRERAIL SYSTEM

The third problem that affects the selection of the prerailroad tariff is the problem of relative costs. The studies of Fogel, Fishlow, and others have assumed that the marginal costs of production in the prerailroad transport system were constant.[11] This means that the prerailroad transport system is assumed to have been able to absorb both passengers and freight from the railroads without experiencing any rise in the unit cost of providing transportation. If all the freight actually conveyed by rail in 1890 had been transferred to water or overland means in the United States, the unit cost of transport might well have risen considerably above what nonrail carriers actually charged in 1890—that is, well above the rate used by Fogel to calculate the railroads' direct savings. To assume constant costs is to assume that millions of ton-kilometers of freight could have been absorbed by the counterfactual nonrail transport system without any effect on marginal costs. The evidence that Fogel cites in his study to

10. McClelland, "Railroads," pp. 114–21.
11. Ibid., p. 120.

support this assumption is not convincing.[12] If the nonrail system had been forced to supply even a part of the transport services actually provided by railroads in 1890, it could well have entered an area of rapidly rising costs. The omission of this possibility clearly introduces a downward bias in the social savings estimates unless evidence can be adduced to demonstrate that the structure of costs in the prerail system was compatible with the constant cost assumption.

In the case of Mexico, this downward bias is probably significant, as has been suggested in the text. The use of an index of prerail transport costs (based on the cost of labor) corrects this bias partially, but does not eliminate it. In constructing our estimates, however, we have been primarily concerned with eliminating *upward* biases. The existence of this downward bias merely reinforces the conclusions reached in the text, viz, that our estimates of the direct social savings due to freight services of the railroads in Mexico are *minimum* estimates.

Perfect Competition?

Even after having taken into account departures from competitive conditions in the transport sectors, the social savings estimates will not measure real resource savings unless competitive conditions exist in all other sectors of the economy, both with the railroad and without it. This point has been made in a number of ways.[13] The actual economy with the railroad may suffer from market imperfections, institutional barriers (legal as well as political), technical external economies, and other similar causes of departures from perfectly competitive conditions. It is not possible to measure the effect of such conditions, nor to project it onto the counterfactual economy without rails. Thus, the social savings measure will always overestimate or underestimate the contribution to gross national product of the railroads. Only in exceptional circumstances, where distortions in both directions exactly cancel each other, will the net bias be equal to zero.

12. Fogel, *Railroads*, p. 28; see McClelland, "Railroads," pp. 115–21; David, "Transport Innovation," pp. 511–13; Hawke, *Railways*, pp. 19–20.

13. Hawke, *Railways*, p. 22.

Fishlow has indicated considerable pessimism as to the possibility that transport innovation can induce increases in the output of presently underdeveloped economies because of structural and institutional obstacles to the efficient allocation of resources. "Underdeveloped countries," he concludes, "afflicted with large and unproductive agricultural sectors, illiteracy, concentration of wealth and state intervention which frequently results in failure can scarcely take hope from the efficiency of railroad investment in the United States before the Civil War."[14]

Market imperfections in underdeveloped societies can create conditions so different from the stupendous efficiency of the nineteenth-century United States that railroads (or any other investment in social overhead capital) fail to produce large social savings despite their superiority over other forms of transportation. In order for potential social savings to be realized, producers must be able to make rational decisions at the margin. As resources are freed from the transport sector, they must be transferred to other uses. As transport costs diminish, entrepreneurs must be able to react swiftly to lower costs with expanded production. If this kind of reaction is restricted or limited by institutional obstacles or market imperfections, the potential savings introduced by the railroads may never be realized.

In the case of Mexico, three considerations make it impossible to discount substantially the effects of such obstacles to competitiveness. First, to repeat a well-known axiom of economic theory, competition does not imply perfect rationality (or even literacy) on the part of the entire population, nor need it be limited (in an "open" economy) to national citizens. So long as entrepreneurs, foreign or national, respond to lower transport costs with appropriate investments and are not prevented from investing by legal or political prohibitions, the necessary degree of competitiveness will be exhibited. Second, no evidence has yet been adduced to prove that Mexican entrepreneurs of the *Porfiriato* were victimized significantly by institutional obstacles to rational investment decisions by any of the factors listed by Fishlow. On the contrary, numerous studies have demonstrated the efficiency and effectiveness of the Porfirian government (and the Liberal movement before it) in eliminating or reducing market im-

14. Fishlow, *American Railroads*, p. 311.

perfections and institutional obstacles. Third, all the evidence that does exist suggests a rapid response to new opportunities by Mexican entrepreneurs during the *Porfiriato,* even in the countryside where custom and tradition are most frequently believed to have impeded progress.[15] A recent work goes so far as to refer to a "technological revolution" in Porfirian agriculture.[16] Even if these considerations were not sufficient, the inflow of foreign capital, induced in great part by the construction of railroads, made the Mexican economy highly responsive to transport development.

Perfectly competitive conditions, as required to satisfy the specifications of full neoclassical general equilibrium, are never encountered in the real world. But they are almost never necessary in their entirety for the fruitful application of economic analysis to historical problems.

The Elasticity of Demand for Transportation

In the studies of Fogel and Fishlow of U.S. railroads, and in most other attempts to measure railroad social savings, the authors have been trying to construct maximum estimates of the railroads' contribution to economic growth. For this reason, these studies have made the convenient assumption that the elasticity of demand for transportation is equal to zero. This means that no matter what the price, the counterfactual economy will use the same amount of transportation as the real economy with the railroads. The assumption of perfectly inelastic demand for transportation introduces an upward bias in the resulting social savings estimates. For any assumed price elasticity of demand greater than zero, the quantity of freight shipped in the absence of the railroad will be less.

15. The growth of railroad freight and passenger traffic, detailed above in chapters 3–5, is evidence enough. See also chapter 6 on the response of landowners to increasing land values through usurpation of village lands and purchases of public domain. The rapid increase in the output of agricultural products for export during the *Porfiriato* (in contrast to the slower rate of growth of domestic foodstuffs) is additional evidence of responsiveness. On the latter point, see John H. Coatsworth, "Anotaciones sobre la producción de alimentos durante el Porfiriato," *HM* 26 (1976):167–87.

16. Meyer, *Problemas campesinas,* p. 24.

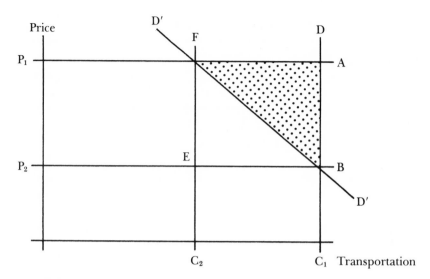

FIGURE MA.3
The Effect of a Positive Price Elasticity of Demand

If the quantity of transport services in the counterfactual economy is less, the transport sector will require a smaller quantity of resources from other sectors of the economy to provide the necessary services. Therefore, the reduction in gross national product without the railroads is less than in the case where elasticity of demand is equal to zero. Figure 3 illustrates this difference. If elasticity is equal to zero, direct social savings are equal to the area P_2P_1AB, as in figure 1. In this case, the demand curve is the line C_1D, perpendicular to the horizontal axis. But if the elasticity of demand is greater than zero, and the demand curve is not perpendicular (as demand curve $D'D'$), then the social savings are smaller. In this case, direct social savings are equal to the area P_2P_1FB. The area ABF represents the exaggeration involved in assuming that elasticity is equal to zero. When elasticity is positive, the amount of transportation demanded declines from C_1 to C_2 as the price increases from P_2 to P_1. ABF resources will not be used for transportation. Instead, the economy will continue to use these resources in other sectors. The reduction in gross national product which would occur without the railroads is not as great as before.

In this study, we have estimated the price elasticity of demand for transportation in Porfirian Mexico in chapter 4. While the estimating procedure is somewhat crude, the result makes it possible to specify the quantity C_2 and thus to estimate the social savings without the substantial bias introduced by the assumption of zero elasticity.

Conclusion

This brief appendix has not discussed in detail all of the methodological and analytical issues that arise from the application of economic theory to the measurement of the railroads' impact on economic growth. The reader who is interested in exploring these questions further may consult the extensive literature on this topic cited in the notes.

One further point may require some emphasis. The positive impact of railroads on economic growth need not result in an equivalent positive effect on long term development. In fact, the argument of chapters 5 and 6 is substantially to the contrary. The railroads reinforced Mexico's comparative advantage in the production of certain mineral and agricultural export commodities. They could not have done so without having had a strong positive effect on national income in the short run. But precisely because railroads made the Porfirian economy more responsive to the world market, they tended to create conditions which made long run development more difficult. "The revolutionary role of the railroad in such a context," Fishlow has remarked, "rests little upon, and perhaps relates even inversely to, social savings."[17]

17. Albert Fishlow, "Comment," American Historical Association Meeting, December 28, 1970 (Xerox, 1970). I am indebted to Professor Fishlow for his comments on earlier drafts of two chapters of this work. The comments referred to here were made in the context of a discussion of my paper, "Porfirian Railroads and Mexican Economic Development."

Appendix I
Aggregate Series Data

The principal source for quantitative information on Mexican railroads during the *Porfiriato* is the voluminous files of railroad materials located in the *Archivo Histórico* of the *Secretaría de Comunicaciones y Transportes* (*AHSCT*) in Mexico City. This archive, which is fully if imperfectly cataloged, contains thousands of *expedientes* lodged in over fifty filing cabinets devoted entirely to railroad materials from the earliest concessions to the 1930s. Every railroad company under federal concession was required during the *Porfiriato* to file an annual report of its finances and operations with the *Secretaría de Fomento* (until 1891) or the *Secretaría de Comunicaciones y Obras Públicas* (from 1892 on). These annual reports, which frequently contained more detailed information than railroad companies cared to include in their published reports to shareholders, have been preserved in this archive almost in their entirety. In addition to the company reports, government inspectors—usually engineers—and government representatives, appointed to sit on the boards of directors of nearly every line, also submitted reports on the railroads to which they were assigned. Most of these reports contain little more than the data already found in the reports of the companies themselves. The reports of the inspectors, however, frequently yield additional data on the engineering and construction aspects of new lines as well as comment on the condition of equipment, roadbed, bridges, safety devices, and the like. Nearly every company was required to submit to the ministry detailed descriptions, engineering specifications, and even blueprints for approval prior to construction, as well as to submit to an official inspection prior to the opening of each section of track to regular traffic. Many of these plans and blueprints have been preserved.

In the reports of the government representatives on boards of directors, company financial and operating statistics are occasionally, and in some cases frequently, accompanied by the representative's personal observations on the financial condition of the company, its difficulties or success in raising additional capital, the mood of the shareholders at their most recent meeting, the fate of the company's stock and bond issues on the New York or London exchange, rumors of financial manipulations involving the company, reports on new equipment ordered or placed in service, and the like. For all of the major lines included in the sample described above (see pp. 80–94) reports of government inspectors and representatives have been checked against company annual reports in the construction of the time series employed in this study. Correspondence between company officials and officials of the *Fomento* (and later Communications and Public Works) ministry, and between ministry officials and government inspectors and representatives was also examined. Whenever companies failed to report as fully as required or discrepancies appeared in their reports, letters and supplementary reports frequently contained the missing data or an explanation of the discrepancy. For all of the major lines in the sample, the appropriate files of the *AHSCT* were examined in their entirety.[1]

The most important source of published data on Porfirian railroads are the four volumes published by the *Secretaría de Comunicaciones y Obras Públicas* (*SCOP*) from 1894 to 1906.[2] The first volume contains data for every line from the date of its first complete report to the ministry. For a number of lines which commenced operations in the 1870s, and for a few others (most notably the Tehuantepec National), the series data in this volume begin some years after the

---

1. It would not be useful to list, by number, each of the more than two thousand *expedientes* from which data was obtained, nor the hundreds more checked for information which did not contain operating information. The Mexican Railway files alone contain more than 700, while the Mexican National and Mexican Central together with the National Railways form a set of files with more than 3,500 separate *expedientes*. Reference is made in the text to specific files, only where direct citation is made or unusual data has been found.

2. *Reseña histórica y estadística de los ferrocarriles de jurisdicción federal desde agosto de 1837 hasta diciembre de 1894* (Mexico, 1895), *Reseña histórica y estadística de los ferrocarriles de jurisdicción federal desde 1° de enero de 1895 hasta 31 de diciembre de 1899* (Mexico, 1900), *Reseña histórica y estadística de los ferrocarriles de jurisdicción federal desde 1° de enero de 1900 hasta 31 de diciembre de 1903* (Mexico, 1905), *Reseña histórica y estadística de los ferrocarriles de jurisdicción federal desde 1° de enero de 1905 hasta 31 de diciembre de 1906* (Mexico, 1907).

company began its operations. For the large number of smaller companies, established from the late 1880s on, the data are usually complete. For each line, the *SCOP* volume reports passenger revenues, "diverse" (including freight) revenues, total revenues, and expenses. The total output series reported in table 2.4 was constructed using this source to supplement the data for the most important lines surveyed in the archive. A comparison of the data in the *SCOP* volumes and the data in the files of the sample lines indicated that the published data contain numerous copying and printing errors. Most of these errors were small, however, and reliance on the published volumes for the output data of only the smaller lines suggests that a high degree of confidence may be placed on the output series in table 2.4.

Some minor difficulties were encountered in constructing the output series. Most of them involved use of the *SCOP* volumes to acquire revenue data for the smaller lines. The *SCOP* volumes contain data through 1906, but no later. The *Anuario estadístico* of the Republic contains the same data as the *SCOP* volumes (as well as additional data on the number of passengers and tons carried for each line) but it ceased publication after its volume for 1907.[3] Revenue data for 1907 for the smaller lines was taken from the *Anuario estadístico* for that year, but for the last three years of the series a somewhat arbitrary procedure was followed. In 1907, the eleven major lines accounted for 88.5 percent of total railroad revenues. The remaining forty smaller lines earned 11.5 percent of the total. For the years 1908, 1909, and 1910, the output of the smaller lines was calculated on the basis of the 1907 ratio. As table A.I.1 indicates, the ratio of sample line revenues to the revenues of the smaller lines had remained quite stable for some years. From 1900 through 1907, the major lines accounted for between 86.9 and 90.7 percent of total railroad earnings. The average for these years, 89.2 percent, is slightly higher than the 1907 ratio of 88.5, but evidence on the number of tons of freight carried and other indicators suggest that the smaller lines were increasing their share of total railroad business,

3. Secretaría de Fomento, Colonización e Industria, Dirección General de Estadística, *Anuario estadístico de la República Mexicana, 1901–1907* (Mexico, 1902–1912).

TABLE A.I.1

Total Revenues of Sample Lines As a Percent of Total Output,
1900–1907
(Thousands of Current Pesos)

Year	Total Revenues of Sample Lines	Total Revenues of Other Lines	Sample Lines As a Percent of Total $\dfrac{(1)}{(1) + (2)}$
1900	44,052.3	5,625.2	88.3
1901	44,045.7	7,066.4	86.3
1902	50,721.0	5,562.0	90.7
1903	60,904.8	6,278.3	90.4
1904	63,381.8	6,688.8	90.3
1905	66,744.0	7,926.4	89.4
1906	74,174.7	9,139.5	89.3
1907	85,771.6	11,131.9	88.5

Source: Appropriate files in the *AHSCT* for sample lines, and Secretaría de Fomento, Dirección General de Estadística, *Anuario Estadístico de la República Mexicana* (1901–1907) (Mexico, 1902–1912), for lines not included in sample.

even if rather slowly, during the last years of the *Porfiriato*.[4] The lower 1907 ratio was therefore used.

Lacunae in the published data for the nonsample lines occasionally required simple interpolation of missing figures. Except for 1894 (and 1908–1910 already discussed) the interpolated data always accounted for less than 1 percent of total output. In 1894, five railroad companies, out of a total of twenty-three, failed to submit annual reports to the government. In this year, interpolated data amounted to 12.1 percent of the total. The failure of these companies to file their annual reports as usual was probably connected to new instructions issued by the *SCOP*, requiring greater detail in reporting on

4. See above table 4.3, p. 84, and text, pp. 86–87.

operations and personnel. All five had submitted reports regularly through 1893, and all five resumed reporting in 1895.[5]

Most of Mexico's major railroad companies shifted from calendar to fiscal year reporting at some point between 1902 and 1910. For consistency, the fiscal year data were converted to calendar year figures according to the somewhat arbitrary procedure described above (p. 86).

The construction of the time series data on total tonnage shipped by rail during the *Porfiriato* also relied most heavily on the manuscript annual reports and other documents and correspondence in the *AHSCT*. All the data for the sample lines was taken directly from *AHSCT* files. The *Anuario estadístico* for 1901 contains historical data on Mexico's railroads, including the number of tons shipped on each line from the date of each company's first complete report.[6] Annual volumes thereafter report the results of each year's operations, company by company. For the smaller lines, the *Anuario estadístico* was therefore employed for tonnage data through 1907. From 1908 to 1910, the tonnage data was taken directly from the *AHSCT* files, as in the case of the major lines. The tonnage series in table 4.1 may be used with confidence (subject to the limitation relating to conversion from fiscal to calendar year data).

Lacunae in the tonnage data were somewhat more common than for revenue statistics. In almost every case where company reports or published data failed to indicate the number of tons carried, freight revenues *were* reported. Interpolation of the missing data could therefore be carried out by assuming that revenue per ton in the unreported year was equal to the average of the years immediately preceding and following. In only two years (1882 and 1894) did the sum of the interpolated tonnage exceed 5 percent of the total. In 1882, the Sonora Railroad, together with the partially constructed Mérida–Peto line, failed to submit complete reports of their operations. Interpolation of the tonnage data for these lines amounted to 8.3 percent of the total for that year. In 1894, the Sonora again failed

---

5. Annual reports are in appropriate files of the *AHSCT*. On new instructions regarding contents of annual reports, see the manuscript annual reports and attached correspondence of the Mexican National and Mexican Central lines, in *AHSCT* *10*/2316, 10/2317, 10/2318, 10/3175, 17/125.

6. *Anuario estadístico*, 1901, pp. 188–201.

to submit a report, as did the more important Monterrey to Gulf line. Together with three smaller lines which also failed to report their tonnage, the interpolated data account for 10.3 percent of the total.

Despite the conversion to calendar years for several important lines after 1902, and the occasional lacunae that required interpolation, no important source of error in the data has been discovered. Railroad companies do not appear to have had any motive for systematically under- or over-reporting the number of tons they carried. Random errors in reporting tonnage data, or revenues, must certainly have occurred, but their impact on the aggregate series is likely to have been small.

Appendix II
Series Data for Sample Lines

The major lines included in the sample were selected on the basis of four criteria: length of line, quantity of freight and passenger service in 1910 (or prior to merger in the National Railways Company), regional importance, and historical significance. Those selected are listed in table 4.2. They include all but three of the steam railroads with more than 200 kilometers of track in 1910. Table A.II.1 lists the length of track, freight ton kilometers, freight revenues, passenger kilometers, and passenger revenues of all of Mexico's railroads in 1910. In volume of freight and passenger service, the most important exclusions from the sample were the South Pacific, the Northwest of Mexico, the Coahuila and Zacatecas, the Nacozari, and the Mexican Northern. These five lines, four of which operated chiefly as mineral feeders to the National Railways, were the only lines not included in the sample which transported more than ten million ton kilometers of freight in 1910. Only the South Pacific, Northwest, and the Nacozari earned more than $1 million in freight revenues, while none earned as much as $1 million in passenger revenues, and only the South Pacific and the Northwest produced as many passenger kilometers as the smallest line included in the sample.

While smaller in some respects than several of the excluded lines, three railroads were of such historical significance and regional importance as to require their inclusion. The Sonora, the Tehuantepec National, and the four companies that merged to form the United of Yucatán were added to the sample, partly because of their size and partly for other reasons. The Sonora and Yucatecan lines were constructed very early in the *Porfiriato* and accounted for a much larger proportion of railroad business in the 1880s and 1890s than in 1910. Their exclusion would have reduced the usefulness of the series data for these earlier decades far more than the exclusion of the mineral lines later on.[1] Together with the Tehuantepec National, they provided the only rail transport available for many years in important

1. In the 1880s especially, the Yucatecan lines together with the Sonora accounted for as much as 5 percent of total railroad revenues in the country.

TABLE A.II.1
Operating Data, Mexican Railroads, 1910

Company	(1) Length of Track (kilometers)	(2) Freight Ton Kilometers (millions)	(3) Freight Revenues ($1,000's)	(4) Passenger Kilometers (millions)	(5) Passenger Revenues ($1,000's)
*Mexican Railway	604.8	175.1	5,681.0	1114	2,153.2
*Tehuantepec National	304.0	207.6	5,470.1	11.3	265.0
*Sonora	442.3	49.1	921.8	17.9	460.9
*National Railways	8,945.9	2,566.8	44,886.5	681.2	12,475.7
*Interoceanic	1,188.6	209.2	6,882.2	120.5	2,047.9
Veracruz–Alvarado	70.4	2.4	176.1	3.1	73.6
*United of Yucatán	813.6	23.2	1,475.1	41.8	821.0
Monte Alto–Tlalnepantla	50.6	.9	59.7	1.2	26.2
Mexican Northern	193.3	13.3	535.0	.3	10.1
Toluca–Tenango	45.7	.8	42.1	4.3	66.1
Esperanza–El Xúchil	26.1	.2	13.9	(a)	.2
Coahuila and Zacatecas	152.9	24.8	910.4	1.9	51.4
Jalapa–Teocelo	31.0	.4	52.4	1.8	46.1
Cazadero–Solís	60.1	1.3	43.2	(a)	1.0
San Juan–El Juile	28.3	(b)	2.0	.1	1.3
San Marcos–Huajuapan	109.0	.6	32.9	1.0	18.0
Occidental of Mexico	60.0	.4	23.9	1.8	21.6
Ixtlahuaca, Mañi and Presa Grande	34.9	.7	44.1	.1	1.2

Torres–Minas Prietas	33.0	.5	44.0	.2	8.7
San Rafael–Atlixco	147.9	4.7	178.0	8.5	129.7
Parral and Durango	101.0	2.3	221.3	1.5	18.1
Mineral of Chihuahua	22.5	1.3	74.2	.9	26.7
Nacozari	123.5	19.1	1,094.6	1.9	78.8
Northwestern	597.1	48.6	1,556.7	13.6	420.1
San Luis Potosí–Río Verde	6.8	5.0	188.1	.1	2.3
Tlalnepantla–Mexico	11.4	1.2	52.3	.8	15.0
Kansas City, Mexico and Oriente	390.6	4.1	195.8	1.7	51.9
Pan American	457.4	8.4	431.1	5.9	169.8
Inter-California	83.1	(b)	25.4	.6	17.9
El Oro Mining	59.0	4.2	398.2	1.2	30.1
Zitácuaro–Joconusco	16.0	.4	23.1	(a)	.9
South Pacific of Mexico	594.5	63.0	1,789.6	23.7	827.8
Minatitlán	10.0	.5	52.0	.3	9.9
Mexican National Construction Co.	47.0	(b)	.2	1.0	13.6
Totals	15,862.3(c)	3,440.1	73,577.0	1,061.6	20,361.8

Notes:
(a) Less than 50 thousand passenger kilometers.
(b) Less than 50 thousand freight kilometers.
(c) This total differs from the total reported in table 2.3 because urban and animal-powered lines were not included. Also, see above, pp. 39–40.
*Sample Line.
Source: Appropriate files in the *AHSCT*.

regions of the republic. Unlike the larger mineral lines, they served for many years without any connection to the rest of the rail system.

The remaining lines included in the sample constituted the backbone of Mexico's Porfirian rail network. The Mexican Railway from Veracruz to Mexico City was the first of the nation's major lines. The Mexican Central, Mexican National, and Mexican International provided the three major north-south trunk lines to the United States border, as well as the most important east-west connections. The Interoceanic competed with the Mexican Railway for traffic between Mexico City and Veracruz, and serviced several major agricultural and manufacturing centers along its route. The Mexican National Construction Company, originally part of the Mexican National, was included chiefly for continuity in the sample data. Two somewhat smaller lines, the Mexican Southern and the Hidalgo and Northeastern, were added not only because they became important carriers, but for other reasons as well. Both were acquired by the National Railways and were added partly to provide continuity in the series. Both were important regional systems, and both did provide a larger volume of services than any of the excluded lines for most of the era.[2]

A number of the companies in the sample were formed as a result of mergers. The United of Yucatán joined four other companies, three in 1902 and the last in 1910. The Interoceanic was formed by the conglomeration of five separate concessions, of which two involved lines already in operation for some years. Most of the larger companies were involved in mergers and acquisitions from the beginning of their activities. In each case, the sample includes series data collected from the annual reports of all of the predecessor companies. As table 4.3 indicates (p. 84 above), the sample companies accounted for between 76.2 and 100 percent of all railroad freight tonnage carried in Mexico between 1873 and 1910.

Construction of the time series for tons carried by sample lines, reported in table 4.3, relied on annual reports and other materials in the *AHSCT*. The tonnage series data are discussed above.[3] *AHSCT* files provided most of the data required for other sample line time

2. See above, chapter 2.
3. See Appendix I.

series as well. Freight revenue data, unavailable in the published compendia, were almost exclusively recorded in annual reports of the companies. As indicated above (p. 90), company freight, for which no charges were entered, were excluded from the tonnage series data, while construction freight was included together with the charge usually reported against capital account in the company reports. While the published data followed the summary tables in each firm's report, these tables frequently included company freight or excluded construction materials charges. While correcting these inconsistencies, it was also possible to eliminate nonfreight charges from the revenue series. The data reported in tables 4.3 and 4.5 are therefore more accurate and more consistent than the data to be found in the *SCOP* volumes of railroad statistics or the *Anuarios estadísticos*.[4]

Major difficulties were encountered in the construction of ton kilometer estimates. In general, Mexican railroads reported only sporadically, if at all, the number of ton kilometers of freight they produced until 1895. Neither the Fomento ministry nor the *SCOP* required this information until that year. Nevertheless, nearly every line did estimate an average length of haul for at least one year in the period before 1895. In addition, a number of companies computed their average revenue per ton kilometer, a datum easily converted into an estimate of ton kilometers whenever freight revenues and total tonnage were also reported.[5] Table A.II.2 indicates the years for which data were available for direct or indirect estimation of the number of ton kilometers of freight shipped.

As the table indicates, five of the lines in the sample failed to report average length of haul, or any other data from which ton kilometer

4. For full reference to *SCOP* volumes and *Anuarios estadísticos*, see Appendix I, notes 3 and 4.

5. Let T = number of tons carried
     D = average haul
     R = total freight revenues
     P = revenues per ton kilometers

Then

$$P = \frac{TD}{R}.$$

TABLE A.II.2
Availability of Data for Computing Ton Kilometer Series, Sample Lines, 1873–1882

Company	1873	1874	1875	1876	1877	1878	1879	1880	1881	1882
Mexican Railway	nd	nd	nd	nd	nd	nd	**	**	**	**
Mexican National (National Railways)	—	nd	nd	nd	nd	nd	nd	nd	nd	nd
Interoceanic	—	—	—	—	—	—	—	nd	nd	nd
Mérida–Progreso (United of Yucatán)	—	—	—	—	—	—	—	nd	**	nd
Sonora	—	—	—	—	—	—	—	—	nd	nd
Mexican Central	—	—	—	—	—	—	—	—	nd	nd
Hidalgo and Northeastern	—	—	—	—	—	—	—	—	nd	nd
Mérida–Peto	—	—	—	—	—	—	—	—	nd	nd
Peninsular	—	—	—	—	—	—	—	—	—	—
Mérida–Valladolid	—	—	—	—	—	—	—	—	—	—
Mexican International	—	—	—	—	—	—	—	—	—	—
Mérida–Izamal	—	—	—	—	—	—	—	—	—	—
Mexican National Construction	—	—	—	—	—	—	—	—	—	—
Mexican Southern	—	—	—	—	—	—	—	—	—	—
Tehuantepec National	—	—	—	—	—	—	—	—	—	—

TABLE A.II.2 (cont.)
Availability of Data for Computing Ton Kilometer Series, Sample Lines, 1883–1892

Company	1883	1884	1885	1886	1887	1888	1889	1890	1891	1892
Mexican Railway	**	**	**	**	**	**	**	**	**	nd
Mexican National (National Railways)	nd	**	**	nd	nd	nd	nd	**	**	**
Interoceanic	nd	nd	nd	nd	nd	nd	nd	nd	nd	nd
Mérida–Progreso (United of Yucatán)	nd	nd	nd	nd	nd	nd	nd	nd	nd	nd
Sonora	nd	nd	nd	nd	nd	nd	nd	nd	nd	nd
Mexican Central	nd	**	nd	nd	nd	nd	nd	nd	nd	nd
Hidalgo and Northeastern	nd	nd	nd	**	nd	nd	nd	nd	**	**
Mérida–Peto	nd	nd	nd	nd	nd	nd	nd	nd	nd	nd
Peninsular	nd	nd	nd	nd	nd	nd	nd	nd	nd	nd
Mérida–Valladolid	nd	nd	nd	nd	nd	nd	nd	nd	nd	nd
Mexican International	nd	nd	nd	nd	nd	nd	nd	nd	nd	**
Mérida–Izamal	—	—	—	nd	nd	nd	nd	nd	nd	nd
Mexican National Construction	—	—	—	—	nd	—	—	nd	nd	nd
Mexican Southern	—	—	—	—	—	—	—	—	—	nd
Tehuantepec National	—	—	—	—	—	—	—	—	—	—

TABLE A.II.2 (*cont.*)
Availability of Data for Computing Ton Kilometer Series, Sample Lines, 1893–1902

Company	1893	1894	1895	1896	1897	1898	1899	1900	1901	1902
Mexican Railway	nd	nd	**	**	**	**	**	nd	**	**
Mexican National (National Railways)	nd	**	**	**	nd	**	**	**	**	**
Interoceanic	nd	**	**	**	**	**	**	**	nd	nd
Mérida–Progreso (United of Yucatán)	nd	nd	**	**	**	**	**	**	**	**
Sonora	nd	nd	**	**	**	**	**	**	**	**
Mexican Central	**	nd	nd	nd	nd	nd	**	nd	nd	**
Hidalgo and Northeastern	**	**	**	**	**	**	**	**	**	**
Mérida–Peto	nd	nd	nd	**	**	**	**	**	**	**
Peninsular	nd	nd	**	nd	nd	nd	nd	**	**	(b)
Mérida–Valladolid	nd	nd	**	**	**	**	nd	nd	nd	(b)
Mexican International	**	**	**	**	**	**	**	**	**	**
Mérida–Izamal	nd	**	**	**	**	**	**	**	**	(b)
Mexican National Construction	**	**	**	**	**	**	**	**	**	**
Mexican Southern	nd	**	**	**	**	**	nd	**	**	**
Tehuantepec National	—	—	**	**	**	**	nd	**	**	**

TABLE A.11.2 (*cont.*)

Availability of Data for Computing Ton Kilometer Series, Sample Lines, 1903–1910

Company	1903	1904	1905	1906	1907	1908	1909	1910
Mexican Railway	**	**	**	**	**	**	**	**
Mexican National (National Railways)	**	**	**	FF	FF	FF	FF	FF
Interoceanic	nd	**	**	**	**	FF	FF	FF
Mérida–Progreso (United of Yucatán)	**	**	**	**	**	**	**	**
Sonora	**	**	**	**	**	**	**	**
Mexican Central	FF	FF	FF	FF	FF	(a)	(a)	(a)
Hidalgo and Northeastern	**	**	**	FF	FF	FF	(a)	(a)
Mérida–Peto	**	**	**	**	**	(b)	(b)	(b)
Peninsular	(b)	(b)	(b)	(b)	(b)	(b)	(b)	(b)
Mérida–Valladolid	(b)	(b)	(b)	(b)	(b)	(b)	(b)	(b)
Mexican International	**	**	**	FF	FF	FF	FF	(a)
Mérida–Izamal	(b)	(b)	(b)	(b)	(b)	(b)	(b)	(b)
Mexican National Construction	**	**	**	**	**	FF	FF	FF
Mexican Southern	**	**	**	**	**	**	**	**
Tehuantepec National	**	**	**	**	**	**	**	**

Key: — Not in operation; nd No data available for estimating ton kilometers; ** Data available for estimating ton kilometers directly or indirectly; FF Fiscal year data converted to calendar year; (a) Merged with National Railways; (b) Merged with United of Yucatán. Source: See text.

estimates might be induced, for more than a decade after beginning operations. Two other lines reported only once in their first ten years of operation. Four of these seven lines were relatively small Yucatecan railways, and another, the Hidalgo and Northeastern, was a small regional system. The two others were major carriers of international freight—the Interoceanic and the Central. The Interoceanic was really composed of several smaller lines which merged in 1888, and it was not until 1891 that the new company completed its track all the way to Veracruz.[6] The Central was, however, the most important railroad system in the country from the first year of its operations. The procedures used for construction of the ton kilometer estimates for that line are therefore described first.

The Central began commercial freight operations in 1881. Its through line from Mexico City to El Paso was completed in 1884. In that year, the company reported its operations in minute detail. It had carried 276,817 tons of freight a total of 84.5 million ton kilometers for an average distance of 341.4 kilometers per ton. Not until 1893 did the Central's report again contain such data. In that year, the line carried 860,186.5 tons, an average of 429.3 kilometers per ton. From 1902 until its merger with the National Railways, the tonnage carried by the company increased steadily from 2.6 to 4.0 million. Average length of haul during those six and a half years remained quite stable despite the increased volume at about 400 kilometers.[7]

To reconstruct the missing data, two different procedures were followed. For the three years 1881 to 1883, reports and communications from government inspectors were scrutinized to determine the average length of track in use during the year, by each section then under construction. For each section, the average haul was estimated at one half the average length of track in use. The final estimate was the result of summing these section estimates. Between 1884 and 1893, with the main line to the U.S. border completed and construction freight accounting for a sharply reduced percentage of the total, average length of haul increased considerably. By 1893, the reported average haul had increased more than 25 percent over 1884. For the

6. See Powell, *Railways*, chapter 8.

7. For these more detailed annual reports of the Mexican Central, see *AHSCT* 10/3173–1, 10/3175–2, and 17/197 covering 1884 and 1894.

missing years 1894 to 1898, ton kilometers were estimated indirectly by interpolating average earnings per ton kilometer. In 1893, the Central earned an average of $0.01815 per ton kilometer. In 1899, the average was $0.02115. With precise data on tons and freight revenues for all the missing years, ton kilometer estimates could be made from the interpolated unit freight earnings. This same indirect method was employed to interpolate ton kilometer estimates for 1900 and 1901, the last two years for which data were missing.

In the case of the Interoceanic railway, quite similar procedures were employed. From 1880 to 1885, the slow progress of construction on each of the independent lines, which later formed this system, was recorded in addenda to the *Memorias* of the Fomento ministry and in the reports of government inspectors.[8] Average length of haul for each separate line was fixed at one half the length of track in use during the year. From 1886 to 1893, average haul was estimated by interpolating from the 1885 estimate to the 1894 figure recorded in the new company's annual report for that year. After reporting its average haul for seven years (1894–1900), the company again failed to do so in its reports for 1901 to 1903. For these years, average haul was estimated by interpolating along a straight line.

Three of the Yucatecan companies operated for more than a decade without reporting their average haul. A fourth recorded an estimate in 1881, and then failed to do so again until 1895. None of these companies operated as much as 200 kilometers of track. All exhibited a high degree of stability in average length of haul after they began reporting these data in the mid-1890s and had finished construction of their lines. In each case, length of haul was estimated at one half of average length of track in use for each year until construction had been completed. In three of the four cases, the lines were completed several years before the companies began to report average haul. In these three cases, average haul after completion of the line was estimated at the average for the first five-year period after reporting began. In all cases, the estimates based on length of track in use tended to converge toward the later known figures.[9]

8. See *MF, 1877–82*, and *MF, 1883–85*. Also, appropriate files in *AHSCT*.

9. See annual reports of the Mérida–Progreso, Mérida–Izamal, Mérida–Valladolid, Mérida–Peto, and Peninsular railroad companies in appropriate files of the *AHSCT*.

For the remaining lines, except the Mexican Railway, the arbitrary assignment of hauls equal to one half the average length of track in use formed the basis of the ton kilometer estimates for the period from the beginning of operation to the first report of average haul. Thereafter, interpolation of earnings per ton kilometer was preferred for estimation of the missing data. The case of the Mexican Railway was unique. For this line, ton kilometer data were available for the eleven years from 1879 to 1890.[10] During those years, the average haul fluctuated between 155.0 and 193.9 kilometers. The mean for the eleven years was 182.5. Since 1873 marked the completion of the Mexican Railway's trunk line from Veracruz to Mexico City, and no new construction had been undertaken in the following years, ton kilometer estimates were based on an assumed average haul of 180 kilometers from 1873 to 1878. Average length of haul reported by the company in 1895 was 155.5 kilometers. For the missing data from 1891 through 1894, average haul was calculated by straight line interpolation.

The estimating procedures employed in constructing the ton kilometer series reported in table 4.4 were frequently crude, and often quite arbitrary. This was especially the case for the seven lines which reported little or no length of haul data for a decade or more before the mid-1890s. In each case, however, the estimates were scrupulously checked against a considerable body of qualitative evidence. Implicit or interpolated revenues per ton kilometer were checked against the comments of company officials in their annual reports and correspondence, and scrutinized with an eye to changes in tariff schedules and freight composition. In every case, the direction of changes in earnings per ton kilometer suggested by these sources was reflected in the series data. As indicated above (p. 86), the data must be used with caution before 1895. As table A.II.2 indicates, there is additional reason for caution after 1902, as a number of companies shifted to fiscal year reporting, and a somewhat arbitrary conversion ratio was employed to convert fiscal year data to the calendar year series. Nonetheless, for most uses of interest to economic historians, the ton kilometer and unit revenue series in tables 4.4 and 4.6 fall well within acceptable error margins.

10. The data were reported to the *Railway Gazette*, 8 June 1883, pp. 364–65; 14 December 1883, pp. 326–27; 4 June 1886, p. 384; and 27 November 1891, pp. 884–85.

Appendix III
Incidents of Conflict
Over Land, 1877–1884

The place name of each incident reported in figures 6.1 to 6.4, together with summary data on distance to nearest railroad, the nature
of the incident indicated, and the source of the information on the
conflict may be found in table A.III.1. In a number of cases, the
name of the district (*cantón* or *municipio*) or district capital was used
in the sources to indicate location, and this practice was followed in
the table. Thus, for example, Córdoba (#39) is indicated because
the source refers to "various *pueblos* in that county" where a "col-
league" reported "symptoms of a coming communist revolution"
after the Supreme Court refused to permit the villages to contest
usurpations by local *hacendados*.[1] Similarly, "numerous usurpations"
were reported in two Morelos districts (Cuautla, #35, and Jonaca-
tepec, #36), and troops were reported to have been dispatched to
Tehuantepec (#40) and Juchitán (#41) districts by the governor of
Oaxaca. In all cases where the district capital and the district had the
same name, the sources clearly indicated the rural character of the
conflict.

Sources for calculating approximate distances to railroad lines
varied considerably. In all but a few cases, information was discovered which made it possible to indicate traveling distance by the
shortest road. In four cases, such information was not available directly and had to be estimated by measuring road links indicated on
contemporary maps located in the Map Library of The University of
Chicago. Three of the four cases were located well beyond forty
kilometers of a rail line.

El Hijo de Trabajo, a socialist newspaper published in this era,
proved the best continuous source for information on rural conflicts
of all kinds. Many of the incidents reported in this source were also
discussed, usually more briefly, in other Mexico City newspapers, but

---

1. See references to reports in *El Hijo de Trabajo* in the table, abbreviated
HT, followed by the date of the issue in which the report occurs.

TABLE A.III.1
Incidents of Conflict Over Land, 1877–1884

Map Number	Place Name	State	Nearest Railroad*	Approximate Distance to Railroad
1	San Bartolo Tepetitlán	Hidalgo	*México–León*	10
2	Zimapantango	Hidalgo	*México–León*	15
3	Texcaltepec	Hidalgo	*México–León*	35
4	Mixquiahuala	Hidalgo	*México–León*	30
5	Jilenautla	Hidalgo	Hidalgo and Northeastern	30
6	Tornacustla	Hidalgo	Hidalgo and Northeastern	10
7	Santiago	Hidalgo	Hidalgo and Northeastern	10
8	San Agustín	Hidalgo	Hidalgo and Northeastern	—
9	Tizayuca	Hidalgo	Hidalgo and Northeastern	—
10	San Luis de las Peras	México	*México–Cuautitlán*	35
11	Alfajayucan	Hidalgo	*México–León*	40
12	San Gerónimo Aculco	Querétaro	*México–León*	10
13	Sta. María de la Loma	Michoacán	*México–León*	100
14	Ahualulco	San Luis Potosí	León–Laredo	40
15	San José de la Isla	Zacatecas	Zacatecas–Guadalupe	20
16	V. Ortega de Río Grande	Zacatecas	León–Laredo	20
17	Colonia Nava	Coahuila	León–Laredo	200
18	Rancho del Sauz	Hidalgo	*Hidalgo and Northeastern*	30
19	Tenopalco	México	*Hidalgo and Northeastern*	15

20	Acayuca	Hidalgo	*Hidalgo and Northeastern*	—
21	Tultepec	México	*Hidalgo and Northeastern*	5
22	Tonanitla	Hidalgo	*Hidalgo and Northeastern*	10
23	Monte Bajo	México	*Mexico–* CUAUTITLAN	5
24	San Bernabé	Distrito Federal	*México–Cuernavaca*	5
25	San Martín Texmelucan	Puebla	San Martín T.–Puebla	—
26	Santiago Tlajomulco	Hidalgo	*Hidalgo and Northeastern*	40
27	San Pedro Tolimán	Querétaro	Celaya–San Juan del Río	40
28	Sta. María Peñamiller	Querétaro	Celaya–San Juan del Río	80
29	San Vicente	San Luis Potosí	León–Laredo	—
30	Chapingo	México	MORELOS	20
31	Tlapacoyan	México	*Morelos*	—
32	Chalco	México	*Morelos*	—
33	Pelagallinas	Puebla	San Martín T.–Puebla	10
34	La Tenería	México	*México–Cuernavaca*	40
35	Cuautla	Morelos	*Morelos*	—
36	Jonacatepec	Morelos	*Morelos*	25
37	Tancanhuitz	San Luis Potosí	*San Luis P.–Tampico*	40
38	Tamazunchale	San Luis Potosí	*San Luis P.–Tampico*	90
39	Córdoba	Veracruz	MEXICAN	—
40	Tehuantepec	Oaxaca	Tehuantepec	—
41	Juchitán	Oaxaca	Tehuantepec	15

TABLE A.III.1 (*cont.*)

Map Number	Place Name	State	Nearest Railroad*	Approximate Distance to Railroad
42	Jilotepec	México	*Cuautitlán–Jilotepec–Maravatío*	—
43	San Juan Bautista	México	MEXICO–IROLO	10
44	San Andrés Tuxtla	Veracruz	TEHUANTEPEC	90
45	Soteapan	Veracruz	TEHUANTEPEC	40
46	Tehuacán	Puebla	TEHUACAN–LA ESPERANZA	—
47	Acayucan	Veracruz	*Tehuantepec*	5
48	San Luis de la Paz	Guanajuato	*Celaya–León/Dolores*	10
49	Milpillas	Guanajuato	*Celaya–León/Dolores*	25
50	Mineral de Pozos	Guanajuato	*Celaya–León/Dolores*	10
51	Ciudad del Maíz	San Luis Potosí	*San Luis P.–Tampico*	35
52	San Lorenzo	Sinaloa	*Altata–Culiacán*	40
53	Quilá	Sinaloa	*Altata–Culiacán*	35
54	Guadalupe de los Reyes	Durango	*Culiacán–Durango*	—
55	Río Yaqui	Sonora	*Guaymas–Río Yaqui*	—

Sources: See text.

*Roman type indicates concession has been issued, but no construction yet underway. Italics indicate railroad is under construction, but has not reached point nearest to incident. Capital letters indicate railroad already in operation at point nearest to incident.

TABLE A.III.1 (*cont.*)

	Nature of Incident	Source
1	Complaints and litigation against local usurpations.	*El Socialista*, 6 IX 77.
2	Petition to President against local usurpations.	*HT*, 11 XI 77.
3	Indian arrested for threatening litigation against adjudication.	*HT*, 18 XI 77.
4	Agitation for return of lands usurped during Juárez administration.	*HT*, 11 XI 77.
5	Violent usurpation by local *hacendado*.	*HT*, 25 XI 77.
6	Violent usurpation by local *hacendado*.	*HT*, 25 XI 77.
7	Agitation for return of lands usurped during Juárez administration.	*HT*, 11 XI 77.
8	Violent usurpation by local *hacendado*.	*HT*, 25 XI 77.
9	Litigation contesting recent usurpation reported.	*HT*, 11 XI 77.
10	Petition against recent usurpation.	Valadés, I, 246.
11	Agitation for return of lands recently usurped.	*HT*, 11 XI 77.
12	Violent repression of litigants against recent usurpation.	*HT*, 30 IX 77.
13	Protest to state government against court-enforced usurpation.	Valadés, I, 245–46.
14	Protests against imposition of new sharecropping arrangements.	*HT*, 12 IX 77.
15	Court orders return of a portion of usurped lands to village.	*HT*, 4 XI 77.
16	Agitation for distribution of usurped lands.	*HT*, 4 XI 77.
17	Violent occupation of hacienda lands.	Valadés, I, 249.
18	Violent usurpation and kidnapping.	*HT*, 14 IV 78.
19	Occupation of hacienda lands.	Valadés, I, 249.
20	Repression of Indians protesting recent usurpation.	*HT*, 9 IX 78.
21	Occupation of hacienda lands.	Valadés, I, 249.

TABLE A.III.1 (*cont.*)

	Nature of Incident	Source
22	Violent usurpation by local *hacendado*.	*HT*, 17 II 78.
23	Letter signed by 2,214 "workers" supporting a "Ley del Pueblo."	*HT*, 8 XII 78.
24	Violent usurpation by local *hacendado*.	*HT*, 24 XI 78.
25	Indian uprising against local *hacendados*.	González Navarro, 241.
26	Violent usurpation by local *hacendado*.	*HT*, 27 I 78.
27	State government mediator resolved land dispute; some land returned.	*HT*, 17 XI 78.
28	State government mediator resolved land dispute; some land returned.	*HT*, 17 XI 78.
29	Violent usurpation by local *hacendado*.	*HT*, 11 VII 78.
30	Violent usurpation by local *hacendado*.	Valadés, I, 256.
31	Agitation against recent usurpation.	*HT*, 1 XI 80.
32	Violent usurpation by local *hacendado*.	*HT*, 24 VIII 79.
33	Attempted occupation of hacienda lands.	Valadés, I, 252.
34	Court decision confirms earlier usurpation.	Valadés, I, 256.
35	Repeated usurpations by local *hacendados*.	*HT*, 9 III 79.
36	Repeated usurpations by local *hacendados*.	*HT*, 9 III 70; Valadés, I, 204.
37	Indian uprising against local *hacendados*.	Valadés, I, 253 ff.
38	Indian uprising against local *hacendados*.	Valadés, I, 253 ff; *HT*, 10 VIII 79.

39	Agitation against Supreme Court refusal to hear case against recent usurpations.	*HT*, 13 IV 79.
40	Troops dispatched to repress violent conflict over land.	*HT*, 19 II 79.
41	Troops dispatched to repress violent conflict over land.	*HT*, 19 V 79.
42	Violent usurpation.	Valadés, I, 257.
43	Imprisonment of attorney preparing litigation against recent usurpations.	*HT*, 17 VII 81.
44	Lands usurped through adjudication returned by court order.	*HT*, 20 XI 81.
45	Indian uprising against local *hacendado*.	Valadés, II, 275.
46	Protest against usurpation.	*HT*, 15 V 81.
47	Indian uprising over land rights and taxes.	González Navarro, 244.
48	Violent usurpation.	Valadés, I, 257.
49	Violent usurpation.	Valadés, I, 257.
50	Violent usurpation.	Valadés, I, 258.
51	Indian uprising against local *hacendados*.	González Navarro, 243.
52	Banditry and pronouncements in conflict over land.	Valadés, II, 70 ff.
53	Banditry and pronouncements in conflict over land.	Valadés, II, 70 ff.
54	Banditry and pronouncements in conflict over land.	Valadés, II, 70 ff.
55	Indian uprising against land-grabbing in area.	Valadés, II, 275.

El Hijo de Trabajo references are used for most of the incidents in the table for ease of presentation. Along with contemporary newspaper sources, information on rural conflict was taken from two secondary works, noted for their thorough accounts, based on government archival materials as well as newspapers, of rural social change in this period. José Valadés' masterly work on the early Porfirian era proved especially valuable, while Moïsés González Navarro's more recent investigations uncovered additional incidents of importance.[2]

It is impossible to say how much rural social conflict is yet to be discovered in sources as yet untapped. Recent works by Jean Meyer and Leticia Reina are based on the work of an entire seminar of researchers sponsored by the Departamento de Investigaciones Históricas of the Instituto Nacional de Antropología e Historia under the direction of Professor Gastón García Cantú and indicate the increasing interest in the rural social history of nineteenth-century Mexico. In the not-too-distant future, a more thorough and systematic test of the hypothesis advanced in this chapter may be possible.

2. José C. Valadés, *El porfirismo, historia de un régimen,* 3 vols. (Mexico: José Porrúa e Hijos, 1941–48), cited in table A.III.1 as Valadés, followed by volume number; González Navarro, *La vida social,* cited in the table as González Navarro.

Bibliography

Archives

Archivo Histórico de la Secretaría de Comunicaciones y Transportes.

Government Publications

Secretaría de Comunicaciones y Obras Públicas. *Ferrocarril Nacional de Tehuantepec. Reseña histórica.* Mexico, 1905.

Secretaría de Comunicaciones y Obras Públicas. *Memorias, 1891–1911.* Mexico, 1899–1912.

Secretaría de Comunicaciones y Obras Públicas. *Reseña condensada de los ferrocarriles de los Estados Unidos Mexicanos.* Mexico, 1910.

Secretaría de Comunicaciones y Obras Públicas. *Reseña condensada de los ferrocarriles de los Estados Unidos Mexicanos, 31 de diciembre de 1910.* Mexico, 1911.

Secretaría de Comunicaciones y Obras Públicas. *Reseña histórica y estadística de los ferrocarriles de jurisdicción federal, 1837–1894.* Mexico, 1895.

Secretaría de Comunicaciones y Obras Públicas. *Reseña histórica y estadística de los ferrocarriles de jurisdicción federal, 1895–1899.* Mexico, 1900.

Secretaría de Comunicaciones y Obras Públicas. *Reseña histórica y estadística de los ferrocarriles de jurisdicción federal, 1900–1903.* Mexico, 1905.

Secretaría de Comunicaciones y Obras Públicas. *Reseña histórica y estadística de los ferrocarriles de jurisdicción federal, 1904–1906.* Mexico, 1907.

Secretaría de Fomento. *Anales, 1877–1898.* Mexico, 1878–1899.

Secretaría de Fomento. *Boletín, 1877–1880.* Mexico, 1879–1882.

Secretaría de Fomento. *Código de colonización y terrenos baldíos de la República Mexicana formado por Francisco M. de la Maza y publicado según acuerdo del Presidente de la República, por conducto de la Secretaría de Estado y del Despacho de Fomento, años de 1451 a 1892.* Mexico, 1893.

Secretaría de Fomento. *Informes y documentos relativos a comercio interior y exterior, agricultura e industria, 1885–1891.* Mexico, 1887–1892.

Secretaría de Fomento. *Memoria de la Secretaría de Estado y del Despacho de Fomento, Colonización, Industria y Comercio de la República Mexicana escrita por el ministro del ramo, C. Manuel Siliceo, para dar cuenta con ella al Congreso Constitucional.* Mexico, 1857.

Secretaría de Fomento. *Memoria presentada a S. M. el Emperador por el Ministro de Fomento Luis Robles Pezuela de los trabajos ejecutados en su ramo en el año de 1865.* Mexico, 1866.

Secretaría de Fomento. *Memoria que el Secretario de Estado y del Despacho de Fomento, Colonización, Industria y Comercio presenta al Congreso de la Unión.* Mexico, 1868.

Secretaría de Fomento. *Memoria que el Secretario de Estado y del Despacho de Fomento, Colonización, Industria y Comercio de la República Mexicana presenta al Congreso de la Unión, correspondiente al año transcurrido de 1° de julio de 1868 al 30 de junio de 1869.* Mexico, 1870.

Secretaría de Fomento. *Memoria que el Secretario de Estado y del Despacho de Fomento, Colonización, Industria y Comercio de la República Mexicana presenta al Congreso de la Unión, conteniendo documentos hasta el 30 de junio de 1873.* Mexico, 1873.

Secretaría de Fomento. *Memoria presentada al Congreso de la Unión por el Secretario de Estado y del Despacho de Fomento, Colonización, Industria y Comercio de la República Mexicana, Vicente Riva Palacio, correspondiente al año trascurrido de diciembre de 1876 a noviembre de 1877.* Mexico, 1877.

Secretaría de Fomento. *Memoria presentada al Congreso de la Unión por el Secretario de Estado y del Despacho de Fomento, Colonización, Industria y Comercio de la ·República Mexicana, General Carlos Pacheco, corresponde a los años trascurridos de diciembre de 1877 a diciembre de 1882.* 4 vols. Mexico, 1885.

Secretaría de Fomento. *Memoria presentada al Congreso de la Unión por el Secretario de Estado y del Despacho de Fomento, Colonización, Industria y Comercio de la República Mexicana, General Carlos Pacheco, corresponde a los años de enero de 1883 a junio de 1885.* 5 vols. Mexico, 1887.

Secretaría de Fomento. *The Main Concession (September 13, 1880) of the Mexican National Construction Company (Palmer-Sullivan Contract) as reviewed and modified by the law of January 11, 1883.* Mexico, 1883.

Secretaría de Fomento. Dirección General de Estadística. *Anuario estadístico de la República Mexicana, 1893–1907.* Mexico, 1894–1912.

Secretaría de Hacienda. *Da cuenta al Congreso de los Estados Unidos Mexicanos del uso que se ha hecho de la autorización concedida al Poder Ejecutivo para consolidar y convertir las deudas de ferrocarriles.* Mexico, 1890.

Secretaría de Hacienda. *Informe del Secretario de Hacienda y Crédito Público a las Cámaras Federales sobre el uso de las facultades conferidas al Ejecutivo de la Unión por la ley de 26 de diciembre de 1906, para la consolidación de los Ferrocarriles Nacional de México y Central Mexicano.* Mexico, 1908.

Secretaría de Hacienda. *Informe presentado al Presidente de la República por el Secretario de Hacienda y Crédito Público sobre los estudios y gestiones de la Secretaría de su cargo en asuntos de ferrocarriles.* Mexico, 1903.

Secretaría de Hacienda. *Memoria de Hacienda y Crédito Público correspondiente al año económico de 1° de julio de 1898 a 30 de junio de 1899 presentada por el Secretario José I. Limantour al Congreso de la Unión.* Mexico, 1902.

Periodicals

Diario Oficial
Economist
El Hijo de Trabajo
Mexican Herald
New York Times
Railroad Age
Railroad Gazette
El Socialista
South American Journal

Books

Aguilera Gómez, Manuel. *La reforma agraria en el desarrollo económico de México.* Mexico: Instituto Mexicano de Investigaciones Económicas, 1969.

Alvarez, José Justo, and Rafael Durán. *Itinerarios y derroteros de la República Mexicana, publicados por los ayudantes del Estado Mayor del Ejército.* Mexico: Impr. de José de Godoy, 1856.

Barcena, Mariano. *Los ferrocarriles mexicanos.* Mexico: Tip. Librería de F. Mata, 1881.

Baz, Gustavo Adolfo, and E. L. Gallo. *Historia del Ferrocarril Mexicano: Riqueza de México en la zona del golfo a la mesa central.* Mexico: Gallo y Cía, 1874.

Bazant, Jan. *Alienation of Church Wealth in Mexico: Social and Economic Aspects of the Liberal Revolution, 1856–1875.* Cambridge: Cambridge University Press, 1971.

———. *Historia de la deuda exterior de México, 1823–1946.* Mexico: El Colegio de México, 1968.

Benítez, J. R. *Guía histórica y descriptiva de la carretera México–Acapulco.* Mexico: Editorial Cultura, 1928.

Bernstein, Marvin. *The Mexican Mining Industry, 1890–1950.* Albany: State University of New York Press, 1965.

Best, Gerald M. *Mexican Narrow Gauge.* Berkeley: Howell-North Books, 1968.

Bitar Letayf, Marcelo. "La vida económica de México de 1825 a 1867 y sus proyecciones." Mexico: Universidad Nacional Autónoma de México, tesis para licenciatura en economía, 1964.

Butterfield, Carlos. *The U.S. and Mexican Mail Steamship Line, and Statistics of Mexico.* New York: J. A. H. Hasbrouck, 1860.

Calderón, Francisco. *La Republica Restaurada: La vida económica.* Historia moderna de México, edited by Daniel Cosío Villegas. Mexico: Editorial Hermes, 1955.

Callcott, Wilfrid H. *Liberalism in Mexico, 1857–1929.* Stanford: Stanford University Press, 1931.

Chandler, Alfred, Jr., ed. *The Railroads: The Nation's First Big Business.* New York: Harcourt, Brace and Company, 1965.

Chapman, John. "Steam, Enterprise and Politics: The Building of the Vera-cruz–Mexico City Railway, 1837–1880." Ph.D. dissertation, The University of Texas, 1972.

Cole, William E. *Steel and Economic Growth in Mexico.* Austin: The University of Texas Press, 1967.

El Colegio de México. *Estadísticas económicas del Porfiriato: Comercio exterior de México, 1877–1911.* Mexico: El Colegio de México, 1960.

———. *Estadísticas económicas del Porfiriato: Fuerza de trabajo y actividad por sectores, 1877–1911.* Mexico: El Colegio de México, n.d.

Díaz Dufoo, Carlos. *Limantour.* Mexico: Eusebio Gómez de la Puente, 1910.

———. *México y las capitales extranjeras.* Mexico: Librería de la Vda. de Ch. Bouret, 1918.

Fishlow, Albert. *American Railroads and the Transformation of the Antebellum Economy.* Cambridge, Mass.: Harvard University Press, 1965.

Florescano, Sergio. "El camino México–Veracruz en la época colonial." Tesis de maestría en Historia. El Colegio de México, 1968.

Fogel, Robert William. *Railroads and American Economic Growth: Essays in Econometric History.* Baltimore: Johns Hopkins University Press, 1964.

———. *The Union Pacific Railroad: A Case in Premature Enterprise.* Baltimore: Johns Hopkins University Press, 1960.

Foster, John W. *Trade with Mexico: Correspondence between the Manufacturers Association of the Northwest, Chicago, and the Hon. John W. Foster, Minister Plenipotentiary of the United States to Mexico.* Chicago: S.P.I., 1878.

Friedrich, Paul. *Agrarian Revolt in a Mexican Village.* Englewood Cliffs, N.J.: Prentice-Hall, 1970.

Fuentes Díaz, Vicente. *El problema ferrocarrilero de México.* Mexico: n.p., 1951.

Germán Parra, Manuel, and Wigberto Jiménez Moreno. *Bibliografía indigenista de México y Centroamérica, 1850–1950.* Mexico, 1954.

Glick, Edward B. *Straddling the Isthmus of Tehuantepec.* Gainesville: University of Florida Press, 1959.

González Navarro, Moisés, comp. *Estadísticas sociales del Porfiriato, 1877–1910.* Mexico: Talleres gráficos de la nación, 1956.

———. *El Porfiriato: La vida social.* Historia moderna de México, edited by Daniel Cosío Villegas. Mexico: Editorial Hermes, 1957.

González Roa, Fernando. *El problema ferrocarrilero y la Compañía de los Ferrocarriles Nacionales de México.* Mexico: Carranza e Hijos, 1915.

Gorsuch, R. B. *The Republic of Mexico and Railroads.* New York: Hosford and Sons, 1881.

Grodinsky, Julius. *Transcontinental Railway Strategy: 1869–1893: A Study of Businessmen.* Philadelphia: University of Pennsylvania Press, 1962.

Gronau, Reuben. *The Value of Time in Passenger Transportation: The Demand for Air Travel.* Washington, D.C.: National Bureau of Economic Research, Occasional Paper No. 109, 1970.

Gurza, Jaime. *La política ferrocarrilera del gobierno*. Mexico: Oficina Impresora de Estampillas, 1911.

Hale, Charles. *Mexican Liberalism in the Age of Mora, 1821–1853*. New Haven: Yale University Press, 1968.

Hanson, Roger D. *The Politics of Mexican Development*. Baltimore: Johns Hopkins University Press, 1971.

Hawke, Gary. *Railways and Economic Growth in England and Wales, 1840–1870*. London: Oxford University Press, 1970.

Hernán Lozano, Sergio Ortiz. "Caminos y transportes en México a fines de la Colonia y principios de la Independencia: su relación con el marco económico y social." Mexico: Tesis, Escuela Nacional de Economía, Universidad Nacional Autónoma de México, 1970.

———. *Los ferrocarriles de México: una visión social y económica*. Mexico: Sría. de Comunicaciones y Transportes, 1970.

Humboldt, Alexander von. *Political Essay on the Kingdom of New Spain*. Trans. and ed. by John Black. 4 vols. London, 1811–1822.

Johnson, Arthur M., and Barry E. Supple. *Boston Capitalists and Western Railroads: A Study in the Nineteenth Century Railroad Investment Process*. Cambridge, Mass.: Harvard University Press, 1967.

Katz, Friedrich. *Deutschland, Díaz und die Mexikanische Revolution*. Berlin: Veb Deutscher Verlag der Wissenschaften, 1964.

Keremitsis, Dawn. *La industria textil en el siglo XIX*. Mexico: Sep Setentas, no. 67, 1973.

Lerdo de Tejada, Miguel. *Apuntos históricos de la heróica ciudad de Veracruz*. 4 vols. Mexico: Imprenta de Vicente García Torres, 1855–1858.

Long, William Rodney. *Railways of Mexico*. Washington, D.C.: U.S. Bureau of Foreign and Domestic Commerce, 1925.

McBride, George. *Land Systems of Mexico*. New York: American Geographical Society, 1923.

Macedo, Pablo. *Tres monografías que dan idea de una parte de la evolución económica de México*. Mexico: J. Ballesco y Cía, 1905.

McGreevey, William. *Economic History of Colombia, 1845–1930*. Cambridge: Cambridge University Press, 1971.

McNeely, John H. *The Railways of Mexico: A Study in Nationalization*. El Paso: Texas Western College Press, 1964.

Metzer, Jacob. "Some Economic Aspects of Railroad Development in Tsarist Russia." Dissertation, The University of Chicago, 1972.

Mexican Yearbook, 1908–1911. London: McCorquodale, 1908–1911.

Meyer, Jean. *Problemas campesinos y revueltas agrarias (1821–1910)*. Mexico: Sep Setentas, no. 80, 1973.

Moses, Bernard. *The Railway Revolution in Mexico*. San Francisco: Berkeley Press, 1895.

O'Brien, Patrick. *The New Economic History of the Railways*. London: Croom Helm, 1977.

Oficina Internacional de Trabajo. *Poblaciones indígenas. Estudios y Documentos,* no. 23. Geneva, 1953.

Peimbert, Angel. *Ferrocarril Nacional de Tehuantepec.* Mexico: Tipografía de la Dirección General de Telégrafos, 1908.

Pérez y Hernández, José María. *Estadística de la República Mexicana.* Guadalajara: Tip. del Gobierno, a cargo de Antonio de P. González, 1862.

Pletcher, David. *Rails, Mines and Progress: Seven American Promoters in Mexico, 1867–1911.* Ithaca: Cornell University Press, 1958.

Powell, Fred W. *The Railroads of Mexico.* Boston: The Stratford Company, 1921.

Powell, T. G. *El liberalismo y el campesinado en el centro de México (1850 a 1870).* Mexico: Sep Setentas, no. 122, 1974.

Ripley, William S. *Railroads: Finance and Organization.* New York: Longmans, Green and Company, 1915.

Romero, Matías. *Geographical and Statistical Notes on Mexico.* New York: G. Putnam, 1898.

———. *Mexico and the United States.* New York: G. Putnam, 1898.

———. *The Railways of Mexico.* Washington, D.C.: H. W. Moore, 1882.

———. *Report of the Secretary of Finance of the United States of Mexico Rectifying the Report of the Hon. John Foster.* New York: G. Putnam, 1880.

Silva Herzog, Jesús. *El agrarismo mexicano y la reforma agraria.* Mexico: Fondo de Cultura Económica, 1959.

———. *El pensamiento económico en México.* Mexico: Fondo de Cultura Económica, 1947.

Solís, Leopoldo. *La realidad económica mexicana: retrovisión y perspectiva.* Mexico: Siglo XXI, 1970.

Téllez Pizarro, Mariano. *Breves apuntes históricos sobre los ferrocarriles de la República Mexicana.* Mexico: Tipografía de la Dirección General de Telégrafos, 1906.

Thompson, Waddy. *Recollections of Mexico.* New York: Wiley and Putnam, 1847.

Turlington, Edgar. *Mexico and Her Foreign Creditors.* New York: Columbia University Press, 1930.

Valadés, José C. *El porfirismo: historia de un régimen.* 3 vols. Mexico: José Porrúa e Hijos, 1941–1948.

Vernon, Raymond. *The Dilemma of Mexico's Development.* Cambridge, Mass.: Harvard University Press, 1963.

Villafuerte, Carlos. *Ferrocarriles.* Mexico: Fondo de Cultura Económica, 1959.

Viollet, Eugène. *Le problème de l'argent et l'étalon d'or au Mexique.* Paris: V. Giard and E. Brière, 1907.

West, Robert C., and John P. Augelli. *Middle America: Its Lands and People.* Englewood Cliffs, N.J.: Prentice-Hall, 1966.

Whetton, Nathan L. *Rural Mexico.* Chicago: University of Chicago Press, 1948.

Articles

Beesley, M. E. "The Value of Time Spent in Traveling: Some New Evidence." *Economica* 32 (1965):174–85.

Berry, Charles. "The Fiction and Fact of the Reform: The Case of the Central District of Oaxaca, 1856–1867." *Americas* 26 (1970):277–90.

Boyd, Hayden, and Gary Walton. "Social Savings from Nineteenth Century Railroad Passenger Services." *EEH* 9(1972):233–54.

Calderón, Francisco. "Los ferrocarriles." In *El Porfiriato: La vida económica.* Vol. 1. Historia moderna de México, edited by Daniel Cosío Villegas. Mexico: Editorial Hermes, 1965, pp. 483–684.

Coatsworth, John H. "Anotaciones sobre la producción de alimentos durante el Porfiriato." *HM* 26 (1975):167–87.

———. "Indispensable Railroads in a Backward Economy: The Case of Mexico." *JEH* 39 (1979):939–60.

———. "Orígenes de autoritarismo moderno en México." *Foro Internacional* 16 (1975):205–32.

———. "Railroads, Landholding, and Agrarian Protest in the Early *Porfiriato*." *HAHR* 54 (1974):48–71.

Coello Salazar, Ermilio. "El comercio interior." In *El Porfiriato: La vida económica.* Vol. 2. Historia moderna de México, edited by Daniel Cosío Villegas. Mexico: Editorial Hermes, 1965, pp. 731–87.

Cosío Villegas, Daniel. "El Porfiriato, era de consolidación." *HM* 13 (1963–1964):76–87.

Cossío Silva, Luis. "La agricultura." In *El Porfiriato: La vida económica.* Vol. 1. Historia moderna de México, edited by Daniel Cosío Villegas. Mexico: Editorial Hermes, 1965, pp. 1–133.

David, Paul. "Transport Innovation and Economic Growth. Professor Fogel on and off the Rails." *EHR*, 2d ser. 22 (1969):506–25.

Davis, Lance E. "Professor Fogel and the New Economic History." *EHR,* 2d ser. 19 (1966):657–63.

Desai, Meghbad. "Some Issues in Econometric History." *EHR,* 2d ser. 21 (1968):1–16.

Dowie, J. A. "As If or Not As If: The Economic Historian as Hamlet." *Australian Economic History Review* 7 (1967):69–85.

Fogel, Robert William. "Notes on the Social Saving Controversy." *JEH* 39 (1979):1–54.

——— "Railroads and American Economic Growth." In Robert William Fogel and Stanley L. Engerman, eds. *The Reinterpretation of American Economic History.* New York: Harper and Row, 1971, pp. 187–203.

———, and Albert Fishlow. "Quantitative Economic History: An Interim Evaluation: Past Trends and Present Tendencies." *JEH* 31 (1971): 15–42.

Fuentes Mares, José. "De la sociedad porfírica." *HM* 6 (1957–1958):433–36.

Goldfrank, Walter L. "The Ambiguity of Infrastructure: Railroads in Pre-revolutionary Mexico." *Studies in Comparative International Development* 11(1976):3–24.
González y González, Luis. "El subsuelo indígena." In *La Republica Restaurada: La vida social.* Historia moderna de México, edited by Daniel Cosío Villegas. Mexico: Editorial Hermes, 1956, pp. 149–325.
Gunderson, Gerald. "The Nature of Social Saving." *EHR,* 2d ser. 23 (1970): 207–19.
Hacker, Louis M. "The New Revolution in Economic History: A Review Article Based on *Railroads and Economic Growth: Essays in Econometric History* by Robert William Fogel." *EEH* 3 (1966):159–75.
Hilton, George. "Review of *Railroads and American Economic Growth.*" *EEH* 3 (1966):237–38.
Iturribarría, Jorge Fernando. "Aspectos sociales del Porfiriato." *HM* 6 (1957–1958):538–41.
Jenks, Leland H. "Railroads as an Economic Force in American Development." *JEH* 4 (1944):1–20.
Knapp, Frank A. "Precursors of American Investment in Mexican Railroads." *Pacific Historical Review* 21 (1962):43–64.
Lebergott, Stanley. "United States Transport Advance and Externalities." *JEH* 26 (1966):437–61.
McClelland, Peter D. "Railroads, American Growth and the New Economic History: A Critique." *JEH* 28 (1968):102–23.
———. "Social Rates of Return on American Railroads in the Nineteenth Century." *EHR,* 2d ser. 25 (1972):471–88.
Mauro, Frédéric. "Le développement économique de Monterrey, 1890–1960." *Caravelle* 2 (1964):35–132.
Mercer, Lloyd J. "Rates of Return for Land Grant Railroads: The Central Pacific System." *JEH* 30 (1970):602–26.
Nerlove, Marc. "Railroads and American Growth." *JEH* 26 (1966):112–15.
Nicolau d'Olwer, Luis. "Las inversiones extranjeras." In *El Porfiriato: La vida económica.* Vol. 2. Historia moderna de México, edited by Daniel Cosío Villegas. Mexico: Editorial Hermes, 1965, pp. 973–1185.
Pletcher, David. "The Building of the Mexican Railway." *HAHR* 30 (1950): 26–62.
———. "The Development of Railroads in Sonora." *Inter-American Economic Affairs* 1 (1948):3–44.
———. "The Fall of Silver in Mexico, 1870–1910, and Its Effects on American Investments." *JEH* 18 (1958):33–55.
———. "México, campo de inversiones norteamericanas: 1867–1880." *HM* 2 (1952–1953):564–74.
Ringrose, David. "Carting in the Hispanic World: An Example of Divergent Development." *HAHR* 51 (1971):30–51.

Rosenzweig Hernández, Fernando. "El desarrollo económico de México de 1877 a 1911." *TE* 32 (1965):404–54.

———. "Las exportaciones mexicanas de 1877 a 1911." *TE* 27 (1960): 537–69.

———. "La industria." In *El Porfiriato: La vida económica.* Vol. 1. Historia moderna de México, edited by Daniel Cosío Villegas. Mexico: Editorial Hermes, 1965, pp. 311–481.

———. "El proceso político y el desarrollo económico de México." *TE* 29 (1962):513–34.

Schmidt, Arthur P., Jr. "The Railroad and the Economy of Puebla and Veracruz, 1877–1911. A Look at Agriculture." Paper delivered at the meeting of the Southwest Social Science Association, Dallas, Texas, mimeo. 1973.

Solís, Leopoldo. "La evolución económica de México a partir de la Revolución de 1910." *DyE* 3 (1969):1–24.

———. "Hacia un analysis general a largo plazo del desarrollo económico de México." *DyE* 1 (1967):40–91.

Weiss, Thomas. "United States Transport Advance and Externalities: A Comment." *JEH* 28 (1968):631–34.

White, Colin M. "The Concept of Social Saving in Theory and Practice." *EHR,* 2d ser. 29 (1976):82–101.

Index